JAMES J. DICENSO is a professor in the De-
partment of Religion at Memorial University
of Newfoundland, St. John's. He has been a
contributor to the *Journal of the American
Academy of Religion*.

HERMENEUTICS AND THE
DISCLOSURE OF TRUTH:
A Study in the Work of
Heidegger, Gadamer, and Ricoeur

JAMES DiCENSO

HERMENEUTICS
AND THE
DISCLOSURE OF TRUTH
A Study in the
Work of Heidegger,
Gadamer, and Ricoeur

University Press of Virginia
Charlottesville

For Wendy

B
3279
.H49
D53
1990

THE UNIVERSITY PRESS OF VIRGINIA
Copyright © 1990 by the Rector and Visitors
of the University of Virginia

First published 1990

Library of Congress Cataloging-in-Publication Data

DiCenso, James, 1957–
    Hermeneutics and the disclosure of truth : a study in the work of
Heidegger, Gadamer, and Ricoeur / James DiCenso.
        p.   cm. — (Studies in religion and culture)
    Includes bibliographical references.
    ISBN 0-8139-1249-0
    1. Truth—History—20th century.   2. Hermeneutics—History—
20th century.   3. Heidegger, Martin, 1889–1976—Contributions in
concepts of truth and hermeneutics.   4. Gadamer, Hans Georg,
1900–   —Contributions in concepts of truth and hermeneutics.
5. Ricoeur, Paul,—Contributions in concepts of truth and
hermeneutics.   I. Title.   II. Series: Studies in religion and culture
(Charlottesville, Va.)
B3279.H49D53   1990
121—dc20   89-37909
                                                                          CIP

Printed in the United States of America

CONTENTS

CONTENTS vii

ACKNOWLEDGMENTS

The development of this work has benefited from the comments, criticisms, and encouragement of many astute readers. I would like to take the opportunity to thank Patricia Cox-Miller, Robert Scharlemann, Nathan A. Scott, Jr., and James Wiggins. In addition, special thanks is owed to David L. Miller and Charles Winquist, each of whom has been enormously helpful in more ways than I can say.

HERMENEUTICS AND THE DISCLOSURE OF TRUTH:

A Study in the Work of
Heidegger, Gadamer, and Ricoeur

INTRODUCTION

The term *truth* usually precipitates one of two sets of associations. The first, as found in most traditional forms of metaphysics and theology, defines truth in terms of the absolute, the complete, and the changeless. The other, represented by much of modern science and by analytical forms of philosophy, defines truth in terms of what is logically or empirically verifiable. With the one, truth is removed from the existential and historical sphere by virtue of its idealization. With the other, the same area of human existence and human concern is neglected because it does not lend itself to precise forms of verification and the conclusive attainment of certainty.

The present inquiry follows neither of these familiar paths. Its concern is to explicate an approach to truth that can address issues on the historical and existential levels. I will argue that an important contribution to the understanding of the experience of truth in an existence-oriented context is found in the approach to truth as *disclosure,* initially formulated by Martin Heidegger. I will further argue that it is the hermeneutical dimensions of disclosure that allow this approach to truth to function in relation to the problems of perspectivalism that trouble traditional approaches. Since the hermeneutical dimensions of disclosure are inadequately developed by Heidegger, I will turn to a selective analysis of the work of Hans-Georg Gadamer and Paul Ricoeur as a means of furthering the inquiry. Naturally, some of the material contained herein will be familiar to the reader who has studied these thinkers, particularly since I have attempted to articulate

my treatment in a manner that argues out the issues without pre-
supposing prior knowledge of or agreement with the material.
However, it seems to me that there remains a great deal that is
unclear about the relationship of Heideggerian ontology to hermeneutics, and the precise nature of the notion of disclosure in
relation to these disciplines has yet to be analyzed. Thus it is my
hope that the present work, while developing an overall argument
concerning truth as disclosure, will also serve to advance in some
ways the understanding of the three major thinkers involved in
the discussion.

An existence-oriented approach to truth applies to the levels in
which human beings actively carry on their lives in relationship
to each other and to their cultural worlds and natural environments. It is in the existential sphere, extended beyond the individualism of some "existentialist" thought to accommodate the historicality of human existence, that people make the decisions and
discoveries that affect themselves and others. The problem of
truth, as applied to this area of concern, will have to do with the
ways in which human beings understand and relate to one another. More specifically, as I shall argue, it will have to do with
the nature of the frameworks of understanding that shape and delimit our capacity to experience the other. Such frameworks are
cultural and historical and hence are linguistically determined.
They operate as "modes of disclosure" that contextualize and delimit our experience of the world and of others.

Because of this attention to the forces that shape human interaction, existential truth will involve an attention to ethical concerns in the tradition of Aristotle's notion of *phronesis*, or practical wisdom. The precedent set by the notion of *phronesis* is
important for the development of contemporary hermeneutics.
However, Aristotle does not treat the problems of history and language with which contemporary theorists must grapple, nor does
he attempt to unify the notion of *phronesis* with the definition of
truth as correspondence formulated in his *Metaphysics*. It is this
latter approach that has had a predominant influence upon the
history of Western thought. Yet, as Chapter 1 will argue, a correspondence approach to truth faces serious difficulties when it
seeks to address existential and historical areas of concern.

The use of the terms *historical* and *existential* to describe the
level of analysis neglected by traditional theories of truth is not
without difficulties. These terms carry a considerable weight of
prior use, and this serves to shape the ways in which they will be

understood. However, as employed in the context of the present
work, these terms indicate an inquiry into the truth of modes of
being. The problem of the ways or modes in which people apprehend and participate in reality, including other persons, is an
existential problem. Likewise, it is a historical problem because
modes of being are determined by long-term collective and cultural forces. In this light, the present use of the word *history* does
not necessitate the positing of a direct access to an uninterpreted
historical reality. History is itself interpretive and takes the form
of cultural reflection upon culturally interpreted steams of
events. From this it does not follow that there can be no historical
truth but rather that the pursuit of truth at this level requires an
attention to hermeneutics.

An inquiry into existential truth is forced to take account of
the finitude and contingency of human experiences. Likewise, it
must attend to the interpretive nature of human perceptions and
judgments. Therefore, in the present work a historical approach
to truth is not developed by historiographical methods or sociological analyses. Rather, the focus of concern will be problems of
language and interpretation. The connection of hermeneutics
with a historical and existential approach to truth is predicated
upon the argument that human beings live in cultural worlds
which are formed by language and which provide contextual perspectives that inform and condition participation in reality. This
interpretive dimension of existence links modes of being to
modes of disclosure, that is, to the manner in which the "other"
is revealed. Therefore, the term *hermeneutics* as employed here
gives expression to an analysis of the interpretive dimensions of
existential and historical structures and is not confined to textual
exegesis per se. This dual usage can be found, in different ways, in
each of the three thinkers who provide the focus of our inquiry.
Obviously, this position is one that will require elaboration as the
analysis proceeds.

Chapter 1 provides an outline and analysis of some of the abiding problems in traditional theories of truth as seen in some characteristic representatives. This survey does not seek to be exhaustive but is oriented specifically toward explicating problems
on the levels of existence and interpretation that remain unresolved by traditional approaches to truth. Mainly, both correspondence and coherence theories fail to resolve the problems related
to the pluralistic, contextual, and intentional aspects of the experience of truth.

The problems discussed in the opening chapter provide the impetus for a movement to the thought of Heidegger, in particular to the disclosure approach to truth he articulates. Chapter 2 is not intended as a general introduction to Heidegger, of which there are already numerous fine examples. Rather, by analyzing some of the central aspects of Heidegger's work, this chapter provides the ontological background necessary to understanding the arguments concerning truth developed not only by Heidegger but by Gadamer and Ricoeur as well. It cannot be sufficiently emphasized that critical attention to ontological questions is inseparable from the reformulation of the problem of truth. Hence, while the second chapter may appear to be a disgression from an explicit treatment of issues concerning truth, it is in fact the foundation for all that follows. Moreover, it should be noted that some of the analyses of Heidegger's ontology will be, by necessity, rather novel in their formulation. This is because the relationship of Heideggerian ontology to the problem of modes of being has tended to be neglected. Without understanding how the inquiry into "Being" is relevant to the problem of the interpretive frameworks that shape our ways of existing, the significance of the approach to truth as disclosure will not be adequately grasped.

Chapter 3 specifically turns to Heidegger's development of truth as disclosure. The point requiring immediate emphasis is that in this context disclosure does not refer to the unveiling of a preexistent Being or Truth but to a creative activity that occurs linguistically and historically. This indicates connections between disclosure and hermeneutics, some of which are not clearly or adequately developed by Heidegger. Critical reflections upon Heidegger's work are introduced, focusing upon deficiencies in his hermeneutics of history and tradition. These deficiencies indicate the need for a turn in the direction of more recent hermeneutical inquiry.

Finally, the fourth and fifth chapters treat, respectively, the work of Gadamer and Ricoeur. Here, far more detailed analyses of the links between language, hermeneutical operations, and "truth disclosure" are developed. I shall argue that the work of these hermeneuticists provides a means of articulating the experience of truth in terms of the ethical problem of modes of being. These modes have to do with the "existential interpretations," that is, the presuppositions and prejudices that affect our judgments and relations but usually remain hidden even from the well-intentioned subject, since they are not produced by the subject. Therefore, hermeneutics is forced to cultivate a *reflexive* approach to truth, one that emerges from the critical interplay of finite forms. The hermeneutical models of Gadamer and Ricoeur operate in such a manner as, potentially, to disclose the limited and distorting paradigms governing our existential modes. Disclosure enables a critical reflexivity oriented toward ameliorating our interpretive relations with others.

The contribution of the present work, with respect to these hermeneutical thinkers, lies in the clarification and refinement of the approach to truth their thinking offers. This involves a presentation of the work of both Gadamer and Ricoeur in light of its basis in Heidegger's ontology and theory of disclosure. To be sure, in addition to a relationship of continuity, there is a relationship of critique and discontinuity operative between Heidegger and these hermeneutical theorists. The formulation of the critical relationship between Heidegger and hermeneutics reveals the problems and limitations in the former's development of truth as disclosure. Likewise, the movement from the work of Gadamer to that of Ricoeur involves a critical element and is not simply continuous and developmental. As the final figure in this triad, Ricoeur provides a corrective to the formulations that curtail the scope of Gadamer's hermeneutics. Reciprocally, Ricoeur requires the work of Heidegger and Gadamer not only to establish a historical basis but to provide the conceptual framework that delineates the set of issues his hermeneutics addresses.

Therefore the progression from Heidegger, through Gadamer, to Ricoeur as articulated here has the structure of an overall argument. The treatment of each of these figures is not simply descriptive but takes the form of a selective critical analysis informed by an inquiry into truth as disclosure. This engenders a style of argument that is itself hermeneutical, employing an analysis of selected works as a means of cultivating a more encompassing understanding. The approach to truth as disclosure as presented in the present work is something to which each of these figures contributes but is not fully developed by any of them individually.

The insights of hermeneutics allow development of the disclosure approach along lines that address the historical-existential level of truth. This provides a model of truth that is confined neither to the realm of the ideal nor to the experience of simple particulars. It addresses problems of relativism and is applicable to the sphere of human relations and modes of being. This approach to truth intends to take account of the interpretive and historical matrices of human understanding and yet retain the ethical and transformative dimensions of practical wisdom. Indeed, it employs the tools of historical hermeneutics as a means of achieving such transformation.

1

ASPECTS OF THE PROBLEM OF TRUTH IN THE HISTORY OF THOUGHT

Correspondence Theories

THE PRESENT CHAPTER seeks to outline some of the diverse approaches to the problem of truth that have been formulated in the Western tradition. The object here is to point to abiding issues and problems evident in various truth theories. Moreover, it is arguable that some of the general lines of development in the history of thought concerning truth have been guided by attempts to respond to these unresolved dilemmas. Tracing such a line of development, therefore, serves to connect the approach to truth as disclosure with a history of problems and issues it addresses.

The selection of issues is governed by the specific problems upon which the present work focuses: the historical, existential, and interpretive dimensions of the human experience of truth. The analyses of the present chapter should establish the need for turning to the more recent thinkers introduced in the following chapters. Naturally, this does not imply that these contemporary thinkers have solved problems that have remained intransigent throughout the history of thought. Rather, the point is to show that a specific form of inquiry—in this case the hermeneutical approach to truth as disclosure,—offers a means whereby certain key issues that have remained problematic to the present day may be approached in a fruitful manner.

When Heidegger develops an approach to truth as disclosure, he does not argue, as does the present work, that it addresses problems that continually reappear in the history of Western thought. He tends to presume that all approaches prior to his own fall under the heading of correspondence theories, and he draws a sharp boundary between these and his own disclosive approach.[1] While this procedure highlights the innovative nature of Heidegger's formulations, it tends to abstract his arguments from the series of historical problems they have a capacity to address. Moreover, Heidegger has oversimplified the matter, and he fails to do justice to the diversity of traditional approaches to truth.

Indeed, if one attends to correspondence theories alone, it is clear that they exhibit a good deal of internal diversity. The great thinkers of the tradition are at odds in many of their positions, and in the present century, with the work of Bertrand Russell, G. E. Moore, Alfred Tarski, and others, the situation becomes increasingly complex, yet a complete analysis of these developments would take us too far afield from our principal tasks. The present discussion of correspondence theory will outline some of its primary foundations and formulations in the tradition. These may generally be seen to inhere within the paradigm of "the mind as a great mirror, containing various representations—some accurate, some not—and capable of being studied by pure, nonempirical methods."[2] Following a sketch of three historically significant discussions of such a theory, we shall turn to the major criticisms that have been made against it. The critique of correspondence leads directly to a discussion of alternate theories of truth, particularly those that can be grouped under the term *coherence*. These will be introduced to illustrate the nature of some previous attempts to offset the curtailments of correspondence approaches.

PLATO

Chapter 3 examines Heidegger's arguments concerning the *covert* or *unthought* origins of correspondence theory in certain developments in Plato's *Republic*. However, the first explicit formulations of a correspondence theory are found in the *Sophist* and the *Theaetetus*. Significantly, in neither of these dialogues is a correspondence theory of truth advocated without reservation or qualification.

For example, in the *Sophist*, truth as correspondence is presented in relation to simple and straightforward instances of judgment. The Stranger, who is in dialogue with Theaetetus and is seated together with him, uses this as an example of a true statement: "Theaetetus sits." As an example of a false statement, he provides: "Theaetetus, whom I am talking to at this moment, flies."[3] Such cases involve direct perceptual apprehension of the present state of specific givens. Here it is relatively simple to determine whether or not statements correspond to what is presented and thus whether or not a statement is true. Therefore the Stranger is able to conclude, with respect to the matter of the truth or falsity of statements, that "the true one states about you the things that are as they are," and "the false statement states about you things *different* from the things that are."[4]

There is an obviousness to such definitions of truth as correspondence with respect to simple and direct, perceptually based observations and judgments. However, the *Sophist* raises a number of problems that become increasingly obtrusive as one moves to more complex problems of truth. It is highly significant that at several points in the dialogue the human capacity to know what is real, what unreal, is brought into question.[5] This problem concerning our knowledge of reality has profound consequences for a theory of truth as correspondence because some accepted understanding of the reality of the referent is necessary to establish adequation or agreement between judgment and thing.

In an example such as "Theaetetus sits," the nature of the object under discussion is given directly to perception, and it is unlikely that Plato is concerned to cast doubt upon *this* level of the apprehension of reality. However, in a great many instances of human dealings with reality the matter is not so simple. Reality, as we experience it on a day-to-day basis, takes the form not only, or even primarily, of simple perceptual givens. Rather, we are involved with a variety of personal and societal realities that presuppose judgments about the nature of what is. In dealing with issues involving the truth of interpersonal activities, ethical and religious judgments, problems of justice, and questions of meaning and value, the simplicity of the given "real" becomes highly complex and problematic.

These points are not made directly in the *Sophist*, yet the problem of the nature of the real is repeatedly raised in terms that have application to the question of the nature of the reality of transient and mutable configurations of experience. In grappling with such issues, the Stranger proposes a definition of the real or "real being" as that which is "so constituted as to possess any sort of power either to affect anything else or to be affected."[6] While this definition may not be universally applicable or completely satisfactory, it does give expression to something essential about the nature of human being and human reality.

As we shall argue at some length, human existence is active, transformative, and interpretive rather than fixed and static. Granting this for the moment, we may see the implications of the Stranger's argument that "if knowing is to be acting upon something, it follows that what is known must be acted upon by it, and so, on this showing, reality when it is being known by the act of knowledge must, in so far as it is known, be changed owing to being acted upon—and that, we say, cannot happen to the changeless."[7]

The final clause of this argument, taken in isolation, might be construed as proposing that reality is in fact the "changeless" that cannot be acted upon by the knower. However, immediately after the above passage the following interchange reveals the orientation of the argument set forth by the Stranger and, it would appear, by Plato: "STRANGER: But tell me, in heaven's name, are we really to be so easily convinced that change, life, soul, understanding have no place in that which is perfectly real—that it has neither life nor thought, but stands immutable in solemn aloofness, devoid of intelligence? THEAETETUS: That, sir, would be a strange doctrine to accept."[8] The definition of reality developed by Plato through the Stranger, therefore, is one that understands reality to be constituted of both "all that is unchangeable and all that is in change."[9]

In the *Sophist*, these arguments are never brought into a state of final resolution with the presentations of truth as correspondence. I would argue that this is not simply a flaw or limitation but rather is consistent with the nature and orientation of many of the dialogues, including both the *Sophist* and the *Theaetetus*. This orientation, which is usually seen to characterize the Socratic dialogues alone, has an interrogative rather than a propositional quality. It consists in opening up problems inherent in a given standpoint or argument and complexifying the issue by presenting a series of counterarguments that enrich understanding without necessarily concluding in a final position.[10] An understanding of the meaning of the dialogues does not emerge through the abstraction of specific arguments from their dialogical context. Rather, understanding is enriched through the cultivation of "a sensitivity to their dramatic implications and ironic nuances."[11] This approach has a direct application to the *Sophist*. There, the presentation of a straightforward correspondence theory is qualified by the accompanying arguments that question the simplicity and self-evidence of perceptual givens as static and determined entities.

There are similar points developed in the *Theaetetus*. There, Socrates states that things are not given in themselves but rather "for each other." This means that "whether we speak of something 'being' or its 'becoming,' we must speak of it as being or becoming *for someone*, or *of something*, or *toward something*." [12] In a similar vein, Socrates develops the argument that "agent" and "patient" are relative to each other. [13] Socrates is quick to note that these arguments raise the specter of relativism. It would seem to be the case that "what every man believes as a result of perception is indeed to be true for him" and therefore that "every man is to have his own beliefs for himself alone." [14]

As a means of counteracting such extreme perspectival relativism, Socrates turns the argument away from perception itself to the mental operations involved in perceptually founded judgments. It is clear, he argues, that knowledge takes place on a level that is at least as much mental as it is perceptual, as is evidenced by the example of knowledge based upon memory. [15] We can have knowledge of some fact even when it is not present to the senses, and we can have knowledge that is derived not from a given sense-experience but from mental operations that transcend sense-experience, as in mathematics. Therefore, following a number of such arguments, Socrates states that "we have advanced so far as to see that we must not look for it [i.e., knowledge] in sense perception at all, but in what goes on when the mind is occupied with things by itself." [16]

Having transposed the problem of truth to the level of mental operations rather than sense perceptions alone, Socrates then proposes that knowing and not-knowing are equivalent to being and not-being. That is, "one who thinks *what is not* about anything cannot but be thinking what is false." [17] Here again we find a simple form of correspondence theory. However, this is immediately called into question by the counterargument that "to think nothing is the same as not to think at all." [18]

This problem leads to the development of a less literal form of understanding of "thinking what is not." Socrates suggests that, if falsehood does not lie simply in "thinking nothing," then perhaps it occurs "when a person interchanges in his mind two things, both of which are, and asserts that one is the other." [19] Falsehood lies in mixing up the correspondences between different thoughts and entities. Here again, however, problems are raised. In confusing two items of knowlege in this manner, it would seem that one is knowing and not-knowing the same thing simultaneously. That is, the individual in question "is thinking that one thing he knows is another thing he knows."[20] Since to know and not know the same thing concurrently is a contradiction, this definition of truth as the confusion of correspondences likewise is found to be unsatisfactory.

For our present purposes, the important point derived from these considerations is that the initial presentations of correspondence theory are situated within a series of arguments that severely compromise them. Two points should be made here. The first is that Plato raises several issues and questions that will continue to plague attempts to apply correspondence theories of truth to an existential level. These problems have to do with the manner in which contextual and interpretive factors affect the possibility of consistently establishing correspondences between thoughts and experiences. The second point, the relevance of which is not immediately evident, is that in many respects Plato anticipates several of Heidegger's arguments concerning the deficiencies of correspondence theories. Because of this, Plato's work does not seem to fit into the conceptual scheme in which Heidegger seeks to place it. The significance of this will become clear in the subsequent analyses of the relationship between historical hermeneutics and the disclosure approach to the problem of truth.

The fact that both the *Sophist* and the *Theaetetus* end in unresolved aporias concerning the problem of the nature of truth may be disturbing to the reader who habitually associates Plato with a theory of ideal forms. One of the greatest of Plato scholars, A. E. Taylor, was so troubled by this problem with respect to the *Theaetetus* that he was led to provide the following explanation. While the *Theaetetus* itself is not considered to be an early work, the time of the dialogue recorded there is too early in the career of Socrates for him to have developed the theory of forms. Although Plato himself had arrived at this theory by the time of his writing this dialogue, he declined to introduce the solution the theory of Forms provides to the problems of truth, knowledge, and reality raised in the dialogue for the sake of "dramatic verisimilitude."[21]

Unfortunately, Taylor's argument represents an imposition of predetermined perspectives upon the dialogue. In fact, the beauty and power of the *Theaetetus* derive from the aporetic nature of its inquiry. This engenders a process of reflection that subverts fixed theories, forcing the reader to struggle with the issues and strive toward deeper understanding. Indeed, there is more than one reference in the dialogue itself to Socrates' role as a spiritual and intellectual *midwife*.[22] This metaphor reflects the function of the dialogue as a whole, which seems to be to assist in the bringing forth of truth on the level of new insight rather than to provide ready-made truths.[23] To anticipate somewhat, the approach to truth evidenced here is one that may be called *disclosive*.

ARISTOTLE

Unlike Plato, Aristotle provides a version of truth as correspondence that is not qualified by its immediate context. In the *Metaphysics*, Aristotle's definition of truth appears in the course of a discussion of the law of the excluded middle. This law states that there cannot be an intermediary between contrary or antithetical statements concerning one thing but that "of one thing we must either assert or deny one thing, whatever it may be."[24]

In this manner a framework of inquiry is established that excludes mediations or both-and cases. Such a framework allows the following clear definition of truth as correspondence: "To say that what is is not, or that what is not is, is false; but to say that what is is, and that what is not is not, is true; and therefore also he who says that a thing is or is not will say either what is true or what is false."[25] The context of this definition again is restricted to clear and simple instances of a correspondence between a mental reflection (expressed in a statement) and a delimited perceptual object. The qualifying middle ground in which things are apprehended in more than one way or in which changes in judgment occur is excluded from consideration. Aristotle makes this point unambiguously in stating that "when things are mixed, the mixture is neither good nor not-good; and so no statement is true."[26] This position rather severely limits the application of Aristotle's definition of truth.

The correspondence or agreement that occurs in the relation of statement and referent is described by Aristotle as based upon a process of combination and separation. Thus, in speaking of the faculty of understanding, he argues that "when, in asserting or denying, it combines the predicates one way, it is right; when in the other it is wrong."[27] Similarly, in *On Interpretation*, it is argued that "combination and division are essential before you can have truth and falsity."[28] In a manner parallel to an argument from the *Sophist*, Aristotle transfers the problem of truth from the level of sense impressions alone to an operation "in thought."[29] Clearly, for Aristotle truth is predicated upon the capacity of the mind to make judgments and hence statements concerning what is and what is not, and to relate these statements through combination and separation to particular instances of perceptual experience.

The Aristotelian definition of truth as correspondence will exert a profound influence upon the subsequent tradition of Western philosophical and theological endeavor. However, it is significant that while Aristotle does not qualify the definition of truth as correspondence *within* his specific presentations of it, he does in fact develop more than one sense of truth. This differentiation of levels or types of truth mitigates the problem of narrowness that characterizes the highly focused arguments for correspondence.

In the *Nichomachean Ethics* Aristotle argues that "there are three elements in the soul which control action and the attainment of truth: namely, Sensation, Intellect (*nous*), and Desire."[30] Of these three elements, sensation cannot be said to "originate action," by which Aristotle would seem to mean rational or intentional action. Therefore this element does not require a theory of truth to suit its function. The theory of truth described in the *Metaphysics*, that is, a correspondence theory, is seen to be adequate to the "truth of intellect." For *desire*, however, another approach to truth is required in order to understand and address the problem of "right desire."

Such an approach to truth will be oriented toward the "practical" realm, that is to the social world in which human beings live out their lives in relationship to one another. It is here that problems of moral choice present themselves, and therefore the practical wisdom or thinking appropriate to the determination of truth on this level will possess a specifically moral connotation. Aristotle describes this practical thinking in stating that "inasmuch as moral virtue is a disposition of the mind in regard to choice, and choice is deliberate desire, it follows that, if the choice is to be good, both the principle must be true and the desire right, and that desire must pursue the same things as principle affirms. We are here speaking of practical thinking, and of the attainment of truth in regard to action."[31] Here, the problem of truth appears on a very different level from that of "combination and separation" in the relationship between conceptions and percipients.

Truth on the level of right desire and right choice is directly related to what Aristotle calls "fore-choice," *proairesis.* "Perhaps

we may define *proairesis* as voluntary action preceded by delib-
eration; since fore-choice occurs with reason and reasoning."[32]
The perfection of this form of "intelligent choice" that precedes
and governs one's actions Aristotle calls *phronesis*, "practical
intelligence."

The relevance of this form of intelligence to the social realm is
indicated in Aristotle's statement that "practical intelligence
(*phronesis*) is indeed the same power of mind (*hexis*) as political
intelligence."[33] However, *phronesis* is not confined to political
knowledge per se, but is reflective of practical (or existential) activity in general. Randall describes *phronesis* as "the highest intellectual excellence of every form of human conduct and action,"
noting as well that Aristotle associates it with conduct (*praxis*).[34]
Randall suggests a comparison with the American notion of
know-how, noting a common application to "what is variable,
contingent, and relative."[35] Therefore the kind of truth evidenced
here will be one that is relevant to the changing realities and relationships of human existence. It is based upon a forethinking that
governs action, and the cultivation of wisdom through repeated
experiences of right thinking and right action.

The importance of *phronesis* for our present purposes is that it
seeks to give expression to a notion of truth that is not based upon
rigidly determined either-or situations. It is not confined to the
apprehension of static and unchanging entities but touches upon
the active realm where things *matter*, ethically, for human existence. "It remains therefore that practical intelligence is a rational habit of mind that attains truth about action in relation to
things that are good and bad for man."[36] This theory of truth is an
acknowledged predecessor of the hermeneutical approach to
truth, especially that of Gadamer. Thus it indicates an area of
concern to which we shall have occasion to return.

Aristotle, by dividing the faculties of the soul into sensation,
intelligence, and desire, circumvents the necessity of developing
a single theory of truth that applies to each of these areas of human existence. While such a division of types of truth is war-
ranted by the pluralism of human functions and pursuits, it may
be seen that the divisions between these faculties are not absolute. *Phronesis*, as we have seen, involves a specific application of
intelligence and is not confined to issues of desire alone.

This raises certain questions concerning the viability of a correspondence theory of truth, even for a circumscribed faculty of in-

telligence. However, before raising these issues, we should examine an additional thinker who develops a correspondence theory and who seeks to incorporate into it areas of concern that remain extrinsic to Aristotle's narrowly focused definitions.

THOMAS AQUINAS

Thomas Aquinas devotes considerable attention to a theory of truth as correspondence after the model of Aristotle. However, when Aristotle's correspondence theory of truth is appropriated by Aquinas, it undergoes a bifurcation because of the theological orientation of the latter's thought.

Thomas begins with a problem posed by the understanding of truth as based on the intelligible grasping of sensible forms. He presents Augustine's argument against this theory, which points out that if the true is "that which is seen," then, for example, "it would follow that rocks buried in the depths of the earth would not be true rocks because they are not seen."[37] From this argument Augustine is led to conclude that "the true is that which is." However, Thomas notes that this assertion contradicts Aristotle's argument that truth is in the mind. Thomas therefore proceeds to resolve the contradiction in the following manner.

Thomas contrasts truth or knowledge with desire. He argues that "the end or term of desire, which is the good, is in the thing desired; whereas the end or term of knowledge, which is truth, is in the mind."[38] The direction or intentionality involved in desire is outward, toward the thing that is the term, or referent, of desire. The direction of knowledge, on the other hand, is from the thing to the mind, since the referent of knowledge is the experience of truth, which is not given in the thing itself but is rather a mental phenomenon.

These arguments indicate Thomas's concurrence with, and development of, Aristotle's position concerning truth as correspondence. But they do not yet resolve the problem derived from the existence of objects that are not presently standing in a perceptual relation to the knower. The resolution of this problem follows from the differentiation between the human and the divine intellects. Thus, "natural things are called true when they bear a likeness to the types in the divine mind."[39] In effect, Thomas has introduced a second standard of truth. Both represent correspondence theories, but the first is based upon the relation of an object to the human mind, while the second is based upon the relation of

the object to the divine mind. Moreover, the divine mind is introduced as the solution to the problem of relativism that ensues
from making human minds alone the standard of truth. Referring
to this problem, Thomas argues that "the difficulties do not arise
if we make the truth of things consist in a relation to the divine
intellect."[40]

Before remarking upon the significance of this bifurcation of
truth as correspondence, it should be noted that Thomas perceives a problem in the transference of a correspondence notion of
truth from human to divine knowing. We have seen that, for Aristotle, the determination of truth involves the processes of combination and separation. Thomas affirms this understanding of
the intellect as "joining and separating concepts in judgment" and
uses this as further evidence that truth lies in the mind and not in
sense.[41] However, in both the *Summa Theologiae* and the *Summa
Contra Gentiles*, Thomas indicates the problem that derives from
the fact that "in God there is no joining and separating."[42] Otherwise stated, the problem of transferring a correspondence theory
of truth to the divine intellect resides in the fact "that the divine
intellect does not understand in the manner of a composing and
dividing intellect."[43] This follows from the definition of the divine intellect as a simplicity that understands all things simultaneously through His essence.[44] How, then, can there be truth for
the divine intellect?

These problems lead Thomas to develop an alternate conception of truth as applied to the divine intellect. This is modeled on
the adequation of thing to mind but does not involve the mediation and division that occur in the human intellect. This alternate notion of truth derives from the proposition that "God
knows other things through His essence."[45] That is, God's essence, in which knowing and being are coexistent, has in itself a
direct knowledge of all things, which are dependent upon the divine essence for their own existence. In fact, it is clear that this
does not represent simply an alternative form of truth but rather
the "perfect" form. Thus Thomas states of God that "His act of
knowing is the measure and cause of all other being and all other
intellect. . . . Hence it follows not only that truth is in God but
also that he is the supreme and original truth."[46] The plurality of
truths the human intellect can experience indirectly through
combination and separation are ultimately referred to the divine
intellect.[47] Unlike the malleable nature of human truth, "truth in
the divine intellect is unchangeable."[48]

With these arguments concerning truth in its relation to the divine intellect, Thomas adds a dimension to the theory of truth that is of more than historical interest. Clearly, he is seeking to incorporate the Aristotelian theory of truth as correspondence into a definite theological framework. Yet at the same time he is also grappling with the problem of providing a comprehensive determination of, and basis for, all partial and relative finite truths. Whether or not one accepts Thomas's postulates concerning the nature of the divine intellect and its position as the final determination of truth, the problem of perspectival relativism this theological doctrine seeks to rectify is unavoidable.

However, the ultimate basis of truth in the divine intellect remains problematic in terms of its access to the finite human mind. This problem is indicated by Thomas's statement that he has presented *two* quite distinct applications of truth as correspondence: one for the human and one for the divine intellect.[49] The first is the correspondence theory as formulated by Aristotle, which will still be acknowledged as fundamentally correct and adequate by Kant.[50] The second, while acknowledging the correctness of the first within the limitations of the experience of truth for finite intellects, sees truth ultimately as based on a correspondence to "the idea preconceived in the *intellectus divinus.*"[51]

The problem, however, is that these two distinct formulations have not been unified in a single comprehensive understanding of truth. There remains a gulf between the human and divine experiences of knowledge and truth. Because of this, the introduction of the divine intellect as the ultimate ground of truth cannot provide a sound conceptual basis for the experience of truth as correspondence on the level of human understanding.

Thomas's bifurcation of truth indicates the need for attending to the problem of encompassing conceptual contexts or frames of reference within which particular and partial experiences of truth take on their meaning and derive their verity. In other words, *without* access to a divine mind to provide an ultimate basis for particular truths, correspondence theories continue to be faced with the problem of perspectival relativism. As discussed, for example, by Plato, this means that truth is simply the experience of a correspondence for a particular finite mind. Understood thus, the term *truth* does not carry much weight, because it provides no determinable way of mediating between particular perspectival experiences of truth. This problem, complicated by an increasing awareness that human minds are not fixed reference points of objective judgment, has provided the focus for a variety of criticisms that have been directed at correspondence theories.

From Correspondence to Coherence

CRITIQUE OF CORRESPONDENCE

In Plato, Aristotle, and Thomas Aquinas, the *relational* nature of truth is emphasized in a number of different ways. Likewise, more recent thinkers have called attention to the pivotal nature of processes of relationship in the experience of truth. For example, D. J. O'Connor, after arguing that the transition from "belief" to "truth" with respect to any given conception depends upon something "external" to the belief itself, concludes that "truth then is a relational property and a theory of truth must spell out the nature of the relation."[52] O'Connor conceives of this problem of "the nature of the relation" involved in truth as something to be solved within a correspondence approach and thus develops his argument within the limits of this approach.

By contrast, H. H. Joachim uses the problem of the nature of this relational process or processes to point beyond correspondence theories. He summarizes many of the arguments of the classical philosophers in stating that "truth, according to all forms of the correspondence notion, is a determinate relation between two distinct factors: and this relation must be 'for' a mind."[53] Following this, Joachim takes a step in his argument that is indicated but not fully developed by philosophers such as Plato.

Joachim argues that the "mind," which determines the relation constituting truth, is not simply an immediately focused discursive faculty that engages in processes of analysis and synthesis. Rather, the human mind brings to bear pregiven conceptual and perspectival configurations upon any apprehension of perceptual givens. These involve past experience and memory, including theoretical training and methodological approaches derived from particular points of departure and intended goals or ends.

One aspect of the prior meanings operative in any act of judgment, and this is the aspect focused upon by Joachim, is the system of relations or overarching framework of conceptual reference within which entities are understood and terms defined.

Therefore, referring to the problem of the relation between "mind" and "object," Joachim argues that "the relation in question depends through and through upon the system of relations— i.e., the plan, cycle of functions, or teleological scheme—within which the *relata* on either side have their being. There is no 'correspondence' between two 'simple beings,' i.e., without respect to the systematization of their wholes."[54] Systems of reference give concrete determination to the mode of relationality through which the truth of an object manifests itself in a particular situation.

Joachim returns us to Plato's caveat that you cannot know the true until you know the real. The real as experienced by human beings is not constituted by particulars impinging upon the sense faculties. Rather, experience of reality occurs within one or more contextual frames of reference that condition the apprehension of any particular within a greater whole. The nature of any experience of correspondence, therefore, will be determined by the context within which the elements of the correspondence are being approached and apprehended. A truth that is determined within the context of a value-free scientific inquiry may appear quite different within the context of an ethical inquiry, and so on. No correspondence can occur without the operation of some prior conceptual frame of reference that provides the standard of measure that makes specific judgments possible. This means that "truth depends primarily on something other than correspondence—on something which itself conditions the being and the nature of correspondence."[55]

As a means of explicating this "something other" that conditions the nature of truth as correspondence, Joachim turns to the type of approach known historically as the *coherence* theory of truth. The central tenet of this approach is that "truth in its essential nature is that systematic coherence which is the character of a significant whole."[56] That is, because the nature of any particular experience is determined in terms of some pregiven system of references, truth does not consist in the simple correspondence of entity and idea, but rather consists in a coherence, or fit, within the larger system of references. Particulars take on meaning and truth in relation to their place in an encompassing structure of ideas. The argument for coherence has been summarized by Brand Blanshard: "What the [correspondence] theory takes as fact and actually uses as such is another judgment or set of judgments, and what provides the verification is the coherence between the initial judgment and these."[57] On the basis of this priority of coherence over correspondence, Blanshard concludes that "coherence is our sole criterion of truth."[58]

The conception of truth as the coherence of judgments within a greater system is not, of course, a twentieth-century development of such thinkers as Joachim and Blanshard. Coherence theories of truth have been formulated systematically by a number of major thinkers in the philosophical tradition. At this point, it will be well to resume our historical survey by examining two thinkers whose work embodies an approach to truth that can be called coherence-based. Such an analysis, however brief, will illustrate the appearance of coherence approaches in practice and will also serve to disclose the specific problems such theories encounter.

Joachim refers to the work of Spinoza as exemplifying a coherence theory,[59] and we shall follow him in this selection. As a second example of a philosophical system that articulates truth as coherence, we shall then turn to the work of Hegel.

SPINOZA

It should be emphasized that coherence theories of truth are not completely distinct from correspondence theories but rather take instances of agreement to be grounded ultimately by a complete system of knowledge. Toward the opening of the *Ethics*, Spinoza presents us with the axiom that "a true idea must agree with its object."[60] This standard expression of correspondence is qualified, however, by the larger scope of Spinoza's work, which incorporates both idea and object in the system of divine knowledge. Thus, somewhat further on Spinoza reiterates the point that "a true idea must agree with its object," but he continues by stating that "what is contained objectively in the intellect must also be in nature. But in nature there is only one substance, viz. God, and there are no affections other than those which are in God and which can neither be nor be conceived without God. Therefore an actual intellect, whether finite or infinite, must comprehend God's attributes and God's affections, and nothing else, q.e.d."[61] It is the reference of all particular objects of knowledge to the system of God's knowledge that provides the final criterion for truth, and this produces an approach to truth significantly different from that described in Aristotle's *Metaphysics*.

At this point the two key terms in Spinoza's philosophy, *Substance* and *God*, require clarification. Spinoza defines the first as "what is in itself and is conceived through itself, i.e., that whose concept does not require the concept of another thing, from which it must be formed."[62] In similar terms, God is defined as "a substance consisting of an infinity of attributes, of which each one expresses an eternal and infinite essence."[63] The two terms are in certain respects synonymous: each is characterized by an infinitude and essentiality that are not determined by or contingent upon any other entity or concept. Thus, as Joachim expresses the matter, the "one Substance, or 'God,' is absolutely single and absolutely concrete; i.e., God comprises, within the indivisible unity of his individual being, all positive characters in which reality is expressed."[64]

The self-givenness of God provides the basis for Spinoza's deductive system. He states that "all things that are, are in God, and so depend on God that they can neither be nor be conceived without him."[65] Thus the complete Substance, God, is first posited, and is then taken to be the basis of and reason for all extant particulars. Moreover, because of the predication of all particulars upon God, "in nature there is nothing contingent, but all things have been determined from the necessity of the divine nature to exist and produce an effect in a certain way."[66] All aspects of reality are included within the cohesive a priori divine reality, which is equally and at once a system of ideas and the order of things.[67] This conception of an encompassing divine nature allows Spinoza to make assimilation to the divine order the ultimate criterion of truth. This is expressed concisely in proposition 32 of Part 2 of the *Ethics:* "All ideas, insofar as they are referred to God, are true."[68] Therefore, the basis of truth will not reside in the human mind's capacity to compare its ideas to perceptually apprehended givens. Rather, truth appears as the inherence of ideas within the a priori system that is inclusive of reality. As Stuart Hampshire, in his analysis of Spinoza's system, summarizes the matter: "To say of an idea that it is true cannot be merely to say that it corresponds to any external reality; to say of an idea that it is true must be to state its relation to other ideas in the system of ideas which constitutes God's thinking."[69]

Unlike Thomas Aquinas, Spinoza does not bifurcate truth into a human and a divine form, which is the product of Thomas's seeking to maintain the insights of Aristotle's definition of truth as correspondence. For Spinoza, there is only one form of truth, and the task of human knowledge is to gain cognizance of this given system. This, to be sure, does not mean that all human knowledge automatically accomplishes this task.

In fact, Spinoza differentiates between three levels of knowledge, of which the higher is inclusive of the lower. The lowest level of knowledge derives from "the mere suggestions of experience," that is, it comes through the senses and is fragmented, confused, and without order. Somewhat more refined than this is knowledge that comes from symbols, memory, or the imagining of things. Both of these are contained under the heading of "knowledge of the first kind, opinion or imagination." What Spinoza calls "knowledge of the second kind" includes "common notions, and adequate ideas of the properties of things," which is also called "reason." Finally, there is the third kind of knowledge, which is called "intuitive." This "proceeds from an adequate idea of the formal essence of certain attributes of God to the adequate knowledge of the essence of things."[70]

The lower forms of knowledge, the first and second kinds as Spinoza defines them, are not independent means of access to truth. They do not even yield partial and finite truths but are instead imperfect and inadequate approximations to the highest form of knowledge. This latter consists in the *scientia intuitiva* that deduces all particulars from the comprehensive system of divine ideas.[71] The third form of knowledge, which alone yields truth, overcomes the barriers between the divine and human minds.

Spinoza's theory of truth must presuppose that "the human mind has an adequate knowledge of God's eternal and infinite essence."[72] On the basis of this access to the divine, human beings are able to have knowledge of particulars through an understanding of their coherence within the system. It is not the human mind as such, in its particularity and finitude, that obtains truth by means of the establishment of correspondences. Only through its access to the preexistent system of divine ideas does the human mind arrive at truth. This introduces a presupposition on a grand scale, which is succinctly if hyperbolically described by Kojève when he states that Spinoza "must *be* God from all eternity in order to be able to write or think his *Ethics*."[73]

In addition to this major presupposition, Spinoza's system is also incapable of allowing irresolvable falsity to exist. The coherent and comprehensive system of truth already exists in God, and therefore human error can produce only "the privation of knowledge, which inadequate, fragmentary, or confused ideas involve."[74] Although Spinoza's system must be complete in order to be valid, it follows from this denial of substantive error, as Joachim points out, "that error will not fit cohesively into his system."[75] Human knowing can attain to greater or lesser levels of coherence within the single order of ideas, indicating the possibility of a "privation" of knowledge. Yet this fails to account for the existence of actual falsity and error. The intractable and inassimilable nature of negativity in relation to absolute systematization is a problem that is unresolved in Spinoza's thought. G. W. F. Hegel, who provides a second example of a coherence approach to truth, will seek to resolve this problem by incorporating negativity into his system.

HEGEL

The guiding maxim of coherence theories appears in Hegel's statement that "the true is the whole."[76] However, Hegel develops his system in the postcritical atmosphere engendered by Kant's explication of the limits of the human capacity to know "things in themselves" and the restriction of our sensible experience to categorically determined "appearances."[77] In light of these developments, Hegel's phenomenology must begin with the partial perspectives derived from experience and attempt to incorporate the limiting factors of temporality, contingency, and negativity into Absolute Knowing.

It is not surprising that Hegel is critical of the Spinozistic conception of substance, which he views as a necessary but crude and undifferentiated stage in Spirit's quest for complete knowledge. In Hegel's philosophy, "substance is the as yet undeveloped in-itself."[78] Hegel also asserts that "substance is still selfless being."[79] The notion of substance, in Spinoza's sense, has not been mediated and differentiated through the dialectical processes of self-externalization and self-alienation through nature and history that characterizes the movement of the *Phenomenology of Spirit.* In Spinoza's system, substance is not itself in process: as God, it is the eternal basis of the being and the verity of all that is. The movement from the plurality of existents to the one substance is necessary and unidirectional. For Hegel, however, the concept of substance remains an abstraction unless it is dialectically mediated through particularity, existence, and negativity. It is only thus that Spirit becomes self-conscious "being-for-self."[80] In Hegel's system, "only this self-*restoring* identity, or this reflection into otherness [*Andersein*] within itself—not an *original* or *immediate* unity as such—is the True."[81]

Hegel graphically expresses the need for the movement from

abstract substance to self-conscious spirit in stating that "Spirit at once recoils in horror from the abstract unity, from this *self-less* substantiality, and against it affirms individuality."[82] Yet we must inquire as to the nature of the conception of individuality Hegel is proposing here. How is this individuality asserted by Spirit?

There are actually two forms or stages of individuality in the developmental movement of Spirit. In contradistinction to the abstract unity of substance, there is an "outward" movement of Spirit, as it were, in which individuality is "externalized . . . in the sphere of culture, thereby giving it an existence."[83] One side of this process of externalization in time and space is "Nature," which is described as the "living immediate Becoming" of Spirit.[84] The other side of the process, however, is "History," which "is a *conscious* self-*mediating* process—Spirit emptied out into Time." This latter process is also described as being a movement in which Spirit becomes "the negative of itself," and here Hegel clearly is attempting to incorporate differentiation and alienation into the self-becoming of Spirit.[85] The form of individuality that is instated in this moment of Spirit's development, then, may be conceived of as a plurality of contingent individualities existing within time and space. This moment of Spirit's becoming may be equated with the consciousness of human individuals as such.

However, the "gallery of images" which this temporal process of externalization produces and which the *Phenomenology* traces does not represent the final and complete form of Spirit as "individuality." In other words, as Jacques Derrida has emphasized, the *Phenomenology of Spirit* should not be read as an "anthropology" but rather as a movement that incorporates the "science of man" into a process that is greater and other than "man" in himself.[86] This is made clear when Hegel describes the notion of selfhood that gives determinate form to any conception of individuality he employs. He states that "the 'I' is not merely the Self, but the *identity of the Self with itself*; but this identity is complete and immediate oneness with Self, or this Subject is just as much Substance."[87]

The dialectical movement of the self-realization of Spirit, then, begins with selfless Substance, moves through a pluralism of alienated individualities, and returns to a higher unity that is *both* Substance and Subject. The plurality of individualities are not "ends" in themselves, but rather "their goal is the revelation of the depth of Spirit, and this is *the absolute Notion.*"[88] It is here, in this unity that incorporates the fragmented existence and knowledge of isolated individuals into "Absolute Knowing, or Spirit that knows itself as Spirit," that one arrives at "actuality, truth, and certainty."[89]

This indicates the manner in which Hegel, at least in the *Phenomenology*, develops an understanding of truth as "the whole." All finite truths are incorporated into a unifying teleological process that has as its goal Absolute Knowing. It is this terminus ad quem that provides the coherent structure through which particulars take on their truth. As Jean Hyppolite expresses this, "Truth is impossible without the reciprocal recognition of self-consciousnesses and their elevation to the universality of thought."[90] It is this "raising to universality" that forms the process of the Hegelian system as a whole. Only within the structure of this whole can there be truth.

For coherence theories, the final determination of truth appears as the incorporation of particulars in a systematic whole. It is on this basis that Hegel's work has been included in this category. However, there have been arguments to the contrary. For example, J. N. Findlay has argued, with reference to the *Science of Logic*, that "a judgment is true in proportion as the moments distinguished in it coincide in their content, in proportion as they represent the conformity of a thing to its notion."[91] On this basis Findlay offers the following definition: "Objective truth is the conformity of objects to their notion."[92] He understands this definition of truth to diverge from that represented by coherence theories and remarks "how little Hegel connects his 'truth' with the notion of systems of coherence, which are so prominent in the teachings of many Hegelians."[93]

The difference between Hegel and "many Hegelians" is a fact worthy of recognition. Emil Fackenheim, for example, contrasts Hegel's system with that of F. H. Bradley. The latter seeks to "dissipate conflict and chance into mere unreality, on the authority of a system and a Reason which, presupposed from the start, do not expose themselves to the world."[94] In contrast to this, Fackenheim understands Hegel to hold that "the system can *be* comprehensive of the world only by means of total self-exposure to it."[95] This interpretation of Hegel does not conflict with the analysis of the *Phenomenology* undertaken here. Hegel's system is not static and sterile but rather seeks to be comprehensive and dynamic by developing a notion of Spirit that necessitates a movement into the world as time, space, and negativity.

Granting the greater complexity and inclusiveness of Hegel's system in comparison to those of Spinoza and Bradley, how then does truth as "conformity to the Notion," which is articulated by Findlay, differ from a coherence theory? The nature of the concept of Notion (*Begriff*) in Hegel's thought is such as to mediate between the particular and the universal. In effecting this mediation, it incorporates specific judgments into a greater totality of logical systematization. Let us examine the manner in which this systematization is achieved.

Findlay notes that Hegel identifies the Notion with the Self or Subject.[96] As in the *Phenomenology*, however, this use of the terms *self, subject,* or *individuality* does not refer to particular extant individuals. Hegel emphasizes that "the Notion is to be regarded not as the act of the self-conscious understanding, not as the *subjective understanding,* but as the Notion in its own absolute character which constitutes a *stage of nature* as well as of spirit."[97] In Findlay's words, the operation of the Notion through the subjective intellect constitutes the process of "the emergence of unity and universality out of the confused mass of sense experience."[98] Likewise, Findlay informs us that "to have a Notion is to think universally of things, to range them under common characters in which their specific differences and crude individual immediacy will be submerged."[99] Finally, we may compare Hegel's description of the Notion as "penetrating, so that all that is particular is determined by this universal itself."[100]

Therefore, it would appear that the agreement of an object with its Notion represents a conceptual process that comprehends the particular by subsuming it under the universal. That is, the particular moments of experience and judgment are understood in terms of a comprehensive system of concepts by means of which they derive their meaning and their truth. The Notion, as such, embraces all particulars. Yet each particular does not conform to the Notion in the way that, for example, a statement corresponds to an observed phenomenon. Rather, the Notion can be universal only because it embraces particulars within a comprehensive ordering process. Thus, particulars are granted their specific significance and verity by being placed within the whole. Isolated experiences of correspondence are subsumed within a universal system that eradicates incompletion and contingency. Despite Findlay's disclaimer, this represents what may properly be called a coherence theory of truth.

The form of coherence Hegel develops, in both the *Phenomenology* and the *Logic,* is dynamic and dialectically inclusive. It does not refer particulars to a static universal but engages in an active mediation and incorporation into a dynamic process whereby the activity of particulars takes on meaning and truth. This truth is predicated upon the systematic inclusion of all particulars as a series of moments within the self-becoming of the universal, whether this latter is called Spirit, Notion, or Absolute Knowing.

The Critique of Coherence

While there are a number of highly significant differences in the nature of the conceptual systems of Spinoza and Hegel, each serves to illustrate the essential characteristic of coherence theories of truth. This is the dependency of all truth-statements upon a process of systematic universalization, which incorporates them into an overriding conceptual framework and which provides the basis for the determination of truth. In this manner the final criterion of truth is transferred from the certainty of the subjective intellect as such to an encompassing system of thought within which the individual intellect is but a moment or aspect. This transfer allows coherence theories to deal with the question of the variability of interpretive matrices that condition subjective apprehension and judgment. Particular existential matrices can each be referred to a single encompassing systematic frame of reference.

In each case the system of ideas is formulated as being necessarily complete and cohesive. The system, therefore, is not simply a subjective or even a "human" construct but reflects the mind of God or the teleological movement of Absolute Spirit. The system is ultimately and finally "objective," that is, it is "ideal." The approach to truth these systems offer has been summarized by Haig Khatchadourian: "To show that a judgment is true is to show that it coheres with a system of judgment which is true— ultimately with the ideal system of truth."[101]

Coherence theories effectively develop a critique of correspondence theories through pointing to the inescapable contextuality of human thinking that informs and conditions all judgments of truth. In response to the problem of interpretive contexts, coherence theories seek to secure judgments of truth from the problems of relativism based upon subjectivity. Hence they conceive of the problem of contexts in ultimate terms.

This causes coherence theories to follow a path of infinite regress, moving to ever-greater contexts of thought and judgment that can only be completed through the positing of an ultimate referent for all truth. This may take the form of the eternal Substance of Spinoza, or it may take the form of the dynamic and dialectical self-completion of Absolute Spirit in Hegel. In any case, however, it is an ultimate and final context that provides the closure necessary to the establishment of truth as coherence. The conceptualization of this ultimacy is necessarily established by a system of thought that, whatever its pretensions to complete objectivity, remains human thought. The certainty of the Cartesian *cogito,* for example, and the certainty of Hegel's Absolute Knowing may appear to be worlds apart (and in some respects, of course, they are). Yet each shares the characteristic of formulating a fixed basis for truth that is the product of human conceptualization and abstraction. With Spinoza and Hegel, the "self-certain self" is projected upon some form of an Absolute, which is by definition other than and greater than human existence and knowledge.

The projection of completeness and certainty upon an Absolute remains a feat of human conceptualization and cannot succeed in divorcing the system from the finitude and subjectivity of its originator. The irreducible presence of human thinking within the system raises a number of problems. Joachim has articulated the nature of one of the central problems which the quest for complete coherence faces.

> A theory of truth as coherence, if it is to be adequate, must be an intelligible account of the ultimate coherence in which the one significant whole is self-revealed; and it must show the lesser forms of experience, with their less complete types of coherence, as essential constitutive "moments" in this self-revelation. . . . It must show, e.g., how the complete coherence, which is perfect truth, involves as a necessary "moment" in its self-maintenance the self-assertion of the final modal minds: a self-assertion which in its extreme form is Error.[102]

The problem raised here is not simply that of finite minds presuming knowledge of the absolute. In addition, Joachim is inquiring as to the possibility of a complete system being capable of encompassing and accounting for the aberrant, contingent, and spontaneous activities of finite individuals.

The Hegelian system, to be sure, claims to include finitude, contingency, history, and hence both error and freedom within the complete process of Spirit's self-development. However, this is accomplished in a rather strained and artificial manner. J. N. Findlay describes this process of incorporation in stating that "in dialectical thought the false must always be in a sense preserved in the truth, not indeed *qua* false, but as overcome in this truth."[103] What this really means, however, is that the Hegelian system ultimately denies the reality of inassimilable error. To give error its place within the system, thereby transforming the negative and the aberrant into a moment within a greater process that is itself ultimately true, is the antithesis of taking error seriously.

Moveover, the denial of error is the counterpart of the system's denial of the finite and conditioned nature of human thinking. The comprehensive inclusiveness that is the requisite factor for giving truth a basis in coherence is precisely that which human thought, by nature, is incapable of attaining. Joachim argues that every metaphysical theory is "the outcome of experience which is partial and so far finite" and therefore at best represents only "a partial manifestation of the truth."[104]

Joachim's argument parallels that made by Kierkegaard against the Hegelian system's positing of the unity of thought and being in a conceptual scheme that claims to represent the nature of ultimate reality. Kierkegaard reminds us that "the subject is an existing individual, and that existence is a process of becoming, and that therefore the notion of the truth as identity of thought and being is a chimera of abstraction . . . because the knower is an existing individual for whom the truth cannot be such an identity as long as he lives in time."[105] Here the point is not that the human mind is incapable of transcendental operations that rise above the specificity of individual existential situations. Rather, the argument is that this transcendence cannot be such as to leave behind finitude altogether, which is precisely what speculation must accomplish if it is to develop a complete and coherent system. As Kierkegaard points out, such systems claim to reflect the nature of reality and not of thought alone, and therefore must take account of the determining characteristics of the existential sphere.

The impossibility of completely absorbing reality into a conceptual system removes the basis for establishing truth by means of coherence. However, granting the insurmountable obstacles to the complete determination of coherence, perhaps a more restricted notion of coherence may be developed. This has been at-

tempted by Blanshard. He notes, in terms similar to Joachim and
Khatchadourian, that "fully coherent knowledge" would entail
the mutual interdependence of all judgments within a single system of thought, and that in fact we never find such a system.[106]
Nevertheless, Blanshard argues that "for all the ordinary purposes
of life, coherence does not mean coherence with some inaccessible absolute, but with the system of present knowledge."[107] The
obvious problem with this revision is that there is no more a "system of present knowledge" as such than there is a system of absolute knowledge. Rather, in any historical period there will be a
plurality of conflicting theories and approaches operating within
a number of distinct fields of research. In an attempt to avoid this
impasse, Blanshard offers a further qualification of coherence theory by arguing that "what the ultimate standard means *in practice* is the system of present knowledge as apprehended by a particular mind."[108]

Unfortunately, these extreme modifications of coherence theory serve to undermine whatever capacity it may claim for solv-
ing the problems inherent in correspondence theories. Blanshard
is correct in stating that any system of knowledge will be the result of historically conditioned possibilities and perspectives, and
that any such system actually will appear only as apprehended by
particular finite minds. In acknowledging these points, however,
he reintroduces the problems of relativism and subjectivism that
theories of coherence initially set out to overcome.

Coherence theories are oriented toward articulating a single
comprehensive system that has objective existence in relation to
subjective minds. Therefore, they provide no solutions to the
problems raised by bringing a plurality of systematic and non-
systematic configurations into relationships of comparison, conflict, and creative interaction. Closed systems that claim compre-
hensiveness are mutually exclusive. Hence one is left with a
plurality of conflicting interpretations of reality with no clear
means of critically weighing the differences between them.

Furthermore, no means of understanding the creative,
emergent, and future-oriented dimensions of the experience of
truth is possible when the criterion is a closed system. Coherence
theories fall into the same difficulties as correspondence theories
in this respect. That is, they look toward some *given* basis for the
determination of truth. In correspondence theories, this determining ground will take the form of the certainty of the judging

mind encountering supposedly raw perceptual data. In coherence theories, it is the judging mind operating within a given coherent system that provides the basis of truth.

In each case there remains little possibility of approaching truth in terms of the active and engaged processes of human existence. There is a strong case to be made for the existence of frameworks of understanding, or interpretive prejudgments, that function *prior* to specific moments of judgment and have a determining effect upon the nature of the truth of judgments. From this, however, it does not follow that the pursuit of truth lies solely in the direction of the clear and comprehensive articulation of pregiven interpretive structures by means of coherent systematization. To direct our attention exclusively back to what is antecedent to any experience is to obscure and deny those aspects of experience, and of truth, that are the result of engaged activity in a human world characterized by possibility as well as contingency.

This point—the active and prospective nature of the experience of truth—has been made by William James. It seems appropriate to examine briefly his perspective on this matter before concluding. James argues that truth does not consist merely in "copying" an extant form of reality or an idea in a statement but rather has to do with the operational verification of modes of conceptualization and activity in the world. "The truth of an idea is not a stagnant property inherent in it. Truth *happens* to an idea. It *becomes* true, is *made* true by events. Its verity *is* in fact an event, a process: the process of verifying itself, its veri-*fication*. Its validity is the process of its valid-*ation*." [109] In this passage James gives expression to a dimension of the experience of truth that is neglected by both correspondence and coherence theories. Ideas are tested out, and therefore verified or falsified, as they are actively applied in practical situations. This relational activity within the exigencies of the practical realm indicates the temporal and relational dimensions of truth. Truth is not simply established on the basis of the static and pregiven but instead takes shape and appears in the midst of human affairs.

Moreover, James's pragmatic approach to truth builds upon the finitude and temporality of human existence and understanding. He sees truth as emerging dynamically within the context of historical determinations. In a different context James argues that "the wisest of critics is an altering being, subject to the better insight of the morrow." [110] Because of this, the pursuit of truth

is best served by a willingness to be engaged by the transformations engendered by personal and historical experience, rather
than by anchoring ourselves to perspectives that are momentarily
safe. "When larger ranges of truth open, it is surely best to open
ourselves to their reception, unfettered by our previous pretensions."[111]

James anticipates some of the important insights of the disclosure and hermeneutical approaches to truth. However, the central
problem of the nature and means of verification processes is not
given a satisfactory treatment by James. The criterion of "usefulness" or pragmatic competency he offers remains vague and
uncritical. For example, James connects truth with belief, and argues that "the true is the name of whatever proves itself to be
good in the way of belief, and good, too, for definite, assignable
reasons."[112] This definition remains inadequate because there can
be an indefinite number of "good" reasons supplied to support the
truth of any given belief. As Bertrand Russell has pointed out,
there is an unwarranted assumption inherent in James's equation
of truth and belief, since the problem of the criteria of what is
good and what is bad is precisely the problem which requires
resolution and which is left open to question.[113] Furthermore, as
Russell illustrates by a number of examples, the statements "it is
true" and "it is useful to believe" have very different meanings in
actual use.[114] These are issues James's pragmatic approach to truth
does not resolve.

Our survey of selected figures in the history of thought has
shown that approaches to the problem of truth reveal significant
diversity. Plato, for example, indicates the complex problems connected with the changing and variable nature of reality. Aristotle
points to the need for a theory of truth on the level of practical
wisdom. Coherence theories highlight the need for attending to
the frames of reference that condition the understanding of particulars. Pragmatism points to the active, engaged, and future-
oriented dimensions of truth. In each of these instances, the limitations as well as the advances evidenced in these formulations
provide guidance for further thinking. The history of thought creates a series of perspectives from which various aspects of the
problem of truth may be surveyed, and these perspectives provide
the grounds for further inquiry. This point will gain in importance
in the light of the issues concerning history and hermeneutics
that appear in the following chapters.

At the same time, a number of central problems remain unresolved in traditional truth theories, and the approaches developed heretofore do not appear to be capable of establishing a line of inquiry that will bear fruitful results concerning these issues. Correspondence theories are functional within the range of immediately verifiable judgments concerning fixed and simple objects of perception. Yet they fail to account for the frames of reference that condition judgments concerning more complex forms of experience, for the active and temporal aspects of truth as it is manifest in the practical realm, or for the conflicts of judgment that inevitably emerge in complex levels of inquiry.

Coherence theories seek to address the problem of the frames of reference that condition specific judgments, but they do so only by establishing antecedent interpretive structures as complete and coherent speculative systems. The coherence approach to truth thus posits objective frameworks of judgment, the existence of which is unwarranted and problematic in the light of the finitude of human experience and the concomitant limitations of thought. Moreover, such comprehensive systems of reference obscure the dimension of truth which is creative and which emerges from the open-ended and exploratory activities of human experience and understanding. Pragmatism, as represented by James, seeks to develop a notion of truth that is adequate to the understanding of these latter issues of experimentation within concrete experience. Here, however, the problem of antecedent frameworks of judgment is ignored, as is the task of arbitrating between conflicting judgments and beliefs.

What seems to be required is an approach to the problem of truth that attends to both the antecedent interpretive frameworks of judgment and to the innovative dimensions of activity within the world. To develop such an approach, it is necessary to conceive of the antecedent interpretive frameworks not as objective systems but as perspectives that emerge from cultural and historical existence. This prevents the reification of fixed interpretive structures that is caused by the quest for complete certainty and objectivity, and it allows for the creative interplay of heteronomous perspectives with each other and with new experience and insight.

The rudiments of such an approach to truth are found in Heidegger's theory of disclosure, which can be critically extended in the direction of more recent hermeneutical theory. To develop this argument, it will be necessary to begin with a preliminary analysis of the ontological formulations that provide the basis and guidelines for the approach to truth as disclosure. The "ontology of disclosure" discussed in the following chapter overturns the presuppositions concerning the mind as mirror for "perceptual givens" that dominate the history of thought and provides a model of the human experience of reality that is dynamic and emergent rather than static. This model shifts the focus from truth as final and apodictic to truth as a mode of participatory disclosure.

2

AN ONTOLOGY OF DIS-
CLOSURE: HEIDEGGER

The Being of Beings

THE FOCUS OF THIS CHAPTER is an analysis of the ontological inquiry developed by Martin Heidegger, for whom the problems of Being and truth are inextricably intertwined. Although an explicit treatment of Heidegger's approach to truth is reserved for the following chapter, the ontological issues discussed here are inseparable from the overall concerns of this work. A rethinking of the problem of Being, particularly in relation to the issue of the modes of being that shape human existence, is inseparable from a reformulation of truth along existential and hermeneutical lines.

The question of Being is the heart of Heidegger's thinking. This question, we shall argue, is significant for understanding human existence and can contribute to the task of providing orientations for the pursuit of truth within the context of historical existence. To do so effectively, however, the definition of Being employed cannot be one that separates and isolates it from the plurality of extant beings. What is required is an inquiry into Being that is capable of addressing issues concerning the *way* things are, that is, their manner or mode of existing.

Although Heidegger has been accused of formulating an isolated and hence irrelevant notion of Being, by Theodor Adorno, for example, he in fact continually stresses that Being must be understood as the "Being *of* beings" (*Sein des Seienden*).[1] To address the question of the nature of Being is at the same time to inquire into the nature and modality of beings. The question of Being emerges whenever one undertakes to inquire into the modes or structures that govern human experience and relations.

"Of such a kind is Being," Heidegger writes, "that it is not one particular kind among others, but the mode of all beings as such."[2] The question of Being (die Seinsfrage) allows for an inquiry into *ways* of being.

If this is the case, why not develop an inquiry that is focused upon *beings* as such? What is gained by introducing the term *Being?* Heidegger's argument for the significance of the inquiry into Being is predicated upon the nonequivalence of beings and modalities of being. Although "Being itself is not something which keeps itself isolated somewhere" and does not separate itself "from the being," nevertheless, "Being persists in a difference with respect to beings."[3] In particular, this means that people understand themselves within the confines of ways or modes of being that are not completely apparent and are not entirely the product of choice. The question of Being shifts the focus of inquiry from the predetermined givenness of beings to the problem of the modalities that condition human experience. It turns from entities as unreflectively presented to the problem of how entities are *disclosed* in human activity and understanding. Hence Heideggerian ontology and the reformulation of truth as disclosure are inextricably linked.

Heidegger argues that "we always conduct our activities in an understanding of Being [in einem Seinverständnis]."[4] Some presupposition concerning Being is operative within any instance of human judgment or activity, and this affects the manner in which beings are presented. Further, Being is accessed only by means of an inquiry into the existential modalities of beings, that is, the ways in which people understand and relate to others and to the world. In Heidegger's terms, on the one hand "there exists no comportment to beings that would not understand Being," and on the other hand, "no understanding of Being is possible that would not root in a comportment toward beings."[5]

In ontological inquiry, as Ray L. Hart has stated, "one cannot start from Being without beings for that would be to start nowhere, from no 'appearance' or presentation of Being."[6] The Heideggerian ontology, in accordance with this argument, seeks to reveal the mode of Being of existing beings. The essential tension in Heidegger's thinking derives from the attempt to articulate the alterity of Being and the reason why Being is not reducible to beings without positing an independent entity called Being.

Because of the unusual nature of Heidegger's understanding of Being, it is important for him to differentiate his use of the term from that of previous thinkers. Such differentiation, in fact, is taken to the point of an "overcoming of metaphysics."[7] This represents an essential deconstructive aspect of Heidegger's work. Yet as chapter 3 will argue, this deconstructive "overcoming" of the past is connected with certain serious limitations in Heidegger's understanding of the historical nature of thinking. At present, the important point to be made is that without such a deconstruction to distance Heidegger's concept of Being from the previous employment of synonymous terms, the innovative nature of Heidegger's formulations is likely to be missed. There are a number of aspects and levels to this new understanding of Being. Somewhat more obvious than, but not unrelated to, the attention to the problem of modalities that has been indicated is the linking of Being with time. This is a point which Gadamer notes and which he develops through a historical hermeneutics. Although Gadamer diverges from Heidegger in equating the temporality of Being with the historicality of tradition, he concurs with Heidegger as to the innovative and seminal results yielded by transcending nontemporal conceptions of Being.

Gadamer notes that Heidegger's understanding of Being in terms of time serves to "burst asunder" the concern of traditional metaphysics with Being as "what is present." Focusing upon what is present, that is, a determined entity or substance, obscures the temporal processes of disclosure that provide the configurations within which any entity is apprehended.[8] A static and nontemporal conception of Being engenders an approach to reality that takes things "as given" in a particular moment of perception and cognition. Linking Being with time displaces the false immediacy of the given and impels an inquiry into becoming. Again, the significance of this latter process is found in the plurality of interpretive structures that shape human relations to things. This pluralism tends to be obscured by a focus upon "presence."

Along similar lines, Werner Marx has analyzed the innovative nature of Heidegger's ontology in terms of its presentation of the dynamic and creative nature of Being. This allows an inclusion, within the problem of Being, of the emergence of the "new" through human activity, as for example in the areas of technology, art, and creative conceptualization.[9] Werner Marx contrasts Heidegger's dynamic and temporal ontology with the characteristics of "selfsameness" and closure that define the Aristotelian *ousia*, as well as with the "teleological self-determination within itself" of the Hegelian *Absolute Geist*.[10] A temporal ontology such as Heidegger's does not subsume the processes of becoming within a predetermined logical and teleological framework. Even a conception of Absolute Spirit as a process of becoming, such as is found in Hegel, remains closed within its own circuit of self-realization. In the Hegelian System, as argued earlier, there is little possibility of seriously accounting for the contingency, finitude, and brokenness of historical experience. In the System, these erratic phenomena are denied and repressed through a continual movement of *Aufhebung*, which abolishes negativity by incorporating it into a cohesive whole.

Being and Time develops a critique of ontologies based on the notion of substance as a means of explicating the central problems in traditional ontologies. This is accomplished primarily by means of an analysis of the formulations of Descartes. An examination of these arguments will help to clarify the nature of the innovations of Heideggerian ontology.

Heidegger's Critique of Descartes

Heidegger argues that substance-based ontologies conceive as primary that which has the distinguishing quality of "remaining constant" (*ständigen Verbleib*).[11] A particular mode of disclosing the world becomes entrenched conceptually in this reification of Being. There is a certain reciprocity between ways of being and the conceptualization of Being. This is evident, for example, in the Cartesian conception of God, which provides the focus of Heidegger's analysis.

This idea of God, in effect, raises the notion of substance to the highest power. On this point, Descartes's definition is very close to that of Spinoza and in fact provides the latter's model. Descartes states that "by substance we can understand nothing else than an entity which *is* in such a way that it needs no other entity in order to *be*."[12] The only entity that completely fulfills this definition is the *ens Perfectissimum*, the perfect being that is a perfect substance. Thus Descartes asserts that there is only one substance that "is in need of no other thing whatsoever . . . God."[13] All other entities are created or produced, requiring God as their ultimate basis and origin.

Created beings, too, are substances, divided into *res cogitans* and *res extensa*, but they are dependent substances.[14] Indeed, the fact that the subject, or *cogito*, is itself defined as a "thinking substance" is determinative for the conceptualization of human nature and its relations to the world. For Heidegger's argument, what is most significant in these formulations is that God and created entities are simply quantitatively different variations of the same mode of Being. As Heidegger expresses it: although God is supposedly "infinitely" different from conditioned beings, "we still consider creation and creator alike *as entities*."[15]

A specific mode of apprehending reality is operative in any such ontology based upon the notion of substance. The Cartesian idea of Being is one that "has been gathered from a definite realm of . . . entities themselves."[16] Moreover, there is a reciprocal operation of ontological conceptions upon existence, serving to reinforce and entrench determined ways of being. This will be the case even when metaphysical and theological conceptions are no longer consciously dominant in the cultural sphere.

Heidegger employs the term *vorhanden* (present-at-hand) to describe the mode of apprehension that is the correlate of substance ontology.[17] Grasped in this manner, things in the world are taken as they present themselves, which includes a hidden interpretation that conditions their appearance. This manner of apprehension is also referred to as *ontical* (*ontisch*).[18] Heidegger employs the term *zuhanden*, ready-to-hand, to describe the use of present-at-hand things such as tools and equipment based on the fixed manner in which they are seen and understood.[19] The "immediate" relationship to things as "handy" is determined by the usefulness of the thing within an established project or set of ends.

The notion of substance is directly related to the interpretive modes of *vorhanden* and *zuhanden*. Heidegger perceives these modes to be founded upon the imposition of a subject-oriented and manipulative state of being upon the world. This is not necessarily because these modes of engaging reality are overtly repressive but because they are unreflective and so incorporate phenomena into predetermined frameworks of activity. Heidegger maintains that this conception of Being, and the mode of existence which is its correlate, is inappropriate and inadequate for determining the nature of human being and the relations between individuals.[20] Moreover, it is also inadequate for the determination of the nature of "things" encountered in the world.[21]

It is this problematic mode of relating to reality, then, that conditions ontologies based on substance, not only in their analyses of human being and world but likewise in their formulations of Being. The perfect substance, God, is modeled after the self-givenness that represents the present-at-hand but is removed from the sphere of contingency and dependency. It is projected to an "infinite" quantitative removal from the world of sense-experience that engenders it. This hypostatization and reification of the Divine or Absolute serves to remove it from the sphere of human concern and obviates the need for an inquiry into Being. Thus "'Being' itself does not affect us . . . the possibility of a pure problematic of Being gets renounced in principle."[22]

In Heidegger's analysis, this renunciation of ontological inquiry has as its concomitant the instatement of the *cogito*, or ego, as the arbiter of truth.[23] This does not simply mean that God is lost and that fallible man replaces him. Rather, it means that the mode of relating to things as present-at-hand, based upon the perspectives and frames of reference that condition the ego's reality, becomes entrenched and dominant. "Because truth now means the assuredness of presentation-to, or *certitude,* and because Being means representedness in the sense of such certitude, man, in accordance with his role in foundational representation, therefore becomes the subject in a distinctive sense."[24] When Being comes to be understood as a distinct and distant entity, the problem of *modes* of being becomes neglected. This serves to inhibit the reflection of the subject upon its own existential modes. Ironically, the privileging of the subject is simultaneously a closure of the subject.

The main conclusions to be drawn from Heidegger's critique of Descartes, and generally of ontologies based on substance, are as follows. There is an intrinsic interrelationship between the conceptualization of Being, world, and human existence. Our modes of apprehending and relating to the world are conditioned by the manner in which Being is preconceived. The conceptualization of Being is congruous with the disclosure of reality within specific interpretive frameworks. If Being is reified and isolated from human existence in the world, then the problem of *how* things are disclosed, determining their immediate presentations, becomes obscured. This "how" is representative not only of conceptual structures but of existential structures, that is, of modes of being. With the repression of the ontological dimension of inquiry, determined frameworks of experiencing others and things in the world become closed and fixed. On this level, when things are taken as present without attention to antecedently operative frames of reference, truth is relegated to the sphere of the adequation of subject and object.

Heidegger's ontology operates at the intersection of two opposing conceptual tendencies. It is essential to overcome the diremption of Being from beings and from the existential sphere in general, yet the *difference* between Being and beings must be maintained. Without overcoming the barrier between Being and beings evident in ontologies based on substance, the former is cut off from human and worldly concern and becomes irrelevant. Without the difference between Being and beings, one loses access to the problem of modes of being. Being is understood as another determinable entity or is simply reduced to beings as present. The alterity of Being, as the modality of the disclosure of beings, opens the possibility of developing a critique of fixed apprehensions of beings based upon entrenched paradigms and worldviews. Therefore, in opposition to ontologies of substance, Heidegger argues that "'Being' cannot have the character of an entity."[25] Being is no kind of substance or entity at all, not some "thing" that can be referred to in itself.

As this point one may follow Theodor Adorno and inquire: If Being is not an entity, and is not simply a concept, what significance does the term have?[26] Adorno's criticisms of Heidegger are, in one respect, more sophisticated than many, for he begins by emphasizing the need for a dereification of the conceptualization of reality and acknowledges that Heidegger undertakes such a de-reification. Yet Heidegger dwells on the term *Being*, which as de-reified and desubstantialized can have no discernible referent and therefore seems to be meaningless. Adorno accuses Heidegger of basing his thought upon a linguistic fabrication which is completely removed from concrete reality and which resists any conceptual clarification.[27]

The premise of Adorno's critique is that Heidegger's notion of Being is one that is radically *choris*, separated from the reality of extant beings or entities.[28] As a self-enclosed term with no application to an entity or a concept, Adorno argues, Heidegger's *Being* leaves "us empty-handed but for the self-sameness of the mere name."[29] What remains is vacuous verbiage that subsists in its own self-referential universe of discourse. Adorno indicates Heidegger's position concerning the "primacy of language" as furnishing the device for maintaining this linguistic pose.[30] These and other such arguments lead Adorno to conclude of Heidegger that "his definitions turn into moments of Being itself, and thus into things superior to [human] existence. Their astral power and glory is as cold to the infamy and fallibility of historic reality as that reality is sanctioned as immutable."[31]

These comments are important for a number of reasons. In general they provide a forceful and apposite indictment of those types of ontology that fix Being apart from the flux of existence. Adorno highlights the necessity of taking history seriously as something intrinsic to the nature of Being and of developing ways of thinking that have existential and historical application. Here, in fact, Adorno parallels Heidegger's critique of Descartes and substance-based ontology and also articulates some of the concerns of the present work. Yet Adorno's criticisms reveal an incomprehension of the central characteristics and orientations of Heideggerian ontology.

Adorno focuses upon one side of an ambivalence that may be discerned in Heidegger's thinking concerning the relation between Being and beings. There is in fact an irrefragable presence in Heidegger's work of a recurring tendency to isolate Being from beings. However, such a tendency is profoundly self-contradictory in relation to Heidegger's ongoing articulation of a temporal and disclosive ontology.[32] Adorno ignores Heidegger's oft-repeated definition of Being as the "Being of beings," which, if understood, provides an interpretive key that places many of his seemingly cryptic statements in a new light. Primarily, it indicates the relevance of the question of Being to the problem of the existential modalities of human beings. If ontological inquiry grants access to the problem of modalities, to the way people shape their activity and experience within the world, then it has *everything* to do with concrete existence, including its historical dimension.

Since Being is the Being of beings, Heidegger's ontology is inseparable from existential inquiry.[33] Yet this attention to the existential does not involve a reduction to the individualism that has come to be associated with existentialism. Rather, ontological inquiry develops by means of an analysis of the existential phenomena that transcend the individual as such. Among these phenomena, as we shall see, language is of uppermost importance. This means that, *pace* Adorno, Heidegger's attention to the nature of language does not represent a flight from reality but instead connects ontological inquiry to historical existence. These points require elaboration, and so first we shall turn to the problem of human existence and its relation to ontological inquiry; then we examine more specifically the problem of language.

Ontology and Existence

Throughout his writings Heidegger stresses that *human* and *Being* are correlational terms. The initial articulations of this interrelationship take the form of the "existential analytic" of *Being and Time*, which is predicated upon accessibility to the question of Being occurring by means of an inquiry into being-in-the-world. Heidegger employs the term *Dasein*, literally "there-being," to express the nature of human being as what is both "placed" in the world and as the "place" where Being is disclosed.[34] Human beings, with their capacity for reflexive consciousness, are the beings for whom Being is an *issue*.[35] This means both that humans ask about "What is?" and that their own being remains open to question by not being given in a fixedly determined form. Therefore, *Dasein* is the "ontological being."[36]

Heidegger states that "only as long as *Dasein is* (that is, only as long as the understanding of Being is ontically possible), 'is there' Being."[37] Noteworthy here is the fact that the German expression *gibt es Sein*, which is normally translated as "is there Being," can be translated literally as "it gives Being." The latter meaning is emphasized by Heidegger in a subsequent comment on the above statement.[38] The dual meaning of the statement counteracts interpretations which conclude that Being is simply the "product" of humans. Rather, human existence provides the location where Being is "given" or where the "lighting" (*Lichtung*) of Being occurs. This lighting is synonymous with a process of active and creative disclosure. Such disclosure, however, is irreducible to the willful productive activity of human beings because we act and are formed within the matrices of modes of disclosure and of worlds that have already been disclosed. Indeed, when human existence becomes locked within fixed subjective frameworks conditioning the relation to reality, our activity constricts and obscures as much as it discloses Being.

In later writings, although the term *Dasein* is dropped, the same intrinsic correlationality of the human and Being is expressed. For example, Heidegger states that "man and Being are appropriated to each other. They belong to each other."[39] Elsewhere he emphasizes that "as soon as I thoughtfully say 'man's nature,' I have already said relatedness to Being. Likewise, as soon as I say thoughtfully: Being of beings, the relatedness to man's nature has been named."[40] This correlationality is not a matter of the subsequent interaction of two antecedently determined entities. Rather, both humans and Being are themselves consituted by means of, and within, active relational processes of becoming.[41]

The relation between humans and Being is not extrinsic to the nature of each, and so we might speak of an *intrinsic* relationality. Schrag, in making a similar point, states that he prefers the term *vectorial* to describe the manner in which human existence is constituted within a series of relations.[42] However, the term *rela-*

tional should suffice so long as it "is divested of the accumulated metaphysical and epistemological underpinnings that have traditionally defined the 'problem of relations.'"[43] What Schrag primarily wishes to avoid is the confinement of human relationality to Being within the subject-object framework, and in this he is closely allied with Heidegger.

What precisely does it mean to say that humans and Being are correlational? This question can best be addressed by means of an inquiry into the ontological dimension of human existence. This dimension can be approached through the analytical distinction between the ontological and the ontic, which permeates Heidegger's work but is given only indirect formulations.

As mentioned earlier, the notion of the ontic is related to the apprehension of things as immediate or present-at-hand. Heidegger also gives expression to this mode of experience by the term *worldview*, which is "a positing knowledge of beings and a positing attitude toward beings; it is not ontological but ontic."[44] This "positing" mode of apprehending and relating to things, and to reality in general, imposes interpretations upon things in a more or less covert manner. The constrictions placed upon the interaction with things will not necessarily be conscious but derive from a lack of reflection upon the interpretive modes governing one's activity. By linking this positing to worldview, Heidegger indicates that there will be a generally interpretive framework of apprehension constricting and determining ontic modes, and this framework will possess a shared or cultural dimension. Things are defined and used only to the extent that they fit into a predetermined world of significance. This worldview provides the parameters of how things will be disclosed.

Heidegger argues that "the ready-to-hand is always understood in terms of a totality of involvements."[45] These "involvements" need not be "grasped explicitly" by the individual concerned, that is, they may be unconscious to a greater or lesser extent. Indeed, this unconscious state of involvement with the ready-to-hand is the "very mode in which it is the essential foundation for everyday circumspective interpretation."[46] Thus, this problem of interpretation is not confined to specialized or unusual instances of experience. All "everyday" engagements with things, and with others, are formed by the operation of interpretive factors based upon the way in which we are involved with those things or persons.

Such antecedently operative interpretive factors are expressed by a number of interrelated terms. "In every case this interpretation is grounded in *something we have in advance*—in a *fore-having.*" It is also grounded by "*something we see in advance*—in a *fore-sight,*" and finally by "*something we grasp in advance*—in a *fore-conception.*"[47] These aspects of antecedently operative interpretations indicate that the level on which Heidegger is speaking is not confined to purely conceptual issues. Being-in-the-world, and the participation with otherness which this involves, is itself interpretive. This interpretive nature will manifest itself not only in the way things are "understood" but also in the way they appear and are used. As Heidegger concludes, "an interpretation is never a presuppositionless apprehending of something presented to us."[48]

The fundamental problem with the ready-to-hand is not that it contains interpretive elements. It is rather that, in taking things as "presented" or as "immediate," the ontic mode represses the function and effects of interpretation. By denying that there is an interpretive and perspectival nature to all immediate experience, the individual who relates to things ontically becomes fixed in a specific mode of being. This does not mean that the individual or group whose activity is determined within a specific ontic mode cannot engage in complex acts of thinking and doing. Rather, it means that this activity operates within predisclosed parameters and channels. Such activity remains valid only so long as the overriding paradigm remains valid, that is, only so long as it has not been shown to be overlimited and distorting or is not misapplied to an inappropriate area of experience.

To question the necessity and legitimacy of ontic modes, to ask if the Being of things might not be otherwise disclosed, is to move from the ontic to the ontological. Such a transition takes its starting point from an analysis of the mode in which Being has been "projected" upon entities. It must inquire into the conditions and restrictions governing relational apprehension on an ontic level, and on that basis it opens the question of alternate possibilities of disclosing Being.

> Entities "have" meaning only because, as Being which has been disclosed beforehand, they become intelligible in the projection of the Being—that is to say, in terms of the "upon which" of that projection. The primary projection of the understanding of Being "gives" the meaning. The question about the meaning of the Being of an entity takes as its theme the "upon which" of that understanding of Being which underlies all *Being* of entities.[49]

This indicates the interrelationship that exists between the ontological and the ontic. The transition from the ontic to the ontological is not like moving from point *a* to point *b*. They are not two distinct realms but rather two modes of experiencing and relating to the world. Any ontic apprehension is founded upon a mode of disclosure, that is, it has an ontological basis. Any comprehension of the ontological, that is, the modality of disclosure of things, must take as its starting point a given ontic apprehension.

Ontological inquiry seeks to undermine the closure of ontic modes through playing upon the "gaps and points of openness" within the ontic. As Hart argues, ontological thinking does not require a determined ground in subject, object, or Absolute but rather emerges from the temporal "recoiling" or play in the disclosure of entities.[50] Heidegger's statements concerning "mirror-play," or *Spielraum*, are applicable within this context.[51]

Ontological inquiry is predicated upon the fact that, as Schrag states, Being is "anisotropic rather than isotropic in nature."[52] That is, Being is such as to be disclosed in different ways in relation to the perspectives brought to bear upon things. Ontological inquiry plays upon the differences inherent in the ontically given to inquire about the constitution of those differences. It seeks to move from the reification of a single ontic perspective to the critical interaction of multiple apprehensions of reality. This creates an "openness," or a "space," in the relation to things in the world, which Heidegger expresses by means of terms such as the *rift* (*der Riss*),[53] and the *open* (das Offene).[54] The latter term is particularly relevant to Heidegger's analysis of the problem of disclosure.

To pursue these matters, it becomes essential to examine more closely the "points of opening" in the worldly existence of human beings. As we know, Heidegger calls *Dasein* the ontological being, and we need now to examine some of the factors that make this so.

Humans and World

EMBODIMENT

Heidegger uses the expression "being-in-the-world" (*in-der-Welt-Sein*) to designate the constitution of human existence and activity within the contexts and relations of inhabited "worlds." Indeed, "a bare subject without a world never 'is' proximally, nor is it ever given."[55] The term *world*, of course, is polyvalent and even ambiguous. A clarification of Heidegger's use of the term is provided by Schufreider, who argues that "'world' is employed to signify the *a priori* nexus of relations which, as a context, must not be confused with any thing within the world nor with things taken as a whole."[56]

There is a general level of being-in-the-world that expresses the embodiment that is a necessary and determining characteristic of human existence. This embodiment has as its correlate the participation, with others, within various forms of natural and artificial environments. More specifically, therefore, the term *world* refers to the structures of meaning that are created through cultural and historical activity. Let us first examine the ramifications of embodiment on a general level and then turn to the more specific formations of worlds as cultural matrices of existence.

The irreducibility of embodiment, and the participation within encompassing existential matrices which this implies, is expressed by the term *thrownness*, or the state of being thrown (*Geworfenheit*). The primacy of the subject is severely compromised by the fact that one becomes an individual only by participation within a world not of one's own making. It is impossible to isolate the nature of human beings from their development within relational contexts. "An entity of the character of Dasein is its 'there' in such a way that, whether explicitly or not, it finds itself (*sich befindet*) in its thrownness."[57]

The term *thrownness* has often been understood to express the meaninglessness and oppressive givenness of human existence.[58] Such interpretations are related to arguments that Heidegger's is "a philosophy of despair" whose logical consequences are "pessimism and nihilism."[59] Certainly thrownness is a matter which, when acknowledged, dampens the self's illusions of unrestricted hegemony. Thrownness indicates an inherent *dependency* on the part of humans, which is all the more disturbing for the lack of a postulated transcendental referent for this dependency. To exist within Being means not to depend upon an alterity that is determined as an entity but to exist within a series of encompassing matrices that are themselves interpretively determined. This means that understanding oneself involves attention to the relations these matrices engender.

To understand the irreducibility of contextuality in its various forms, however, is the antithesis of nihilism. The latter, it may be argued, derives from the unilateral domination by the subject in relation to posited "objects," which denies the autonomy of the other.[60] By contrast, *die Geworfenheit* means that the authority of the subject is inadequate to the determination of Being and truth. Human existence, and the human capacity for truthful disclosure, are constituted within matrices of alterity. "The world, Dasein-with, and existence are *equiprimordially disclosed*" (*gleichürsprunglichen Erschlossenheit*).[61] We come to know ourselves, and indeed *become* ourselves, by active relationships with others in the world. An awareness of this impels the subject beyond herself or himself, potentially leading to relationships of reciprocity rather than domination.

One of the irreducible characteristics of existence as thrownness within the world is temporality. The visions of Being and truth as eternal or at least extratemporal, and of time as a trap or fetter, which tend to characterize traditional metaphysics, add to the apparently pejorative connotations of thrownness. However, as we have noted, temporality and Being are closely linked in Heideggerian ontology. Indeed, it is temporality as a governing quality of being-in-the-world that makes possible a transition from ontic to ontological forms of inquiry.

TEMPORALITY

We have argued that the ontic mode of apprehending reality "fixes" entities in the world as objects present-at-hand. This clearly does not mean that ontic modes of Being are not also temporal but rather that the form of temporal experience endemic to these modes will be constituted by what Heidegger refers to as the "succession of a calculable sequence of nows."[62] In ontic modes of experience, time is experienced within the determined framework of the means-end relationship governing the matter at hand. A determined subject deals with a determined object that is present to it in a serial-temporal manner. This makes of time something extrinsic to existence and to the constitution of entities within existence.

Heidegger, however, articulates an alternate form of the experience of temporality that does not simply place ontically apprehended objects within a process of succession. In developing this latter notion, which he refers to as "primordial" temporality, Heidegger argues that "temporality is the primordial 'outside-of-itself' in and for itself."[63] It is this being "outside of itself" that indicates the connection of temporality with a distanciation from an immersion within the immediacy of ontic interpretations. This removal from immediacy is predicated upon the human experience of time as something not simply given as a linear succession of "nows" but as incorporating an inherent complexification of experience by the admixture of modes of past and future within any "present." This complexification allows for an *ecstasis*, or "standing outside," of immediacy. "We therefore call the phenomena of the future, the character of having been, and the Present, the *'ecstases'* of temporality."[64] The expression *threefold* (*dreifach*) is also used to indicate the codetermination of the three temporal *ecstases*.[65] Any experience of presence is interlaced with and mediated by elements of "absence" derived from the persistence of what has been and the anticipation of what may be.

Because of the abiding quality of the past, "Dasein . . . *is* as having been."[66] The past, as something that is both personal and cultural, is not simply left behind like a set of tracks. It continues to have an efficacy in the present in a variety of ways, for example, by conditioning and focusing one's perceptions, interests, and biases. This efficacy should not be understood in a causal-deterministic manner, both because the influences of the past are manifold and variable and because the past is itself only one of the three temporal *ecstases*. The abiding of "what has been" adds new dimensions of interpretation to the participation in the present. That is, "what has been presences, but in its own way. In what has been, presencing is extended."[67] It may be seen that the notion of "what has been" is relevant to a treatment of the problem of history, although Heidegger does little to develop this side of the matter. We shall defer a discussion of what he does have to say until we address the issues of the collective and cultural dimensions of existence.

Of the three temporal *ecstases*, the one to which Heidegger gives priority is the future.[68] He emphasizes that the "not yet" is constitutive of *Dasein* to such an extent that, without this futural dimension, human beings would not be what they are.[69] In other words, the nature of human being is to have a forward-looking and uncompleted character. There is an element of the "still outstanding" which makes of human existence a creative and disclosive activity. "It is essential to the basic constitution of *Dasein* that there is constantly something still to be settled."[70] Again, such futurity, potential, and concomitant incompleteness are not simply extrinsic to human being. Rather, as Hart expresses it, "man's *being* is unfinished."[71] Futurity is a defining characteristic of human nature.

The futurally constituted nature of human existence provides an integral part of Heidegger's arguments concerning the ontological dimension of existence. Futurity means that the individual possesses the potential to be distanced, to a greater or lesser degree, from an immersion in the present. The plans and goals that shape our participation in the present remove us from immediacy, and serve to introduce an active dimension to being-in-the-world. One's vision of what may be induces a shaping and transforming of what is. There is a noncoincidence of human existence with its immediate environment that Heidegger expresses as "transcendence."[72] This is not an otherworldly transcendence but is rather a capacity for distance and freedom *within* the finitude of existence. Richardson's term *finite transcendence* is apposite in this respect.[73]

COLLECTIVITY

The "being ahead of itself" of human being is something that "does not signify anything like an isolated tendency in a worldless subject, but characterizes Being-in-the-world."[74] This does not mean that the individual is not characterized by autonomy, uniqueness, and creativity but rather that the individual is not "self-constituted." The "transcendence" *Dasein* exercises in relation to ontically given things is not based upon the presumed superiority of the alienated individual subject. It is a transcendence of immediacy and of the closure of the subject based on the relational activities of being with other. Heidegger emphasizes that the world of *Dasein* is a *Mitwelt*, a "with world," and that "*Dasein* in itself is essentially being-with [*Mitsein*]."[75] The very constitution of human beings, Heidegger argues, is based upon cultural interaction, and here he is in agreement with a variety of social theorists.[76] The participatory nature of human existence does not designate the grouping of fully formed beings, for the human self is shaped only in relation to others. "Being-with is an existential characteristic of Dasein even when factically no Other is present-at-hand or perceived."[77]

Because being-with is endemic to human existence, that is, because individuals are constituted through their reaching out toward others, "care" (*Sorge*) is an essential human characteristic. "If Dasein-with remains existentially constitutive for Being-in-the-world, then . . . it must be interpreted in terms of the phenomenon of *care*; for as 'care' the Being of Dasein in general is to be defined."[78] Although care is a general characteristic of human being, Heidegger limits it, along with the term *solicitude* (*Für-sorgen*) to the description of human relationships. He uses the term *concern* (*Besorgen*) to describe the relations of humans to things.[79]

While the term *care* generally has a positive connotation, it tends to be more value-neutral and inclusive in Heidegger's use. It primarily serves to indicate that human existence is characterized by participation and interaction, a reaching out beyond the self in some form, and an interest in others. Thus, while care and solicitude certainly can be positive attributes indicative of altruistic relations to others, they can also indicate an interest that represses and uses others. Speaking of solicitude, Heidegger argues that "it can, as it were, take away 'care' from the Other and put itself in his position in concern: it can *leap in* for him."[80] This form of being-with-others appears when an ontic mode of apprehension determines one's relations to others, limiting them to the form of "handy" items which one encounters and makes use of: "In such solicitude the Other can become one who is dominated and dependent, even if this domination is a tacit one and remains hidden from him. This kind of solicitude, which leaps in and takes away 'care,' is to a large extent determinative for Being with one another, and pertains for the most part to our concern with the ready-to-hand."[81]

These various inimical manifestations of care provide an indication of the contradictions inherent in *Mitsein*, that is, in sociocultural existence. While socialization is essential to human existence, it is also the source of pervasive distortions and constrictions in the experience of reality. A number of commentators have noted that while Heidegger strongly emphasizes the participatory and relational constitution of the human as an irreducible "being-with," he fails to develop the implications of this argument.[82] Instead, Heidegger focuses upon the pejorative aspects of social reality as repressive and constrictive of the human disclosure of Being.

Heidegger employs the term *das Man* to represent the "leveling out" tendencies of social reality. This expression, translated by Macquarrie and Robinson as the "they" or "they-self," is literally rendered as "one." The meaning of this "one," as well as its constraining influence, has been well expressed by John Fowles in his description of a British embassy dinner: "It was symptomatic that the ubiquitous person of speech was 'one'—it was one's view, one's friends, one's servants, one's favorite writer, one's travelling in Greece, until the terrible faceless Avenging God of the Bourgeois British, One, was standing like a soot-blackened obelisk over the whole evening."[83] This passage provides a graphic example of the force exerted by the anonymous "one," a force that will operate differently in various cultural-historical locales but seems to be a general characteristic of modern societies.

In Heidegger's analysis, the influence of *das Man* is directly connected to the closure of interpretive frameworks of existence. "The 'they' prescribes one's state-of-mind, and determines what and how one 'sees.'"[84] How the individual interprets reality has to do not only with understanding on an abstract level but with action and existence. Thus "the 'they' prescribes that way of interpreting the world and Being-in-the-world which lies closest," and this creates the "referential context of significance" that governs our interaction with the entities we encounter.[85] Heidegger refers to the immersion within the interpretive modes of Being prescribed by *das Man* as "the '*falling*' of Dasein."[86] This expression conveys the ethical dimension of the problem of closed interpretive modes of existence.

The interpretive constraints of *das Man* are manifest in the very forms of language-use in which individuals participate. Heidegger uses the term *Gerede*, or "idle talk," to describe the form of language that falls prey to the givenness of accepted interpretations and continues to foster those interpretive modalities. He makes clear that idle talk is not meant to describe an isolated tendency within everyday language-use but is reflective of a dimension of language in general. "In language," he argues, "as a way things have been expressed or spoken out [*Ausgesprochenheit*], there is hidden a way in which the understanding of Dasein has been interpreted."[87] Idle talk, however, has a specific association with the "fallen" mode of *das Man* because it wards off alternate possibilities of discourse. It creates a closed interpretive world that excludes the possibility of being challenged by the unfamiliar and alien. When discourse becomes "idle talk," Heidegger argues, "it serves not so much to keep Being-in-the-world open for us in an articulated understanding, as rather to close it off, and cover up the entities within the world."[88]

Moreover, this delimitation of existential interpretations places constraints upon the nature of the self as much as it conditions the way the self interacts with the world. "The Self of everyday Dasein is the *they-self* [*das Man-selbst*], which we distinguish from the *authentic Self*."[89] The interpretive determinations exercised by *das Man* upon the individual repress the potential for an "authentic Self" by delimiting and curtailing existential possibilities. The standards of "what one does" and "what one thinks" become determinative of the individual's mode of being, closing off other possible modes. "The 'they' has always kept Dasein from taking hold of these possibilities of Being. The 'they' even hides the manner in which it has tacitly relieved Dasein of the burden of explicitly *choosing* these possibilities. It remains indefinite who has 'really' done the choosing."[90] The determining force of *das Man* has a pervasive character, and precisely because of this it is difficult to determine the source of the dominant modes of being in a given culture. The individual is relieved of the burden of making decisions on fundamental (i.e., ontological) levels, and yet it is not some other individual who assumes this burden. An inertia of reified cultural forms delimits the existential sphere.

What is the nature of the authenticity *das Man* subverts? *Being and Time* develops the notion of authenticity by means of the quality of *Entschlossenheit,* or "resoluteness." This term, particularly in its English translation, appears to indicate a self-sufficient and determined assertiveness that counteracts the dissolution of the "they-self." However, Heidegger emphasizes that resoluteness, as he employs the term, is "a distinctive mode of Dasein's disclosedness."[91] Therefore, authenticity does not describe a self-certain individuality but rather "the opening up of human being."[92] There is an illuminating relationship between the German terms *Entschlossenheit* (resoluteness) and *Erschlossenheit* (disclosure) that supports the interpretation. As Albert Hofstadter has pointed out, *"Entschlossenheit,* if taken literally, would mean 'unclosedness.'"[93] Thus, the dispersion in *das Man* represents a closed ontic mode of Being, which Heidegger describes as "perverting the act of disclosing [*Erschliessen*] into an act of closing off [*Verschliessen*].[94] By contrast, the authenticity that is its antithesis is a disclosive and "opening" mode of Being.

From the fact that authenticity is not indicative of a closed mode of selfhood but of a disclosive openness, it follows that "others" are essential to its cultivation. Heidegger does not seek to formulate an antithesis between dispersed collective existence and authentic "individuality." Authenticity, as well, is a mode of *Mitsein.* Although this follows directly from Heidegger's arguments concerning the constitution of *Dasein* as necessarily a *Mitsein,* he has difficulties articulating the basis for the latter form of existence. Heidegger dwells upon the pejorative aspects of the public realm as it functions to circumscribe existential possibilities. This leads him to neglect his own arguments that authenticity will not have its basis in the isolated individual but in an alternate form of relational mode.

One possible means of addressing these issues is indicated in Heidegger's discussion of historicality. The inherently temporal and collective nature of being-in-the-world indicates, by extension, the historicality of existence. As Heidegger emphasizes, "historicality is a determining characteristic for Dasein in the very basis of its Being."[95] As with the analysis of temporality, the phrasing indicates that historicality is not extrinsic to *Dasein* but is essential to our ontological constitution.

The ontological nature of historicality, which includes the reflection upon history as well as the activity that constitutes historical events, makes possible a distanciation from the immersion in the "present." Thus, "the temporality of authentic historicality . . . *deprives* the 'today' of its character *as present*, and weans one from the conventionalities of the 'they.'"[96] Historicality and historical understanding provide a complexification of existence and understanding that acts critically to liberate one from an ontic immersion. Thus Heidegger indicates the connection of historical inquiry with ontological inquiry. A reflection upon the alternate modes of understanding and Being derived from historical existence provides a possibility for counteracting the closure of *das Man*. This is a point that will be developed extensively by Gadamer.

The significance of historical understanding, or "historiography," is that it permits a distanciation from an immersion in immediacy. When historiography is neglected, *Dasein* becomes immersed within the trajectory of specific interpretive schemes that lead to the entrenchment of the closed public world of *das Man*. Yet while Heidegger's analyses of this problem are apposite, they remain undeveloped, and this leads to serious problems in the understanding of the relationship between history and social existence, on the one hand, and ontological inquiry, on the other.

For example, Heidegger expresses a mistrust of cultural forms that are historically transmitted and may be called "traditions." Here his approach parallels that found in the analysis of *Mitsein*. That is, while stressing the irreducibility of the social and the historical, Heidegger tends to focus on the manner in which these phenomena obstruct understanding and constrain existence, and

hence his treatment of the problems of culture and history are formulated in almost entirely pejorative terms. He argues that *Dasein* "falls prey to the tradition of which it has more or less explicitly taken hold." This falling results in the determining and
limiting of the possibilities of human existence. The freedom to
fulfill the potentiality of *Dasein* is diminished because "tradition
keeps it from providing its own guidance, whether in inquiring or
in choosing."[97] While this argument is sound, it expresses a specific one-sided focus of concern within the complex phenomena
associated with tradition. This tends to curtail Heidegger's analysis of historically and culturally transmitted forms.

We have argued that the authenticity that counteracts the closure of *das Man* is characterized by an openness that permits the
disclosure of Being. This openness likewise is representative of a
transition from an immersion within an ontic interpretation to
an awareness of the ontological, by which alternate interpretive
modes may be disclosed. Here it becomes essential to turn to an
aspect of being-in-the-world that is fundamental both to the constitution of the ontic and to the liberation by means of ontological inquiry. This is the problem of language, which becomes increasingly important to Heidegger's ontological inquiry as his
work develops and provides the basis for the conjoining of hermeneutics with an approach to truth as disclosure.

Language

Being and Time formulates a distinction between two modes of
language-use that provides a guide for our inquiry. In section 33 of
that work, Heidegger distinguishes between the apophantic, or
assertive, use of language, on the one hand, and the hermeneutic,
on the other. It should be noted that this differentiation does not
parallel that made between *langue* and *parole* by Ferdinand de
Saussure. The latter differentiates between the systematic and
structural nature of language as a whole (*langue*) and the specific
utterances or instances of linguistic expression (*parole*).[98] Heidegger, however, differentiates between two modes of discourse that
are operative on the level of *parole*. Both the apophantic and the
hermeneutic modes refer to ways in which language is actively
employed.

Heidegger analyzes three significations contained in the notion
of assertion: pointing out, predication, and communication.[99] Although each of these forms has a different function, they share the

quality of focusing upon a determined object of discourse. When something is pointed out it is immediately approached from a particular point of view based upon the subject who is pointing, and possibly as well by the one to whom the pointing out is communicated. Predication serves to clarify and further determine the act of pointing out. Hence Heidegger offers a general description of assertive language as "a pointing-out which gives something a definite character and which communicates."[100]

Assertive discourse represents the everyday mode of language that is indispensable for practical affairs. Heidegger does not attempt to challenge its validity as such but rather seeks to uncover what remains presupposed and "unthought" in assertive usage. He argues that any such apophantic determining of an object in an assertion necessarily occurs within the framework of pregiven views and perspectives: "When an assertion is made, some foreconception is always implied; but it remains for the most part inconspicuous, because the language already hides in itself a developed way of conceiving. Like any interpretation whatever, assertion necessarily has a fore-having, a fore-sight, and a foreconception as its existential foundations."[101] Pregiven perspectives and modes of relational apprehension, which are determinative of the ontic, are revealed as functioning within language itself.

Assertive language, while essential for practical purposes, is incapable of elucidating its interpretive foreconceptions. Assertive language is closely allied with the mode of apprehending things as ready-to-hand, that is, as objects determined by their utility within a specific means-ends scheme.[102] Because the ends that govern it are both predetermined and, to a greater or lesser extent, covert or unconscious, assertive langauge has an obscuring effect. It does not permit a transgression of its interpretive frameworks or an inquiry into the manner in which they constellate objects. The most extreme form of such limitation and distortion is represented in idle talk, but this is not its only form.

Because apophantic discourse is founded on interpretation, Heidegger argues that hermeneutical language possesses ontological priority. "The assertion cannot disown its ontological origin from an interpretation which understands. The primordial 'as' of an interpretation (hermeneia) which understands circumspectively we call the 'existential-hermeneutical "as"' in distinction from the 'apophantical "as"' of the assertion."[103] It is in this sense that the apophantic use of language may be said to be "derivative" of the hermeneutic. Apophantic language always points to something *as* this or that, that is, as interpretively delimited and determined. Hermeneutical language inquires into the manner or mode in which things are grasped *as* this or that, that is, into the frameworks governing the disclosure of beings.

It is significant that Heidegger speaks of an existential-hermeneutical *as*, thereby indicating that the form of interpretation to which he refers has to do with being-in-the-world. The hermeneutical *as* articulates the modality of our existence and relationships. As Otto Pöggeler has stated, "The hermeneutic *as* . . . is proper to our concernful dealing with what is."[104] Hermeneutical language is relevant to our care, to the modes in which we understand and relate to others. It probes beneath the surface of the ontically given and provides a means of disclosing, and potentially transforming, the manner in which our relations are interpretively constellated. Precisely how such transformation may be effected is a matter that occupies the remainder of this work.

After *Being and Time,* the distinction between hermeneutic and assertive language-use receives no further attention. However, it remains informative for the subsequent development of Heidegger's thinking concerning language. For the most part, Heidegger's later work on language simply is not concerned with assertive language-use, and he tends to ignore the more immediate aspects of language as they are manifested in everyday communication. Rather, it is the level of inquiry here designated as hermeneutic that remains the focus of concern.

The actual use of the term *hermeneutic* becomes infrequent in Heidegger's later work. In one instance, he states that his use of the term *hermeneutics* does not denote interpretation theory in the strict sense, but rather expresses "the bearing of message and tidings."[105] Hermeneutics, Heidegger emphasizes, has to do with the disclosure of Being, rather than with the merely technical processes of textual exegesis. This is based on the understanding that being-in-the-world is itself linguistic. "Language has the task of making manifest in its work the existent, and of preserving it as such."[106] The extrapolation of hermeneutical inquiry beyond the technical rules of exegesis, and the turn to language as relevant to ontological-existential concerns, is highly significant. Yet Heidegger's explicit statements concerning hermeneutics indicate a neglect of the relationship between the ontological and disclosive nature of hermeneutics and its more traditional function in relation to texts. Conversely, in practice Heidegger participates extensively in textually based hermeneutics as a means of pursuing ontological inquiry.

There are two main forms of this applied hermeneutics. One of these is an ongoing critical analysis of moments in the history of philosophy, which is related to a project of "overcoming metaphysics." This project will be discussed in some detail in chapter 3. The other is what Heidegger calls the "dialogue between thinking and poetry," which takes the form of hermeneutical reflection upon a number of poetic works.[107] Many of Heidegger's most important insights into the nature of language appear within the context of these reflections.

For example, Heidegger uses an interpretation of a Stefan George poem as a basis for exploring the relationship between language and Being. Each has to do with the appearing and "showing" of things, yet neither can be grasped as things themselves. "A thing is not until, and is only where, the word is not lacking but *is* there."[108] Yet the "is there" of the word, or language, is not of the same order as the "is there" of the thing. This is where the linguistic and the ontological are conjoined. "As with the word, so it is with the 'is.' It belongs no more among the things that are than does the word."[109] Therefore, as we said earlier of Being, so we should say of language that "it gives" (*es gibt*).[110] Language allows things to be presented, to appear *as* something, and it is formative of the modality of this *as*. This is not, as Adorno would have it, a form of linguistic idealism. Rather, it means that human beings interact with things in the world by means of interpretations. Things are not given in a purely objective manner, but through language and, more specifically, through culturally formed worlds of discourse.

This indicates an additional point that requires elaboration. That is, language is not simply a human "product" or "tool." The most obvious sense of this is that language is not the product of the individual: it is historical and cultural by nature and therefore transcends any instance of individual use. As Cassirer points out, "Language arises not in isolated but in *communal* action. . . . Language as a *sensorum commune* could only grow out of the sympathy of activity."[111] The communal or collective development of language through the course of time also indicates its *historical* nature. Heidegger argues that "all language is historical," emphasizing that this is the case "even where man does not know history in the modern European sense."[112] The cultural and his-

torical character of language means that it shapes the worlds inhabited by human beings. It is formative of the matrices within
which the individual lives and is shaped.

If we accept these views, does it remain possible to view language as the product of a series of individuals interacting over the
course of time? This would still make of language a human tool
that functions to enable communication between constituted
subjects. However, since the individual is formed within a series
of interactive relationships within the world, and since language
is constitutive of the modalities of these relations, it cannot be
reduced to a merely functional item. In other words, the development of language in the course of cultural-historical activity is
formative of the subjects who engage in that activity. "The ability
to speak is what marks man as man. This mark contains the design of his being. . . . Language, in granting all this to man, is the
foundation of human being." [113]

Human existence involves relations to the "other than human," that is, to the "world" as such and to things within it as
well as to other human beings. Because language is formative of
our active relations, it is disclosive of being-in-the-world. "Language, then, is not a mere human faculty." [114] It transcends the human as such and grants access to the relational modes in which
worlds have been disclosed, that is, language grants access to ontological inquiry. Stated otherwise, "language is the precinct
(*templum*), that is, the house of Being," [115]

The fact that language is formative of modes of Being, and
opens the possibility of transforming those modes, indicates, for
Heidegger, the need for a "listening" to language. [116] This allows
for an exposure to alterity that expands and enhances our understanding of what is, allowing a release from closed ontic modes.
Listening means being open to the aspects of language that sur-
pass subjectively intended uses. It means attending to the nonliteral, suppressed, and "unthought" dimensions of words, texts,
and traditions.

Heidegger attempts such forms of listening in his readings of
poets and philosophers, but he neglects many of the technical
considerations that are essential to these hermeneutic endeavors.
Language, in any of its forms, is not transparent in its meaning,
but rather is polysemous, frequently obscure, and lends itself to
multiple interpretive disclosures. Indeed, the anisotropic nature
of language parallels the nature of Being and allows for the transcendence of closed ontic interpretations. However, this semantic

pluralism, its relationship to interpretive perspectives, and the conflicts of interpretation which this produces are issues not addressed by Heidegger. His work indicates the relationship between Being and language but neglects the specifically hermeneutical considerations that arise from this relationship.

For the moment, these explicitly hermeneutical issues must be deferred. The ontological underpinning of Heidegger's theory of truth as disclosure has now been articulated. In the following chapter, as this theory of truth is analyzed, hermeneutical questions will once again come to the fore. Following this, we shall be able to develop a more detailed analysis of the issues and problems concerning the relationship between hermeneutical inquiry and truth as disclosure.

3

TRUTH AS DISCLOSURE: HEIDEGGER

Correspondence and Disclosure

"ONCE KNOWN, truths acquire a utilitarian crust; they no
longer interest us as truths but as useful recipes. That
pure, sudden illumination which characterizes truth
accompanies the latter only at the moment of discovery.
Hence its Greek name *aletheia*, which originally meant
the same as the word *apocalypsis* later, that is, discovery,
revelation, or rather, unveiling, removing a veil or cover."[1]

This passage was written by Ortega y Gasset in 1914, and it anticipates many of the insights that were developed more extensively
and systematically by Heidegger. Like Ortega, Heidegger draws
upon a particular etymological rendering of the Greek *aletheia* as
a means of explicating the disclosive dimension of truth. *Aletheia*, Heidegger argues, means "unhiddenness," and this tells us
something essential about the nature of truth.[2]

Approaching this disclosive dimension serves to articulate the
creative nature of the experience of truth. Moreover, it renders access to the problem of the operation of conceptual and existential
contexts in the delineation of the frameworks within which particular truth-statements subsist. The strength of the approach to
truth as disclosure is found in its capacity to bring to light these
constitutive dimensions of disclosure while maintaining a basis
in lived experience or being-in-the-world. This, as we shall see,
permits a critical and transformative approach to the problem of
truth.

Heidegger introduces the argument for truth as disclosure by indicating the limitations of correspondence theories, which are determined by "the kind of relation that obtains between the statement and the thing."[3] In the light of the problem of "modes of relation," the complexity of these issues should be evident. Relations to things are mediated and directed in a number of possible ways because of the interpretive effects of foreconceptions.

One of the main ways in which Heidegger describes the relationship to things and to worlds is in terms of the form of openness to what is presented. He makes reference to the open region within which the appearance of things becomes manifest, "the openness of which is not first created by the presenting but rather is only entered into and taken over as a domain of relatedness."[4] This open region designates the interpretive stance that informs the perspectival apprehension of any given object. A somewhat pedestrian example of this would be the different modalities of interest, openness, and contextualization brought to bear upon the same piece of landscape by a tourist, an artist, and a real estate developer. Each of these modes allows for the disclosure of the given reality in a different manner, highlighting different aspects of the nature of the thing. The problem of the region of openness within which reality is encountered and determined manifests itself in a variety of such relatively uncomplicated instances. However, in matters of human concern, where less obvious and more elusive perspectives and biases are involved, the problem becomes increasingly complex.

Modes of relationality, or being open, antecede any specific and determinable existential encounter or experience. That is, the open region is a necessary dimension of the human capacity to relate hermeneutically to a world and to others and hence to have any form of experience. The specific determinations that any given region exhibits, however, are not given a priori in the Kantian sense. As Kockelmans points out, these determinations are formed within a "matrix of relationships."[5] The perspectives and interests that constitute modalities of openness and relationality are themselves formed within existential relations. They are cultural and historical as well as individual and biographical and therefore appear to operate naturally and independently. Nevertheless, they are actively constituted within temporal reality and therefore are subject to potential transformation.

Heidegger's argument is that prior to any possible experience of truth as the correspondence of entity and idea there must be a constitutive region of disclosure that informs the specific mode of apprehension of the given. In other words, no judgment can be made in a manner that is purely objective and context-free. This is especially relevant to the question of truth as applied to human relations, where a great many interpretive factors are formative of the open region involved. To address this issue, the focus of inquiry must be shifted from the truth of objects as ontically given to the truth of the interpretive bases of disclosure. "A statement is invested with its correctness by the openness of comportment," argues Heidegger. Therefore, "what first makes correctness possible must with more original right be taken as the essence of truth."[6]

The "more original" essence of truth appears as the modality in which things are disclosed. When entities present-at-hand are judged in terms of correspondence or agreement, they have already been subjected to an interpretive process that presents them *as* this or that. Schürmann develops this point with specific reference to its social-historical dimensions in arguing that "*aletheia* is to be understood in terms of economies of presence."[7] The originative nature of *aletheia* has to do with its expression of the mode in which things come to presence: "origination means multiple presencing."[8] Hence "disclosure" has the same relationship to "correspondence" as the ontological does to the ontic, and as hermeneutic language has to assertive language. In each case one does not shift from one type of givenness to another but rather from an unreflexive representation of things to an inquiry into the interpretive modes by which things are presented.

The relationship between disclosure and the ontological has been developed by Richardson. In explicating Heidegger's argument that "truth as conformity presupposes another type of truth," Richardson points out that conformity, or correspondence, "does not make its object accessible but presupposes its accessibility."[9] This presupposition entails the rigidification of a specifically determined framework of disclosure, producing what Richardson terms *ontic comportment*. This mode of comportment remains within a predisclosed region of openness, and establishes truth within the confines of this disclosure, resulting in *ontic truth*. By contrast, Richardson employs the term *ontological truth* to refer to the process of disclosure itself, within which ontic truths are conditioned. Ontic truths are not necessarily invalidated by ontological truth. They are both clarified and relativized

by the process of attending to the presuppositions upon which
they are based. Ontological truth refers to the validity of the "unveiling" that antecedes ontic modes of comportment. Therefore,
"this unveiled-ness is the truth of Being, sc. ontological truth."[10]
Richardson's analyses help to clarify the significance of Heidegger's statements concerning "the ontologically derivative character of the traditional conception of truth."[11]

Heidegger argues that truth, like Being, must not be reified, for
this serves to obscure the processes of disclosure. To reify "disclosure" as itself the "nature" of truth would be to make of it another of those "useful recipes" of which Ortega y Gasset speaks.
We should follow H. Pietersma, then, and understand Heidegger
as developing "a theory about the nature and conditions of the
search for truth" rather than as providing a fixed "theory of
truth."[12] This inquiry into "conditions" is also an inquiry into
"modalities," since the constituent elements of disclosure are
ways of being rather than fixed categories.[13]

Human existence is not such as to remain in encounters determined by immediacy and presence but involves elements of distance, temporality, activity, and interpretation. These distancing
factors allow for freedom to disclose reality creatively. However,
Heidegger's arguments concerning the ontic and the present-at-
hand indicate that forms of disclosure can become ossified and
obstruct further disclosive processes. Perspectives and judgments
concerning entities in the world emerge from the relations of human beings with those entities. This relational process discloses
or "uncovers" a partial aspect of the thing involved. Once such
disclosure has occurred and has become culturally functional and
accepted, the emergent process tends to become forgotten or denied. Thus a specific interpretive disclosure comes to be apprehended in a mode of "presence," repressing its representational
nature. "The relation itself now acquires the character of pres-
ence-at-hand by getting switched over to a relationship between
things which are present-at-hand. The uncoveredness of something becomes the present-at-hand conformity of one thing which
is present-at-hand—the assertion expressed—to something else
which is present-at-hand—the entity under discussion."[14] Both
the object and the assertion concerning it are frozen in a static
referential relation that obscures the *mode* in which the object is
being disclosed. Hence although an element of ontic truth may be
found within the confines of the presuppositions of a specific

mode of disclosure, the deeper question concerning the truth of the frameworks and interpretations governing that disclosure remains unasked.

The Nature of Disclosure

To develop these points, we need now to pursue some of Heidegger's central arguments in the essay "On the Essence of Truth." Following the discussion of the "more original" form of truth as the "open region," Heidegger directly turns to the problem of freedom. He expresses this in what may initially appear to be a paradoxical manner by arguing that "to free oneself for a binding directedness is possible only by *being free* for what is opened in an open region." [15] From this it is concluded that "*the essence of truth is freedom.*" [16] The paradox here lies in the connection of freedom with a "binding directedness," which would appear to represent a contradiction in terms. What type of freedom is Heidegger referring to, and what is the significance of the relation of this freedom to truth?

The matter is clarified by recalling that human existence is characterized by an intrinsic relationality, that is, by a being with others that requires some form of care. From this it follows that truth appears as a relational process. It involves a self-limitation and a compromise of one's limited standpoints based upon sensitivity and openness to other beings and to alternate modes of Being. "All human actions and attitudes," argues Macomber, "involve an intrinsic reference to an 'other.'" [17] Freedom, therefore, does not exist in a vacuum but manifests itself within the context of a world in which the individual develops and gains understanding only in relation to others. This is why one frees oneself for a binding directedness. Freedom involves becoming aware of one's modes of relationality to others so that these are not locked within conditioned frameworks of disclosure. This awareness facilitates the development of choice concerning those modalities and opens possibilities of ameliorative transformation.

The connection of freedom with an openness to alterity is emphasized by Heidegger's statement that "freedom for what is opened up in an open region lets beings be what they are. Freedom now reveals itself as letting beings be." [18] Freedom is irreducible to acts of self-assertion and domination that repress others. Rather, freedom appears as a mode of being that cultivates self-awareness and the fruition of selfhood as it allows others to become what they are. Freedom is connected to an authentic selfhood predicated upon openness and disclosure. In many respects Heidegger's notion of freedom as letting-be may be understood in the light of Erikson's notion of "mutuality."[19]

Nevertheless, this notion of "letting beings be" may have a disturbing quality, particularly when taken out of context. Does it not seem to advocate a passive and accepting stance toward reality, abrogating the task of critically transforming things as they are? Commentators such as Palmer, for example, have argued that Heidegger's work reveals a tendency to view human being in too passive terms.[20] More pointedly, Fackenheim has derided the Heideggerian philosophical and existential position as "a 'composure' that 'lets things be.'" Such a stance, argues Fackenheim, is particularly inauthentic and harmful given the demonic nature of twentieth-century history. Such a letting-be indicates an acquiescence and a complicity in these events.[21]

These criticisms of Heidegger, in relation to his work in general, are at least partially accurate and apposite. This is because of the ambivalence noted in the previous chapter, one side of which expresses tendencies in Heidegger to despair of any willful human activity and to turn to "Being without reference to beings." This despair in itself is not groundless given that the evils emphasized by Fackenheim and others are the product, to some extent, of the will to dominate and to repress others. Yet a passive stance does little to transform things for the better. Perhaps, however, we need not remain trapped within a simple antithesis between willfulness and passivity. There may be modes of willing which do not involve the negation of alterity but which foster the growth of individual freedom and directedness in terms of mutual relations. It is this latter interpretation that best describes Heidegger's particular statements concerning the freedom to "let be."

Letting-be, as it appears in the context of Heidegger's analysis of truth and freedom, has little to do with a passive acceptance of what is and what has been. Letting-be applies to the manner in which things are "allowed" to be disclosed, that is, to the modality of relational comportment by which one participates in reality. Macomber has addressed this issue, although perhaps he turns too much in the opposite direction in stating that "letting beings be in this sense does not entail a passive or disinterested attitude toward them; it is not synonymous with letting *alone* but with the letting-be of the fiat."[22]

While Macomber's rejection of the identification of letting-be with "letting alone" is essentially correct, his reference to a fiat on the part of humans courts subjective idealism. This loses sight of the contextual and relational bases of human existence Heidegger emphasizes and addresses. Heidegger's argument seeks both to establish the need to allow a space, or open region, for things to disclose themselves and to analyze the active manners in which this openness is conditioned and informed by interpretive factors. "Letting-be, i.e., freedom, is intrinsically exposing, ek-sistent. Considered in regard to the essence of truth, the essence of freedom manifests itself as exposure to the disclosedness of beings."[23] Objects have their own reality, and to speak of a fiat on the part of humans is inaccurate. Yet people will always be engaged in letting beings be because for us the nature of things becomes manifest only in relation to our activity and understanding. Therefore, rather than attempting to deny and suppress the active human element in the disclosure of beings, Heidegger is calling attention to it and indicating the need for a clearer understanding of its interpretive nature.

Actually, Heidegger is more concerned with being misunderstood as developing a subjective idealism rather than a realism characterized by a passivity in the face of "things as they are." He raises the possibility that his statements might entail the subjectivization of truth and argues vehemently against this interpretation.[24] The disclosure of reality through human interpretations does not entail the subjective *determination* of truth.[25] The orientation of Heidegger's work leans neither toward the subject nor toward the object but to the relational processes of disclosure. Yet this is not to say that, in practice, he has resolved the difficult problem of ensuring that this middle way of openness is always maintained.

The relational nature of truth, which results neither from the "positing" activity of the subject nor from the apprehension of the object "in itself," is evidenced by the "eventful" nature of the experience of truth. An event involves the "discovery" of something in the course of active engagement with things in the world and is predicated upon the differentiation of entities inherent in the relation. An illustration of this appears in Heidegger's discussion of "brokenness," which indicates how the subject becomes trapped within fixed relational modes and may be liberated therefrom by unintended and accidental encounters or turns of events.

Heidegger uses the term *referential context* to describe the encompassing projects or assignments within which human beings relate to things. This term parallels the notion of worldview mentioned in the previous chapter. The referential context will be determinative of the manner in which a thing, in this case a tool, will be implemented as ready-to-hand. As long as the tool is in its proper place and functions normally, the frame of reference operative in one's relation to it will remain automatic and unconscious. However, "when something ready-to-hand is found missing, . . . this makes a *break* in those referential contexts which circumspection discovers."[26]

The pattern or framework within which a tool normally operates is suddenly disturbed, and a gap appears in one's immediate world of activity. The usual reaction to such an occurrence is often simply frustration or anger. One wishes to reinstate the normal functioning of implements as rapidly as possible in order to get on with things. Yet Heidegger stresses that *"when an assignment has been disturbed*—when something is unusable for some purpose—then the assignment becomes explicit."[27] This "making explicit" is related to a process of "laying open" or "disclosure."[28] In this way a habitual mode of relational activity that conditions the manner in which things are disclosed is itself disclosed. This occurs not through willful activity but by coming up against the "worldliness" of things when, by hazard, they disrupt the pattern of activity in which they have been incorporated. This example is instructive in a more far-ranging manner than its commonness might indicate. It illustrates the function of differentiation and otherness in disclosive processes, although naturally it does not follow that "accidents" are the only means whereby this can occur.

Heidegger develops an understanding of truth-disclosure that places it firmly within the context of finite human existence. Truth appears as a relational process whereby aspects of reality continue to be disclosed through being-in-the-world. This means that truth as experienced by human beings is not finalized and closed. This lack of finality means that there is always an element of "hiddenness" remaining in any disclosure. "Untruth" (*Unwahrheit*) abides in any finite experience of truth, and so "Dasein is equiprimordially in the truth and in untruth."[29]

There are two senses in which a dimension of untruth is present in any human experience of truth. One of these is that "precisely because letting-be lets beings be in a particular comportment which relates to them and thus discloses them, it conceals beings as a whole. Letting-be is intrinsically at the same time a concealing."[30] Here, untruth is associated with the concealing that abides in any revealing, because of the necessarily partial nature of the latter. Unlike coherence-oriented theorists, Heidegger is not arguing that truth is found only in the "whole." Rather, truth has the form of an ongoing process. We cannot grasp things in a final and total manner because there remain alternate perspectives and frameworks of interpretation that evoke further disclosure. "Each being we encounter and which encounters us keeps to this curious opposition of presence in that it always withholds itself at the same time in a concealedness."[31] Truth does not appear as the certainty of immediate presentations of a thing because this illusory certainty freezes a specific ontic mode of apprehension. The "otherness" that remains endemic to the thing stimulates the continual supersession of closed relational modes.

The first form of untruth derives from abiding concealment and indicates that even valid interpretations of a phenomenon will not be final and definitive. From this it follows that truth is not found in closed certainty but in continual inquiry and openness. The second form of untruth is somewhat more obvious and lies in the fact that a thing often "presents itself as other than it is."[32] Heidegger distinguishes the first sense of untruth as the "not yet disclosed" from this second sense of untruth as a false presentation, or "dissembling" (das Verstellen).[33] This distinction allows Heidegger to maintain a critical dimension in his thinking concerning truth. The containment of untruth within truth and concealment within disclosure do not make all presentations of a thing equally valid.

An awareness of "abiding concealment" functions to maintain a critical relationship to finite forms of disclosure. It allows representations of a thing that are dissembling, or simply inaccurate, to be checked in terms of their capacity to further or to inhibit meaningful disclosure. Heidegger speaks of an "inappropriate certainty" functioning to block openness to new disclosure and reifying inadequate representations of a thing. "In inappropriate certainty, that of which one is certain is held covered up."[34] This form of certainty freezes a particular interpretive apprehension of an object, blocking ontological inquiry into the modality conditioning that form of disclosure. To offset this tendency, Heidegger calls for the continual reappropriation of "what has already been uncovered," which serves to "defend it against semblance and disguise."[35] Here semblance and disguise are not merely the undisclosed remainder of any disclosure but refer to the artificial closure of a determined mode of representation.

We can see how truth as disclosure is inseparable from both on-tological inquiry and hermeneutic language-use. Each requires a transition from a closed mode of relating to things as given to an inquiry into the mode of openness that conditions this giveness. Just as assertive statements are founded upon interpretation and just as ontic representations are founded upon ontological modes, so too is the experience of truth as correspondence founded upon a framework in which entities are disclosed. We need now to in-quire more closely into the problem of gaining access to modes of disclosure.

Disclosure and Artwork

Thus far, the phenomenon of disclosure has been discussed in terms of the interpretive modes of relational comportment that delimit the manner in which reality is actively engaged by human beings. On this level of inquiry, disclosure refers to the nexus of interpretive foremeanings that are operative in all interactions with others. Admittedly, it is difficult to grapple with the prob-lem of the explication and transformation of modes of disclosure on this abstract level. There is a need to concretize the inquiry by attending to objectifications of modes of disclosure in order to gain access to those modes. It may be recalled that the inter-pretive and disclosive frameworks articulated by Heidegger oper-ate on a cultural and historical, rather than a purely individual, level. This means that cultural or collective products may grant access to the modalities of disclosure that are operative in their formation.

In general, the concern of the present work is with linguistic embodiments of cultural activity. Our approach to the problem of modes of disclosure focuses upon a hermeneutic of language and linguistic works. This is clearly in accordance with Heidegger's emphasis on language as the place where Being is disclosed. How-ever, along with his inquiry into language, Heidegger has also de-voted attention to the problem of truth in the graphic arts. Since a number of seminal insights emerge in these aesthetic reflections, it will be helpful for the more general inquiry into hermeneutics to pursue briefly some aspects of the relationship between truth-disclosure and the artwork.

In his essay "The Origin of the Artwork," Heidegger asks: "How does truth happen?" He responds that there are a number of essential ways in which truth happens and then introduces his immediate line of inquiry by stating that "one of these ways . . . is the work-being of the work."[36] The expression *work-being*, with its active verbal quality, expresses the creative and emergent nature of the occurrence of truth Heidegger perceives in the work of art. This active nature has more than one dimension of significance. Heidegger tends to focus upon the struggle involved in the processes of artistic production. The activity here occurs between the artist and the materiality of the work. However, there is an additional active dimension to the experience of truth in the artwork that occurs in the relation of the work to the one who experiences it. The work remains actively disclosive once it has been completed. Art provides us with an "objectified" or "projected" focus of disclosure, but it does not fix the disclosure in a final manner. Instead, "the work opens up a *world* and keeps it abidingly in force."[37] The "abiding" and "preserving" accomplished by means of the artwork should not be confused with a static maintenance of fixed representations of reality. It is the keeping open of a place or world that engenders transformative experience.

What is the significance of the work of art as an abiding place of disclosure for the problem of the interpretive nature of the relation to reality? The mode of openness that is determinative of specific apprehensions of things is not something to which the individual or the group has immediate access. This openness takes the form of interpretive foremeanings that condition the mode of being of the subject so that the individual is unable to distance himself or herself from this manner of interpreting. As Kockelmans argues, "The opening of the open and the clearing of beings come to focus only when the openness is . . . projected."[38] He further argues that art provides one such form of projection. This point has also been made by Weinsheimer, who states that "in order to interpret ourselves we need to interpret art." Since we are not "present to ourselves, we need an other through which to understand ourselves."[39]

It would be misleading to conceive of the projection or objectification that occurs in the artwork simply in terms of the concretization of pregiven modalities of disclosure. While both Kockelmans and Weinsheimer are correct in emphasizing the need to work through the alterity of art in order to gain access to disclosive modes, this alterity must not be conceived simply as a "mirror" of the self. Just as art is inadequately understood as a "mirror of nature," so is it equally diminished and deformed if seen as an exteriorization of subjectivity (whether of the artist or the interpreter). Disclosure occurs actively, in relations, and art is a relational process.

"The artist is the origin of the work," yet equally "the work is the origin of the artist."[40] Insofar as art is a *doing*, it is itself a means whereby disclosure *happens*. The coming-to-be of the artwork involves a tension between the human and the nonhuman, between the disclosive capacities of the artist and the medium and subject matter of the work. Indeed, in this relational activity there emerge aspects of the artist's being that are not present to consciousness. What the artist is, *qua* artist, appears and articulates itself by means of the creative activity of art. The otherness of the artwork is the product of this conjunction of diverse aspects of reality. The world that is disclosed in the artwork appears *between* human and other. Schufreider sheds light on this matter by arguing that the artwork provides a place for the "instantiation" of ontological truth in the "midst of beings."[41] It allows the mode of disclosure, that is, the ontological level of truth, to appear ontically among beings. The artwork creates an "ontological" place that is "thinglike" and so maintains disclosure in an abiding and accessible way.

There is a struggle and tension inherent in the work-being of the artwork, and this parallels the creative tension between truth as disclosure and untruth as the not-yet-disclosed. Heidegger does not express this in terms of an encounter between ontological and ontic. Instead he states that "truth is present only as the conflict between lighting and concealing in the opposition of world and earth," arguing further that this conflict is "established in the work."[42] The term *earth* expresses that which is both sheltering and concealing, that is, whatever in a given instance acts as the ground or basis for emergent disclosure.[43] This would include given cultural formations upon which the creative work draws, "as of drawing water from a spring."[44] The term *world*, in this case, specifically refers to the creative disclosure that occurs in the artwork.[45] Creative disclosure requires an existential basis in cultural worlds that have become established. Yet it also challenges the fixity of given forms of cultural reality by means of an innovative and transformative opening of previously unknown vistas. This creates a tension that provides the dynamics for disclosure. The particular work of art will not, as Hofstadter emphasizes, "express" its solution to that tension but will itself *be* the solution.[46] The tension is not dissolved but is creatively articulated in the production of new visions of reality.

One may refer to the creative results of the tension of the artwork, as does Biemel, as an "excess" or "surplus" that is a "granting" and "bestowing."[47] Similarly, Hofstadter argues that artistic expression "is always an activity in which more is arrived at than is possessed to begin with and in which the point is to arrive at this more."[48] Here the "futural" dimension of the disclosure of truth is found to be intrinsic to the artwork. Its truth does not lie in the reproduction of reality but in extending it beyond the limitations of extant ranges of vision and understanding. The creative and productive qualities of the artwork should not be reduced to the literal fact that henceforth something new exists. This point has been made by Scharlemann, who argues that truth as disclosure transforms one's apprehension of what is and serves to awaken one "from an amnestic state in which what is there is not seen or noticed."[49] This provides a further clarification of the relationship between earth and world. Creative disclosure, whether effected by means of the artwork or otherwise, occurs through the interpretive transformation of what is there. Art provides the vision whereby repressed and unknown aspects of reality are unveiled, and this acts reflexively upon established worlds of meaning.

Some instructive examples of the artistic transformation of reality appear in Loren Eiseley's reflections on artistic genius. He points out that the artist has the power to illuminate dimensions of reality that are opaque or unknown to others. Through this illumination of the artwork, these realities can become at least partially opened and accessible. Eiseley evokes "the fairyland of *The Tempest*, the midnight world of Dostoevsky, . . . the blackbirds on the yellow harvest fields of Van Gogh."[50] Those who partake of the worlds made manifest in such works as these are granted an illumination that may continue to be active within their own experience. The opening of perception that may occur, for example, while standing before a Van Gogh painting may abide in one's subsequent perceptions of things. Without Van Gogh, states Eiseley, "we would have seen blackbirds and endured the depravity of our hearts, but it would not be the same landscape that the act of genius transformed."[51] Artistic vision is not simply a cosmetic gloss upon reality. Rather, artistic transformation of things reveals the constricted and distorting effects of practical everyday modes of interpretation.

The "sharable" character of the world disclosed by art indicates that it "extends into the interpersonal" and gives rise to "a world inhabited by human beings and constituted as such by meanings accessible to their minds."[52] Artistically disclosed worlds are not mere abstractions but relate to the existential worlds in which we live out our lives. As culturally produced, existential worlds share

with artistic worlds an origin in human relational activity. Therefore the truth disclosed by the artwork creates "a clearing which
is itself historical and governs the manner of unconcealment
which belongs to all beings in a historical age."[53]

These considerations provide an indication of the relations between disclosure, historical existence, and the interpretation of
inherited cultural forms. Theorists such as Gadamer and Ricoeur
draw upon Heidegger's work to develop an approach to disclosure
along more specifically historical and hermeneutical lines. However, Heidegger also introduces historical and hermeneutical elements directly into his analysis of disclosure, with rather different results from those obtained by Gadamer and Ricoeur. The
conflict between these latter theorists and Heidegger centers
around the issue of original truth and its devaluation of history.

Aletheia *and Original Truth*

PRE-SOCRATIC THOUGHT

An important dimension of Heidegger's thinking concerning
truth is articulated in his interpretations of the meaning of *aletheia* as it appears in some of the fragments of the pre-Socratics.
Heidegger views these texts as providing precedents for his own
arguments concerning truth as disclosure. As noted earlier, Heidegger follows Ortega y Gasset in arguing that *aletheia* (truth)
originally had a meaning close to "unveiling," and we saw that
this process could be understood as a mode of "origination." However, there is a significant difference between explicating an *unthought* dimension of a text and claiming that one has discovered
its historically original meaning. Heidegger indicates an awareness of this difference, yet in practice he does not consistently ad-
here to it.

Access to Heidegger's hermenuetical approach may be obtained
by following the line of inquiry he develops in analyzing the nature of early Greek thinking. In one instance he inquires into the
relationship between contemporary thought and the fragment of
Anaximander. He asks whether we are "latecomers" in the history of philosophy who can only catch glimpses of antiquity as we
head toward "an increasingly sterile order of uniformity." He continues: "Or does there lie concealed in the historical and chrono-
logical remoteness of the fragment something unsaid, something
that will speak out in times to come?"[54]

In asking this question, Heidegger touches upon a matter of

central concern to historical hermeneutics. Does the interpretation of works of the past simply highlight the paucity of contemporary thought and reinforce the status of contemporary thinkers as epigones? Or does the historical distance of present thinkers from the texts of the past provide the opportunity for a creative disclosure of new meaning and insight? Heidegger's affirmation of the latter possibility is pivotal and yields seminal results. Yet it should not be allowed to obscure the significant risks involved in attempting to disclose the new by interpreting the old.

An example of Heidegger's creative retrieval that is directly relevant to the issue of truth appears in his inquiry into the meaning of *Logos* in the fragments of Heraclitus. He asks the reader to consider the possibility that it is unwarranted to presuppose "that whatever Heraclitus says ought to be immediately obvious to our contemporary everyday understanding."[55] Perhaps the interpretations contemporary usage imposes upon terms is inappropriate to the divergent historical context from which the text emerges. Heidegger points out that a number of interrelated interpretations of *Logos* have prevailed in the cultural history of the West: *Ratio, Verbum*, cosmic law, the logical, reason, and so forth.[56] In contrast to these he develops an alternate angle of interpretation by exploring the connections between the Greek words *Logos* and *legein* (talking, saying). Such connections are not novel, they are also found in traditional interpretations. "*Logos* means *legein* as a saying aloud."[57]

However, Heidegger argues that an even "more original" meaning of *legein* is "to lay down and lay before."[58] Further connections of laying with "gathering" and "sheltering" are developed, pointing to the concern humans have for what lies before us.[59] The convergence of the two sets of meanings associated with laying and saying leads to a novel interpretation. "The saying and talking of mortals comes to pass from early on as *legein*, laying. Saying and talking occur essentially as the letting-lie-together-before of everything which, laid in unconcealment, comes to presence."[60] Hence *Logos*, as "laying before" and as language, expresses a process in which aspects of reality are brought into a state of meaningful presentation, or letting-be. *Logos* expresses a process of disclosure.

Being and Time provides an explication of the word *aletheia* that parallels the interpretation of *Logos* given here. *Aletheia*, truth, expresses a process of disclosure and indicates the existence of an inherent relationship between "being-true" and "being-

uncovering."[61] This provides the background for the connection
Heidegger establishes between the Greek terms *aletheia* and
Logos. "Because the *Logos* lets lie before us what lies before us as
such, it discloses what is present in its presencing. But disclosure
is *Aletheia*. This and *Logos* are the same."[62] Therefore "truth" and
"language" are interrelated: each represents processes whereby
Being is disclosed.

The Greek terms also lend themselves to an expression of the
dynamic tension between revealing and concealing in any process
of disclosure: "*Logos* is *in iteself and at the same time* a revealing and concealing. It is *Aletheia*. Unconcealment needs concealment, *Lethe*, as a reservoir upon which disclosure can, as it were,
draw. *Logos*, the Laying that gathers, has in itself this revealing-
concealing character."[63] Heidegger argues that the presence of
Lethe, concealment, within the term *Aletheia*, truth, expresses
something vital about the nature of the latter. Attention to the
concealment that abides within any moment of disclosure and
any presentation of truth serves to counteract the tendency to reify partial truths.

These points are further developed in the essay entitled "*Aletheia*," which examines the Heraclitus fragment normally translated as "How can one hide himself before that which never
sets?" Heidegger understands this question to contain a number
of insights related to *aletheia* as disclosure, despite the fact that
the term does not appear within the fragment.[64] The *lethe* within
aletheia is forgotten because of the common tendency to focus
upon what is present, that is, upon what has "come forward into
appearance and left concealment behind."[65] In relation to the fragment that is the focus of inquiry, Heidegger argues that the phrase
"not setting ever" (his rendition of "that which never sets")
points to the concomitance of revealing and concealing.[66] Furthermore, the relation of human apprehension to this disclosive process is pondered. This points to the revealing-concealing nature of
any human encounter with that which is disclosed or which
emerges into presence.[67] Translated into the terms of the present
work, this indicates that the interpretive grasp of anything "present" is necessarily partial and perspectival.

What needs to be attended to most carefully in these hermeneutical analyses is the application of a disclosive approach to
truth. By explicating the richness of the language of the text,
Heidegger displaces and augments standard interpretations of its
meaning. He is practicing a hermeneutic that allows the text to

disclose itself in new ways, thereby illustrating something of the manner in which disclosure occurs. Heidegger's interpretations seek to uncover meanings in the texts that are concealed by other forms of exegesis. This indicates the relationship of disclosure to the "angle of approach" or interpretive standpoint.

Like any interpretation, Heidegger's will conceal as it reveals. To approach the text in terms of its disclosive capacities is to abandon the paradigm of a one-to-one correspondence between an interpretation and the "thing itself." Heidegger need not claim that he has provided the definitive presentation of what Heraclitus, for example, "really meant." He asks whether Heraclitus intended his question to be understood "as we have been discussing it." Heidegger's response ("Who knows? Who can say?") expresses the autonomy of the text in relation to its author and the polysemy of its disclosive capacities in relation to the interpreter. He need only argue that "the fragment does say it."[68]

These hermeneutical considerations indicate that the validity of Heidegger's exegesis is not predicated upon his having arrived at the original meaning of the text. It is rather the case that the historical lateness of the present provides a hermeneutical vantage point that facilitates the disclosure of repressed and unthought dimensions of the text. The fragments of Heraclitus and other pre-Socratic thinkers can reveal insights into truth as disclosure. Yet this does not mean that the literally original notion of truth in Greek thought is identical with Heidegger's interpretation.

PLATO AND METAPHYSICS

As it turns out, Heidegger is inconsistent concerning the literal nature of his interpretations of the Greeks. In his essay entitled "Plato's Doctrine of Truth" he attempts to instate his interpretations of the pre-Socratics as reflective of the historically original meaning of truth in Greek thought. He perceives the displacement and subsequent falling into oblivion of this original notion of truth as occurring in Plato's *Republic*. This displacement is not carried out explicitly but appears in the "unthought" significance of the text. "What remains unsaid in Plato is a shift in the definition of the essence of truth."[69]

What is the nature of this transformation? Briefly, the core of Heidegger's argument is that the allegory of the Cave contains a hidden transition from a notion of truth (*aletheia*) understood as disclosure to a notion of truth as correspondence to the idea of the good. Heidegger quotes the *Republic* to the effect that the idea of the good "is itself master, dispensing both unhiddenness (to what emerges) and the ability to perceive (the unhidden)."[70] Here, truth is understood to be determined by a correspondence of action and thought to the transcendent given of the idea. This means, in Heidegger's interpretation, that "*aletheia* comes under the yoke of the idea. . . . The essence of truth relinquishes the basic feature of unhiddenness."[71]

In traditional interpretations of Platonic idealism, to which Heidegger here subscribes, the ideal forms exist independently of and antecedently to any human activity or conceptualization. Human pursuits, therefore, cannot be creatively disclosive of reality and truth but are only true insofar as they correspond to the pregiven idea. Heidegger accepts this standard interpretation of the *Republic*. He also commits himself to the postulation that before the development of idealism in the *Republic*, truth was quite literally understood as disclosure. A definite historical transformation is seen to occur in Plato's work. "Truth becomes *orthotes*, correctness of the ability to perceive and to declare something."[72] This orthodoxy takes the form of the reduction of truth to conformity with the heteronomous ideal. This provides the model for all subsequent developments of theories of correspondence, which are based upon the perception and declaration of what is in its apparent immediacy.

In the transition from *aletheia* to *orthotes*, the locus of truth is displaced from the *relational* disclosure that emerges through the interaction of human and world to the *positing* of the subject. This is because "as correctness of 'looking' truth becomes the label of the human attitude towards beings."[73] To be sure, in the type of idealism that is commonly perceived in the *Republic*, truth does not reside in the subject but in the idea itself. However, it is the subject who has access to the truth of the idea and determines which modes of Being conform thereto.

Because idealism incorporates a covert projection of the subject's attitudes and perspectives, Heidegger sees a continuity between Platonism and the positing of truth in the correspondence of object to subject in, for example, Descartes and Kant.[74] Indeed, the turn that occurs in the *Republic* is determinative for the history of Western metaphysics. This is summarized in the following passage, which explicitly indicates that an original notion of truth antecedent to Plato has been lost.

> Truth no longer is, as unhiddenness, the basic feature of Being itself, but it is, in consequence of having become correctness by

being yoked under the Idea, from this time forth the label of the recognizing of beings.

Since then there has been a striving for "truth" in the sense of correctness of looking and the position of the glance.[75]

Heidegger's remarks concerning the nature of idealistic theories of truth and their relationship to immediate (i.e., ontic) apprehension are cogent. Yet his interpretation of the *Republic* as presenting truth as correspondence to the idea is limited and closed. Moreover, the presupposition of a literally original notion of truth as disclosure in pre-Platonic philosophy is unfounded. In his hermeneutical analyses of the pre-Socratic fragments, Heidegger carefully distances himself from such a conclusion, yet here he resorts to it as a necessary component in his argument for a loss that is traced to Plato.

Two divergent hermeneutical approaches to the history of thought are evident in Heidegger's work. He articulates one form of hermeneutics in approaching the pre-Socratics and another in approaching Plato (and indeed all subsequent Western thought).[76] With the first, a contemporary perspective allows the disclosure of unthought dimensions of the text, drawing upon the richness of the language to ascertain meanings repressed by standard approaches. With the second, while also seeking to elucidate the unthought, Heidegger maintains a standard metaphysical interpretation of Plato. He uses this to illustrate the loss of the *contemporary* interpretation of pre-Socratic thought, which is now projected back as the historically original meaning.[77]

In the case of the *Republic*, some recent theorists have presented interpretations that shed new light on the text and qualify the standard interpretations in terms of idealism. For example, both Randall and Wolz point to the series of clearly *impossible* requirements necessary to the construction of the "Ideal state." The Guardians must be able to "apprehend the eternal and unchanging."[78] They "must have in their soul . . . a clear pattern of perfect truth."[79] They must shape themselves and other members of the state into conformity with "the vision of the ideal."[80] Other ludicrous requirements include "scraping clean" the canvas of society and human character,[81] and sending all citizens above the age of ten into the country and taking over their children.[82]

With respect to these stipulations Randall remarks that "here is obvious irony."[83] He further argues that "to the audience for which the *Republic* was first written, the perfect city of Socrates' ironical criticism could have had but one meaning: it was the Spartan ideal."[84] Similarly, Wolz argues that the absurdity of these requirements indicates the "mock seriousness" of Socrates' statements and should serve "to warn interpreters against taking the discussion of the *Idea of the Good* and its accessibility at face value."[85]

Another indication of the ironic nature of the *Republic* appears in the myth of Er, which appears in book 10. There we find the story of a recently deceased man who is given "first choice" from among a number of possible reincarnations. He immediately makes the horrible error of choosing "the greatest tyranny," having failed to observe that this "involved the fate of eating his own children, and other horrors."[86] The individual who makes this sorry choice is described as having "lived in a well-ordered polity in his former existence." He views this previous form of life as the *cause* of his woes, since the orderly state allowed him to participate in virtue "by habit and not by philosophy."[87] The "ordering from above" that characterizes the perfect state modeled upon the idea has the effect of inhibiting the individual's capacity to make wise decisions and to act responsibly.

The inclusion of the myth of Er at the end of the *Republic* reflects back upon the text in a critical and deconstructive manner. As Wolz notes, this ironic conclusion to a dialogue that presumably constructs a blueprint of a "perfect state" dramatically questions the value of such a state. "Instead of advocating the rule of philosopher-kings who would disburden us of the need to make vital decisions," Wolz argues, "we find Socrates trying to sharpen our wits so that we might learn to make such decisions ourselves."[88] In other words, as Randall states, the myth serves to make us "see."[89]

These analyses reflect upon Heidegger's arguments in at least two significant ways. First, they indicate that the statements concerning the hegemony of the idea cannot simply be accepted at face value without attention to the context of the work as a whole. If certain key characteristics of the work deconstruct the literal presentation of the ideal state, then the specific arguments associated with that state are subjected to reversal. Secondly, the ironic and deconstructive qualities of Plato's text are not didactic but are the result of a dramatic interplay that opens vision. The truth that emerges in the *Republic* is not based on conformity to the idea but has a dialectical, tensive, and relational nature.[90] We may accurately express the matter by saying that "Plato conceives of truth as an event."[91] Given the benefit of a careful hermeneutical retrieval, the *Republic* can itself present a theory of truth as disclosure. This interpretation would also be consistent with the arguments concerning the *Sophist* and the *Theaetetus* in chapter 1.

For our present purposes, Heidegger's attempt to instate disclosure as the original meaning of *aletheia* is of concern only insofar as it affects his hermeneutics of history and tradition. In itself, this attempt has been questioned by the close analyses of Paul Friedländer, who argues that the term *aletheia* is polysemic from its earliest use, with "unhidden" representing only one of several possible meanings.[92] Indeed, this criticism caused Heidegger to retract his arguments concerning unhiddenness, or disclosure, as the original meaning of *aletheia*.[93] Nevertheless, the *hermeneutical* value of Heidegger's interpretations of the pre-Socratics remains unaffected by this controversy. The analysis of these texts is not predicated upon the establishment of its definitive original meaning but rather occurs as the disclosive interaction of the text with contemporary thought.

CONCLUDING REMARKS

In his analysis of the *Republic,* Heidegger contradicts his own hermeneutical approach and lapses into a form of literalism. In so doing, his thinking becomes determined by a paradigm of "origins" that locates truth at the most incipient possible moment in the development of thought. All subsequent thought, beginning with Plato's *Republic,* takes the form of a "falling away" from the original insight into truth as disclosure. Thus, in contradicting his own hermeneutics, Heidegger simultaneously contradicts his arguments concerning the inextricable linking of Being with time, disclosure, and action. This is the point where the *ambiguity* that characterizes Heidegger's work profoundly affects the development of the hermeneutical and historical dimensions of truth as disclosure.

A severely curtailed hermeneutic of history is evident in Heidegger's reduction of the Western conceptual tradition to a closed metaphysics. In presenting his interpretation of metaphysics, Heidegger argues that, traditionally, "because Being itself remains unthought, the unconcealment of beings remains unthought."[94] This indicates that there has been an inattention to the problem of Being, that is, to the modes of disclosure of beings, in the history of thought. Yet this lack of explicit articulation and treatment of truth as disclosure does not mean that tradition is not itself disclosive. In other words, one can turn to Heraclitus, Plato, or to a variety of other seminal figures, and in the hermeneutical encounter disclosure can occur. Language has been, and continues to be, "disclosive of Being" in a manner that may supersede the intentionality of authors and the accepted interpretations of the history of thought. It is such an approach Heidegger exhibits in his exegeses of the pre-Socratics as well as in his interpretations of poetry.

However, in his arguments concerning original truth and the falling away from this origin, Heidegger blocks access to disclosure by means of hermeneutical inquiry. Rather than disclosing the potential dimensions of meaning that remain unthought in tradition, Heidegger inscribes truth *prior* to the bulk of historical and cultural developments in the Western world. "The omission of Being itself in the thought of beings as such is the history of the unconcealment of beings as such. That history is metaphysics."[95] Here we find a subtle but highly significant change in Heidegger's language and thinking. Being seems to be set apart as something that is not inherent in the process of the unconcealment of beings. This change means that Being is no longer conceived as the dynamic mode of disclosure that occurs through relational activity in the world. Being is hypostatized and somehow located *outside* history and language. It becomes something wholly other than beings. "As history, metaphysics keeps the truth of Being concealed in the unconcealment of beings as such. As the promise of its truth, Being keeps to itself with its own essence."[96]

Yet when "Being keeps to itself," we lose access to ontological inquiry into modes of disclosure. We are left with a mysterious nonentity subsisting apart from beings, as appears in Heidegger's later attempts to "think Being without beings."[97] This indicates the area where the forceful criticisms of Adorno become relevant, not in relation to the entirety of Heidegger's thought but to one of its two conflicting tendencies. Similar criticisms of Heidegger's ahistoricism, in relation to hermeneutics and tradition, have been formulated by diverse hermeneutical theorists. Gadamer, Ricoeur, and Habermas each have critiqued in different ways the closed and constricted interpretation of tradition that Heidegger constructs.[98] Gadamer, for example, describes Heidegger's quest for an "original" disclosure of Being in Greek thought as a "teleology in reverse."[99] In the same vein, a contemporary critic has argued that Heidegger's thought is characterized by "a persistently nostalgic orientation."[100] It is this nostalgia for an atemporal and ahistorical revelation of Being that contradicts, rather strikingly, Heidegger's emphases upon Being as the ground of temporal and relational disclosure.

Heidegger's hermeneutics of tradition is split by a conflict between disclosive and ahistorical tendencies. These contradictory tendencies likewise affect Heidegger's approach to truth as disclosure, since this is intimately linked to hermeneutics. It follows that the approach to truth as disclosure may be developed further by an attention to hermeneutical issues. Heidegger undertakes some work in this direction, but it becomes curtailed by his ambivalent relation to history and tradition. This ambivalence is at the heart of a number of related problems in Heidegger's work. Chapter 2 noted the undeveloped state of Heidegger's reflections on *Mitsein*, or collective existence. Here, and in some of his reflections on history, there is a tendency to confuse society and history with their present manifestations. Society is reduced to the closure of *das Man*, and history is reduced to the immediacy of twentieth-century trends. The latter form of reduction can lead to a conflation of history with a "destiny" that is taking shape in the contemporary world. If such a contemporary unfolding of destiny comes to be rejected rather than affirmed, then history in itself takes on a pejorative character because of its conflation with this rejected destiny.[101]

Heidegger loses sight of the potential sources of *alterity* embodied in the forms, particularly the linguistic forms, of historical-cultural existence. Considered in terms of the potential disclosure of alterity, history can become the catalyst for a critical reflexivity in relation to the forms of conceptual and social closure that dominate any mode of the present. The task of the remainder of this work will be to articulate and develop this critical dimension of historical inquiry. This is accomplished by attending to the hermeneutic dimension of truth as disclosure, which involves the creative and reflexive engagement with cultural forms.

4

HISTORICAL HERMENEUTICS AS A PROCESS OF DISCLOSURE: GADAMER

Ontology and Historicity

HEIDEGGER'S ONTOLOGY provides seminal articulations of the temporal-historical, linguistic, and disclosive nature of truth. Yet, in a self-contradictory manner, he describes the historical embodiments of language in tradition as a falling away from a historically original truth. One side of Heidegger's work focuses on Being and truth as the mode of presencing or disclosure, as the way that things "originate" for us in time and action. The other side focuses on Being and truth as "original," as something that is lost or forgotten in the course of time and in the disclosure of beings. These represent antithetical conceptual tendencies that maintain an uneasy relationship throughout Heidegger's work.

Hans-Georg Gadamer, whose work is greatly influenced by his onetime teacher, extends and develops Heidegger's insights into the temporal and linguistic nature of ontological disclosure. At the same time, Gadamer questions the countertendencies that appear whenever Being is posited as a suprahistorical and original source of truth.

Toward the center of *Truth and Method*, Gadamer formulates an argument that enables us to ascertain some of the parallelisms between his hermeneutics and ontological inquiry. Gadamer is discussing the nature of our understanding of historical realities, and he argues that within such processes of understanding "neither the knower nor the known are present-at-hand in an ontic way."[1] It will be recalled that the term-*ontic* refers to a mode of apprehending objects as "immediately" (i.e., unreflexively) given. To encounter something ontically is to hypostatize a particular interpretive standpoint in relation to that object. This usually will be a standpoint that has become entrenched through personal and social habituation. One relates to the matter at hand, which may be an object, a conceptual formation, or another human being, in a manner that is determined by an antecedent interpretive framework.

Where Heidegger uses the term *ontological* to designate the movement beyond closed ontic modes of seeing and acting, Gadamer employs the term *historical*. The above-quoted statement concludes with the argument that, rather than being "ontic" in nature, both knower and known "are of the mode of being of historicalness."[2] In the same vein Gadamer refers to Yorck's statement that "everything depends on 'the generic difference between the ontic and the historical.'"[3] The nature of historical understanding is not adequately conceived after the manner of the apprehension of determined substances, that is, ontically. For Gadamer, historical understanding is itself the means of transcending immediately given ontic apprehensions of a subject matter. The historicity of human understanding counteracts tendencies to view truth as a fixed representation of a perceptual given.

The focus of Gadamer's concern is texts as cultural and historical expressions, and so for him *historical inquiry* refers to text interpretation. Texts are historical both because they are produced within cultural frameworks, and because their meaning discloses itself in relation to historical-cultural standpoints. Moreover, attention to the historicality of the text contributes to the disclosure of the interpreter's own historically-related frameworks of interpretation. It is in a qualified sense, that is, in terms of hermeneutics, that Gadamer may be said to be engaged in historical inquiry.

While interpretation is historical, it is equally the case that access to history is necessarily interpretive. Gadamer is very close to Heidegger in arguing that "all experience in the world" is itself interpretive and so comes under the purview of hermeneutics.[4] This is why he maintains that "interpretation is not an occasional additional act subsequent to understanding, but rather understanding is always interpretation."[5] Throughout our analysis of hermeneutics, therefore, two interrelated senses of the term will appear. Hermeneutics refers both to acts of textual exegesis per se and to an inquiry into the interpretive nature of human self-understanding and modes of being. The former activity provides a means of revealing the latter. Because we are cultural and historical beings who exist within linguistically formed worlds, the interpretation of texts can disclose modes of being-in-the-world.

Gadamer distinguishes historical inquiry from the form of inquiry that seeks to establish definitive "historical objects." He argues that "true historical thinking must take account of its own historicality. Only then will it not chase the phantom of an historical object which is the object of progressive research, but learn to see in the object the counterpart of itself and hence understand both."[6] The interpretive nature of understanding is directly related to both the inquirer and the topic of inquiry necessarily being historically located. To posit a "historical object" which the inquirer can grasp as such presumes a completed or perfected understanding of history.[7] Because of the relational constitution of knower and known and because of the unfinished nature of the historical processes that shape each, "the true historical object is not an object at all, but the unity of the one and the other, a relationship in which exist both the reality of history and the reality of historical understanding."[8] An awareness of the codetermination of knower and known serves to keep historical inquiry open, since specific interpretations are not presumed to be objective. By contrast, the model of a historical object functions to reify a specific interpretive grasp and to inhibit further inquiry.

These arguments differentiate Gadamer's hermeneutics from traditional epistemologies. In the latter, the separation of epistemology from ontology sustains the notion of a context-free subject as the basis of knowledge. Both Gadamer and Heidegger challenge the validity of maintaining this separation, particularly when the object of knowledge is related to the existential and historical sphere. Gadamer notes that in Heidegger's work the disclosure of temporality as the "hidden ground" of *Dasein* results in "transcending thinking from the position of subjectivity," and he adds that this process of transcending is "an experience that Heidegger calls 'Being.'"[9] Ontological inquiry reveals that the subject is "in" time. This being-within-time is formative of the subject's modes of apprehending reality.

In Gadamer's work the reconnection of thinking and being, or epistemology and ontology, takes the form of historical inquiry. This inquiry addresses the problem of modes of Being by linking understanding to active, temporal, and linguistic being-in-the-world on a collective level, that is, to historicality. Hence the focus upon the terms *Being* and *truth* in Heidegger is shifted to *history* and *understanding* in Gadamer. These terminological shifts may serve to obscure the rootedness of Gadamerian hermeneutics in Heidegger's ontology of disclosure. Yet Gadamer remains concerned with developing an approach to truth as disclosure, accomplishing this by means of the interpretive processes of historical understanding.

This transposition of terminology explains why, as Bernstein notes, Gadamer never presents the reader with a "theory of truth." [10] Bernstein is correct in rebuking Gadamer for the lack of a clearer exposition of his approach to truth. However, the oversight is mitigated when we note that Gadamer's articulation of the nature and task of hermeneutical understanding *is* his theory of truth. Understanding is a process that occurs in relation to what has been disclosed through past cultural activity: it is historical. It functions within the linguisticality that characterizes historical knowledge and self-knowledge: it is hermeneutical. It provides a means of disclosing and transforming the finite perspectives of the inquirer: it is critical.

Gadamer uses the term *effective history* (*Wirkungsgeschichte*) to describe the process of cultivating an awareness of the ways in which understanding has been shaped by historical forces. Likewise, he refers to the dialogical form of understanding that emerges from such an awareness as "an effective-historical relation" (*ein wirkungsgeschichtlicher Vorgang*). [11]

> If we are trying to understand a historical phenomenon from the historical distance that is characteristic of our hermeneutical situation, we are always subject to the effects of effective-history. It determines in advance both what seems to us worth inquiring about and what will appear as an object of investigation, and we more or less forget half of what is really there—in fact we miss the whole truth of the phenomenon when we take its immediate appearance as the whole truth. [12]

The principle of effective history gives expression to the limiting forces that operate in any act of understanding. Gadamer historicizes the Heideggerian conception of foremeanings, arguing that such antecedent interpretive frameworks develop through historical existence. Effective history includes both the creative production of cultural forms, such as texts, that shape the worlds we inhabit, and the history of the *interpretations* of those texts. When we encounter a historical phenomenon, our perceptions will be influenced by the dominant modes of interpretation by which it has been culturally articulated.

An exhaustive knowledge of effective-historical processes is unattainable.[13] Therefore, the point of hermeneutics is not to attempt to transcend finitude altogether and grasp the whole nature of a subject without remainder. Rather, like ontological inquiry, historical consciousness disrupts the ossification of fixed ontic modes of apprehension by revealing the interpretive nature of understanding. The image of the whole functions heuristically to impel an ongoing supersession of specific finite perspectives.

Because of his attention to the diverse ways in which understanding is historical, Gadamer rejects any attempt to predicate truth upon a fixed origin. Unlike hermeneutical versions of the quest for original truth, which focus upon the author as the basis of a text's meaning, Gadamerian hermeneutics attends to the dynamic and reflexive dimensions of the process of understanding. Gadamer's critique of author-oriented hermeneutics emphasizes the importance of attending to historicality and its relationship to language as the key to developing reflexive understanding. A discussion of these issues provides a means of clarifying the nature of the problems that hermeneutical inquiry seeks to address.

Author and Text

SCHLEIERMACHER

Gadamer focuses upon Friedrich Schleiermacher in analyzing author-oriented hermeneutics, which he associates with a psychological approach.[14] Schleiermacher's work is enormously important for the development of modern hermeneutical theory, and Gadamer himself acknowledges a great debt to him. For our present purposes, however, the discussion of Schleiermacher will be confined to the problem of authorial intent.

As Kimmerle has argued, Schleiermacher's hermeneutics has generally been seen through the lens of Dilthey's "psychologistic" approach to understanding, which focuses upon the mind of the author.[15] Yet Kimmerle notes that there are also indications of a less psychologistic and more historically oriented hermeneutical approach in some of Schleiermacher's earlier writings. This point provides a more balanced understanding of the

Schleiermacherian corpus, which does not express a uniform position on the matter of the centrality of the author. At the same time, Kimmerle acknowledges that throughout his work Schleiermacher's conception of a universal hermeneutics "was linked to a . . . questionable view that hermeneutical method should not be concerned at all with the historical particularity of the item to be understood."[16] One may conclude that while Schleiermacher's hermeneutical work includes exceptions, the prevailing orientation is one that privileges the author over historicality.

The focus upon the psychology of the author is evident in Schleiermacher's repeated emphasis upon the need for the interpreter to "step out of one's own frame of mind into that of the author."[17] The hermeneutical task, for Schleiermacher, consists in working *through* the language of the text to the thoughts of the author, which are both the source of meaning and the goal of understanding. Hermeneutics consists of a "retracing" of the movement from thought to language. That is, "every act of understanding is the reverse of an act of speaking, and one must grasp the thinking that underlies a given statement."[18]

The view of language to which Schleiermacher gives expression makes of it a duplication of an ideational reality that is antecedent to and independent of linguistic expression. Yet it does not follow that for Schleiermacher hermeneutics is unnecessary. On the contrary, since "speaking is the outer side of thinking, hermeneutics is a part of the art of thinking."[19] However, Schleiermacher does not conceive of the object of hermeneutical inquiry as being attained *within* the encounter with language. The goal is already preestablished outside of linguisticality. Hermeneutics is merely the tool that is put aside when one has arrived at the non-linguistic origin and goal of understanding. For Schleiermacher, notes Palmer, "the task of hermeneutics came to be that of transcending language in order to get at the inner processes."[20]

In displacing language in this manner, Schleiermacher also displaces history. The truth of a text is found in the author's thoughts, which remain untouched and unaffected by the reception of others through the course of time. Historical change may affect the contexts of interpretation and the perspectives that are brought to bear upon the text, but it cannot alter the author's thoughts. Moreover, Schleiermacher presupposes "that the individuality of the author can be directly grasped" through a transhistorical meeting of minds.[21] Not only must the author's thoughts remain untouched by historical reality, but the inter-

preter is also characterized as an ahistorical being capable of transcending cultural and historical vantage points. The text and its
historical effects simply become stepping stones in this intersubjective process. As Gadamer argues, "Schleiermacher's problem is
not historical obscurity, but the obscurity of the 'Thou.'"[22]

In opposition to this approach, Gadamer points out that "not
occasionally, but always, the meaning of a text goes beyond its author."[23] Therefore, "the artist who creates something is not the
ideal interpreter of it." Once a work is produced, it becomes objectified, and is independent of its author. Hence the creator of the
work becomes one interpreter among others.[24] It is this historical
objectification that Schleiermacher and the romantics neglect,
and so "they oust the critique based on the understanding of the
object from the sphere of scientific interpretation."[25] With the
dismissal of the role of history in the understanding of language,
which is the "objectification" under consideration, the possibility
of critically transcending subjective standpoints is relinquished.

HIRSCH

In criticizing Schleiermacher for attempting to base "true understanding" of a text upon the thoughts of the author, Gadamer
opens himself to the charge that he forgoes the possibility of establishing correct interpretation. This critique has been leveled
by E. D. Hirsch, Jr., whose position represents a contemporary
version of author-oriented hermeneutics.

Hirsch's general approach, as well as his argument against
Gadamer, is summarized when he states that "to view the text as
an autonomous piece of language and interpretation as an infinite
process is really to deny that the text has *any* determinate meaning."[26] In Hirsch's view there are two possible approaches for hermeneutics, and these are antithetical and incommensurable. Either the text is seen to possess a single determinable unchanging
meaning, or the text is likely to mean "just anything."

Hirsch's position operates within the paradigm Bernstein characterizes as a dichotomy between "objectivism" and "relativism."
As Bernstein argues, this paradigm is determined by a specific
outlook and mode of thinking that receives an exemplary presentation in the work of Descartes. However, if we do not follow the
"Cartesian persuasion," then "the very opposition of objectivism
and relativism loses its plausibility."[27] Hirsch's dichotomizing approach eliminates the possibility that multiple interpretations of

the same text might each be capable of disclosing valid meanings. For Hirsch, in order to have valid interpretation, the text must be univocal.

Of course, arguing that Hirsch frames his criticism of Gadamer within a questionable either-or paradigm does not necessarily refute that criticism. We must examine Hirsch's position more closely in order to determine whether or not he can establish a means of arriving at the exclusive truth of a text.

Hirsch expresses a preference for the term *validation* over the term *verification* to express the goal of interpretation. The manner in which he defines the former term is significant. He emphasizes that "a validation is achieved only with respect to known hypotheses and known facts."[28] Thus, Hirsch acknowledges that there is no possibility of objective understanding "in itself" and that valid understanding emerges through the interaction of text and interpreter. Since the interpreter is not omniscient but rather is representative of a finite perspective, a particular validation is subject to the possibility of being superseded or refuted by the appearance of better-informed perspectives. That is, "as soon as new relevant facts and/or guesses appear, the old conclusions may have to be abandoned in favor of new ones."[29]

In these statements, Hirsch's argument bears a close resemblance to Gadamer's. In essence, Hirsch points out that there never can be a final determination of the meaning of a text, and hence there will be a series of valid interpretations rather than a single verified reading.[30] It seems, despite Hirsch's disclaimers, that understanding is indeed historical in nature. As new facts and hypotheses emerge through cultural-historical developments, so too are the insights into given texts altered and enriched.

However, when similar arguments are formulated by Gadamer, Hirsch attempts to refute them. In opposition to a historical hermeneutics, Hirsch devotes the main body of *Validity in Interpretation* to an attempted establishment of definitive methods of understanding. The determination of the true meaning of the text is based upon the self-identity of language[31] and the willed meaning of the author.[32] There is a clear correlation between these two principles. If meaning is to be founded upon authorial intent, then the language in which the author inscribes that meaning must not be capable of plural significations. Therefore it must be the case that the self-identity of verbal meaning "always remains the same from one moment to the next—that it is changeless."[33]

While this is the position Hirsch claims to hold throughout the work, it may be wondered if he has contradicted himself. Has he not refuted his own argument by allowing that valid interpretations are subject to the knowledge available at a given time and to a given individual? Does it not follow from this variability that the meaning of the text is subject to change? While Hirsch cannot fully resolve these difficulties, he avoids blatant self-contradiction by establishing a number of interrelated rigid dichotomies. In opposition to Gadamer, Hirsch asserts that "understanding is prior to and different from interpretation."[34] He preserves the classical distinction between *subtilitas intelligendi* and *subtilitas explicandi*, which Gadamer rejects.[35] Likewise, Hirsch formulates a parallel distinction between a text's "meaning" and its "significance." Meaning is defined as what "is represented by a text" and also as "what the author meant by his use of a particular sign sequence. It is therefore constant and unchanging."[36] "*Significance*, on the other hand, names a relationship between that meaning and a person, or a conception, or a situation, or indeed anything imaginable."[37]

The series of related dichotomies Hirsch develops all share the common binary structure of opposing the constant to the changing. *Subtilitas intelligendi* is the process of understanding, whereby the fixed meaning intended by the author is apprehended. *Subtilitas explicandi* is a secondary process, dependent upon the first, in which the fixed meaning of a text is brought into some form of relation. The latter represents an interpretive process in which the significance of the text for a specific situation is articulated. These binary structures allow Hirsch to separate the meaning of the text in its originally intended and intrinsic form from the extrinsic interpretations that appear in different contexts. "All understanding is necessarily and by nature intrinsic, all interpretation necessarily transient and historical."[38]

The obvious problem evident in these dualistic structures is that they represent a hermeneutical version of the Kantian "thing-in-itself," or noumenon. Hirsch establishes a "meaning in itself" which exists prior to and apart from any relation to an interpreter and which is presumed as the solid basis upon which transient interpretations are constructed. To be sure, Hirsch does not follow the Kantian formulation that the thing-in-itself is as inaccessible as it is necessary. Rather, Hirsch seems to be saying that the process of understanding a text "in itself," in an uninterpreted and context-free manner, is straightforward and self-evident. That is, if the meaning is *not* self-evident, we continue to be faced with the problem of *interpreting* the text in order to understand it.

Unfortunately, there is no basis for presuming that the intrinsic meaning of a text is self-evident. The more complex the text, the more problematic will be the establishment of a single agreed-upon meaning. How might one even attempt to establish the intrinsic and exclusive meaning of a text? Since, according to Hirsch, meaning is directly related to authorial intent, perhaps one can arrive at the former by means of the latter. If this is the case, then we are faced with a further regress to the problem of establishing the author's intent in a comprehensive and definitive manner. Hirsch approaches this problem by arguing that the task of interpretation is to determine the type or genre within which the author intended the text to be understood. He states that "verbal meaning can be defined . . . as a *willed type* which an author expresses by linguistic symbols and which can be understood through those symbols."[39] An important shift has occurred here, and it is one which has profound implications for Hirsch's argument.

Hirsch has shifted from a Schleiermacherian approach that seeks meaning in the very thoughts of the author to a more complex formulation. Authorial intent is inaccessible in any direct, self-evident, and certain manner. Instead of reexperiencing the author's thought processes, the interpreter must operate within the framework of the more loosely defined *type* the author intended. Moreover, this "willed type" can be determined only by means of the "linguistic symbols" of the text. The broader scope of the willed type and the focus upon language as the locus of that type allow Hirsch to include within "verbal meaning" an intentional object that can "transcend (as it does) the actual contents of consciousness."[40] Therefore, not only is the intentionality of the author accessible only in the language of the text, but moreover that intentionality supersedes the author's own awareness! This serves to eliminate the author as an independent source that can serve as a fixed reference point for the determination of meaning.

Hirsch makes a further attempt to maintain the rigid dichotomies between author and text, as well as between text and reader. He does this by altering his emphasis upon "author's will" to that of "shared type."[41] As Hirsch states, this serves to transform the criterion of meaning "from the type willed by the author to a type experience that is common to author and reader."[42] However, in making what he calls a "small alteration," Hirsch has taken a step that forever separates him from his goal of determining authorial intent, or the authorial intention of a genre, apart from the reader's engagement with the language of the text.

Hirsch posits the author's intended genre as the basis of the text's intrinsic meaning. This genre cannot be clearly distinguished from the generic conception through which the reader encounters the text. Yet the reader's genre, by Hirsch's definition, should not be capable of producing an "understanding" of the text, but only an "interpretation" of it.[43] Nevertheless, because of the shared nature of the genres of author and reader, any rigid distinction between understanding and interpretation, or between meaning and significance, is undermined. Hirsch's categories have become hopelessly intermingled.

The failure to isolate a level of meaning and understanding based on authorial intent from the interpretive act derives from the very nature of language. In order for the text to possess a single determinable meaning that corresponds to the intentions of the author, language would have to be a pliant tool that is imprinted by the author's mental processes. It would have to fixedly retain this impression and unambiguously present it to the reader.

However, it is not only the case that language displays a richness and polysemy that makes of it more than a technical system of signs manipulable by the authorial intellect. It is also arguable that no such anterior ideational meaning can become fully formed without the author's participation within language. Language's function transcends the subjective processes of the individual, and it makes those processes possible because the subject is formed within linguistically constituted cultural worlds. Language is a collective and historical development operating referentially within a shared universe of discourse. It is not simply a tool of subjectivity but an intersubjective and transsubjective cultural reality. From this it follows that linguistic meaning will be intersubjective in nature. This is a point Hirsch acknowledges in stating that "speech is not simply the expression of meaning but also the interpretation of meaning, each pole existing through and for the other, and completely pointless without the other."[44]

Because meaning is shared, it becomes necessary for hermeneutics to raise into consciousness the manner in which the interpreter shapes its disclosure. This cultivation of awareness will not eliminate the reader's contribution to the disclosure of the text's potential meanings. It will, however, allow for the continuing development of more critical and insightful forms of interpretive understanding. By contrast, in attempting to isolate meaning and understanding from the interpretive process, Hirsch abrogates the task of developing critical reflection. Any attempt to posit "original" or "authorial" meaning and truth leads to the instatement of particular interpretations in this privileged role. In the final analysis, Hirsch is reduced to arguing that "the root problem of interpretation is always the same—to guess what the author meant."[45] Since this means that the reader's guesses are taking the place of authorial meaning, Hirsch is led to the very subjectivism he sought to circumvent.

The Problem of Method

The reification of fixed interpretive perspectives is one of the central problems Gadamer's work addresses. He argues that this is a problem that is exacerbated by attempts to posit "original" meaning, as well as by attempts to establish "objective" methodologies that regulate our engagement with phenomena.

This leads to Gadamer's critique of "method," which he defines as a process of enframing a subject matter within a predetermined systematic approach. For example, when he criticizes Dilthey's employment of the "Cartesian method of doubt" in the human sciences, what Gadamer opposes is the entrenchment of a fixed mode of investigation that constricts the scope of an inquiry. He argues that Cartesian doubt represents an approach that does not maintain the openness necessary to a reflexive doubting of its own points of departure. Rather, it establishes a model of certainty that "is always anterior to any process of being doubted."[46] The method is what determines what kind of questions will be asked and what will be subjected to doubt. Yet the method itself conceals a standpoint or set of standpoints. These operate to delimit and determine the nature and results of an inquiry without themselves being subjected to question. "Just as when Descartes set up an artificial and hyperbolical doubt, . . . so methodological science fundamentally doubts everything that can be doubted, in order to achieve in this way the certainty of its results."[47]

Gadamer rejects the closure of frameworks of understanding that accompanies the application of method. His criticism parallels that leveled by Heidegger against modern technology, which subjects reality to an "enframing" (*das Ge-stell*) that represses its alterity.[48] "Method" is like an "enframing" because it only allows things to be disclosed in accordance with specific means-ends orientations. The relation to the matter at hand occurs within previously determined attitudes, projects, and goals, and the validity of those governing frameworks remains exterior to the range of questioning.

By focusing on such pejorative significations of the term *method,* Gadamer creates the impression that he is denouncing careful scientific inquiry in favor of a vague openness. Because of this, a number of scholars have taken issue with him on this matter, opposing his "strained polemic against all 'method.'"[49] Furthermore, Weinsheimer points out that "some of [Gadamer's] characterizations of the method of the natural sciences are now no longer tenable."[50] He makes this statement on the basis of contemporary developments in scientific theory and methodology that transcend the paradigm of the subject-object dichotomy. In the same vein Bernstein has explicated some of the points of contact between hermeneutical theory and the contemporary philosophy of science developed, for example, by Feyerabend and Kuhn.[51] He concludes that in strictly segregating truth from method, "Gadamer tends to rely on an image of science which the postempiricist philosophy and history of science have called into question."[52]

These arguments do not seek to challenge the validity of hermeneutical inquiry: in fact they extend it into the scientific realm. Indeed, it may be that it is not only contemporary science that parallels hermeneutics and transcends Gadamer's narrow definition of method. For example, Dewey explicitly contrasts scientific method with the type of "false certainty" attacked by Gadamer. Dewey argues that "scientific conceptions are not a revelation of prior and independent reality. They are a system of hypotheses, worked out under conditions of definite test."[53]

In speaking of hypotheses, Dewey indicates that there must be an initial methodological standpoint or set of conceptions brought to bear upon a given problem or phenomenon, but that this initial standpoint remains open to development and transformation in relation to the process of inquiry. Dewey characterizes scientific method not in terms of a nondialectical application of fixed categories but rather as the unfolding of knowledge based on an interaction with the emergent results of experience. "There is no *a pri-*

ori test or rule for the determination of the operations which define ideas. They are themselves experimentally developed in the course of actual inquiries."[54]

Dewey seeks to apply the procedures of scientific method to all fields of inquiry; and for him this means cultivating a form of reflexive experiential approach similar to that which Gadamer articulates for the humanistic disciplines. In each case the results of an inquiry emerge from a process of interaction with previously undetermined and unforeseen factors inherent in the subject matter. Because of this emphasis upon experiential interaction, Dewey shares with Gadamer an opposition to "the notion that certainty is attained by attachment to fixed objects with fixed characters."[55] Verification of an inquiry does not derive from maintaining fixed points of departure and from determining relationships of correspondence of these starting points with fixed objects. Rather, according to Dewey, "verification, or the opposite, is attained only because experimentation effects a transition of a problematical situation into a resolved one. In this development new individual objects with new features are brought to light."[56]

Remarks such as this indicate formulations of scientific method that share common features with hermeneutical inquiry. Nevertheless, Gadamer's critique of method remains relevant in relation to what may be called *methodological objectivism*. This represents the imposition of a fixed method, as in many pseudoscientific "isms," that does not retain the reflexive openness Dewey perceives in the best examples of scientific inquiry. Gadamer's error lies in failing to qualify his statements and to provide a clear differentiation between scientific method in general and the methodological objectivism that displays the conceptual closure that is the focus of his critique.

At the same time it must be emphasized that hermeneutics, because of the nature of its field of inquiry, cannot be absorbed into the natural sciences. Part of the impetus behind Gadamer's polemic against method derives from the need to provide the humanistic disciplines with the requisite autonomy from the natural sciences. This is required because of the essential points of divergence between the two sets of disciplines. For example, while Dewey and Gadamer both seek to develop approaches to understanding that emphasize a reflexive relationship between theory and experience, the type of experience differs radically in each case.

When Dewey argues for "practical" and "active" approaches to knowledge, he has in mind primarily the model of the controlled experimental situation. By contrast, for Gadamer it is historical experience that forms the basis and focus of hermeneutical understanding. Gadamer argues that "the main lack in the theory of experience hitherto" is that "it has been entirely oriented toward science and hence takes no account of the inner historicality of experience."[57] Scientific knowledge is founded upon the objectification of experience attained through the controlled situations which allow for the "fundamental repeatability" of scientific experiments.[58] Historical experience, by contrast, with its unique and innumerable psychological and cultural variables, is characterized by contingency and nonrepeatability. Therefore human existence and its cultural forms cannot be subjected to controlled observation after the manner of scientific experimentation.

Historical experience differs from scientific experience in another essential way. In historical experience the knower is implicated in the subject matter by nature of the historical constitution of the individual. As Weinsheimer notes, the aim of objective knowledge in the natural sciences "requires a consciousness maximally transparent to itself, one without any alien forces influencing it unawares toward a given conclusion or directing it outside its own control."[59] Such self-transparency of consciousness, to the extent that it is attainable in the sciences, is predicated upon the methodological controls that minimize the role of the observer. Since historical knowledge is not subject to such controls and since the empirical subject is already and necessarily constituted within historical-cultural realities, a value-free and self-transparent standpoint is unattainable.

The hermeneutical inquirer is a finite cultural being whose understanding is shaped by historically formed vantage points and perspectives. Because of this, hermeneutics is most effective if it involves a process of disclosing the fore-meanings and prejudgments that derive from these historical perspectives. Hermeneutical inquiry must be reflexive upon the *methodological* presumptions of the inquirer, as must sound scientific inquiry. Moreover, since the nature of the selfhood of the hermeneutical thinker is part of the historical reality that comes into play in understanding, hermeneutics precipitates a transformation in the very modes of being of the self. This is to say that there is an ethical dimension to hermeneutical inquiry that is lacking in the natural sciences.

In Gadamer's analysis, the author-oriented approach to hermeneutics of Schleiermacher or Hirsch and the methodological objectivism of nonreflexive inquiry share a common problem.[60] The pursuit of an objectified apprehension of truth, whether this is conceived of as the truth of an author's thoughts or the certainty of correct method, serves to suppress the historical nature of hermeneutical understanding. This suppression means that the task of critical reflection upon the biases of the interpreter is abrogated.

Speculation and Experience

Gadamer seeks to develop an approach to understanding that is thoroughly reflexive and interactional. He finds a general model for such a dynamic approach to understanding in the speculative and dialectical thinking of Hegel. Gadamer notes that the term *speculation* as employed by Hegel "refers to a mirror reflection."[61] The reflection involved here requires a differentiation of standpoints so that any particular interpretation of a subject matter encounters alternatives against which it may be compared. Potentially, this reflexivity based upon differentiation leads to the ongoing critical transformation of the initial standpoints involved. Thus Gadamer argues that "in speculative idealism the concept of the given, of positivity, has been subjected to a fundamental critique."[62]

In speculative thought, the "positivity" or "immediacy" represented by a particular apprehension of things is reduced to a moment in a greater dynamic process. It follows from this that "'speculative' is the antithesis of the dogmatism of everyday experience."[63] Speculative thought seeks to penetrate beyond the immediacy of unreflected experience (i.e., the ontic level), to an encompassing process of which such immediate apprehensions are but partial aspects. What was initially taken to be an objective representation of a thing comes to be seen as an interpretation determined by a particular context of apperception. In Hegelian terms, as Gadamer notes, this means that one comes to see "that the 'in-itself' is a 'for-me.'"[64]

The model of reflective thought that Hegelian speculative philosophy provides leads Gadamer to favor it over the nondialectical approach to understanding represented by Schleiermacher.[65] Nevertheless, Gadamer insists that hermeneutics must "free itself from the embrace of the synthetic power of the Hegelian dialectic."[66] Despite Gadamer's debt to Hegel, it appears that the differences between the two thinkers are more significant than are the similarities.

Dialectical reason transcends the focus upon the immediacy of perceptual judgments, which is characteristic of correspondence theories of truth, by calling attention to the greater contexts within which specific moments of knowledge are defined. The reflective process of dialectical reason, which seeks to move beyond limited moments of knowledge to absolute knowing ends, however, by being merely a "reflection" of the subject's logically formulated teleological structures.

In order to articulate complete teleological structures, Hegel must posit a system that permits no extrinsic elements, no inassimilable alterity that might challenge and transform it. "This is why," in Hegel's thought, "the dialectic of experience must end with the overcoming of all experience in absolute knowledge, i.e., in the complete identity of consciousness and object."[67] Therefore, Hegel's speculative philosophy is not fully reflexive. The system teleologically conditions the movement beyond particular moments in the process of knowing. On this basis Gadamer argues that "Hegel's dialectic is a monologue of thinking that seeks to carry out in advance what matures little by little in any genuine conversation."[68]

In contrast to Hegelian thought, Gadamerian hermeneutics does not presuppose teleological ordering in the development of knowledge, nor is it premised upon the certainty and closure of a complete system. Rather, Gadamer predicates the reflexive and dialogical processes of understanding upon human experience as characterized by finitude, historicality, and linguisticality. Because the empirical self is historically formed, because it cannot attain a state of complete self-transparency, and because it cannot reach the objective overview of absolute knowledge, it is *forced* beyond itself in its quest for understanding. The reflexive processes of hermeneutics require an inassimilable other and engender a transformation in the structures of the self. To this extent Gadamer's hermeneutics resembles what Gasché calls "heterology," that is, "a confrontation with Otherness that would no longer be *its own*."[69]

For Gadamer, such an encounter with otherness occurs dialogically.[70] A true dialogical experience will be a process whose outcome cannot be foreseen because it involves the interaction of finite yet autonomous perspectives. Gadamer uses the term *negativity* to convey the quality of experience that requires an encounter with the unfamiliar and antithetical. "Every experience worthy of the name runs counter to our expectations. Thus the historical nature of man contains as an essential element a fundamental negativity that emerges in the relation between experience and insight."[71] For Hegel the negative is simply a moment in the synthetic process of absolute knowing. For Gadamer specific experiences of negativity lead to insight and growth and involve mediation and transformation. However, this does not terminate in a final unity, and negativity continues to be understood as contingent and heteronomous.

The finitude of human beings and the negativity and alterity that characterize human experience form the basis for Gadamer's critique of the "omnipotence of reason." The operations of pure reason that are effective in some specialized disciplines cannot be transferred to an inquiry into history and language. Therefore, hermeneutics seeks insight into the limitations and determinations within which historical reason functions. "Real experience is that in which man becomes aware of his finiteness. In it are discovered the limits of the power and self-knowledge of his planning reason. It proves to be an illusion that everything can be reversed, that there is always time for everything and that everything somehow returns."[72]

Gadamer looks to Hegel for an approach to understanding that will counteract tendencies to posit truth as an origin to which understanding must somehow return or as the product of a method that rigidly controls experience. From Hegel he derives an approach that is speculative and future-oriented, seeing truth in an emergent process that is reflexive and dialectical. Yet after this initial insight Gadamer has moved very far indeed from Hegel's teleological system.

In fact, it is the Heideggerian conceptions of *Geworfenheit* and *Befindlichkeit* that are reflected in Gadamer's inquiry into the finitude and historicality of experience and understanding.[73] Reason does not dominate historical reality, and it cannot legitimately find within history a rational order of development. Rather, reason finds itself placed, or "thrown," within antecedent and encompassing historical realities.

Prejudgments, Legitimation, and Fusion of Horizons

In discussing Gadamer's notion of effective historical consciousness, we noted that this involved the disclosure of the historical

and cultural determinants operative within the inquirer's interpretive activity. We now have seen that various attempts to repress or circumvent the historicality of understanding inevitably
lead hermeneutics into a conceptual cul-de-sac.

Because the inquirer is shaped by historical realities, hermeneutical understanding must begin with standpoints that are not
fully conscious or chosen. This is because "reason exists for us
only in concrete historical terms, i.e., it is not its own master, but
remains constantly dependent on the given circumstances in
which it operates."[74] This dependency of reason means not only
that rationality derives from history the disciplines within which
to operate and the problems to address. In addition, Gadamer argues that the modes of rationality by which human beings pursue
and develop knowledge are themselves historically formed. History is not simply an external environment in which rationality
functions; it has been effective in the shaping of modes of thought.

Such observations lead Gadamer to a further argument that initially seems questionable. He states that "the prejudices of the individual, far more than his judgments, constitute the historical
reality of his being."[75] The point is that rational judgments develop and function within pre-disclosed interpretive frameworks
derived from cultural-historical existence. Judgments have been
"anticipated" by a series of cultural developments that are not of
a purely rational order, and in this sense judgments have a secondary quality. Gadamer employs two terms to describe the antecedent perspectives that condition judgments: *prejudgment* (*die
Vorentscheidung*) and *prejudice* (*das Vorurteil*). As long as the
term *prejudgment* is used carefully to describe the existence of
historically produced interpretive frameworks, Gadamer's argument remains cogent and compelling. However, in interchanging
the term *prejudice* with the term *prejudgment,* as he frequently
does, Gadamer opens himself to the interpretation that all human
understanding is hopelessly and inevitably biased.

He reinforces this view with the accompanying argument that
"the overcoming of all prejudices, the global demand of the Enlightenment, will prove to be itself a prejudice."[76] With this critique of Enlightenment rationalism, Gadamer appears to be advocating a form of irrationalism. This is the interpretation arrived
at by Hirsch, who understands Gadamer to be saying that " 'pre-
disposition' or 'prejudice' connotes the idea of a preferred habitual
stance," and that "the interpreter cannot alter his habitual attitudes even if he wants to."[77] To be sure, *this* position would rep-

resent a hopeless determination of reason by unreason. In Hirsch's interpretation, prejudgments become both arbitrary and indissoluble.

Gadamer is not advocating irrationalism. To the contrary, he seeks to develop a form of rationality that includes an awareness of the cultural-historical factors that both influence reason and provide standpoints and structures for thought. His critique of the Enlightenment is based on a rejection of its desire to posit reason as fully autonomous and self-aware. This positing merely serves to rigidify cultural and personal perspectives and biases rather than overcome them.

Gadamer seeks to "rehabilitate" the term *prejudice*, for example by referring to its meaning in German legal terminology as "provisional legal verdict" or its French and Latin meanings as "adverse effect." He notes in passing that "the German *Vorurteil*, like English 'prejudice' and even more than the French *préjugé*, seems to have become limited in its meaning."[78] In this argument, Gadamer de-emphasizes the reality and significance of current uses of terms in favor of archaic or specialized uses. In doing so, he contradicts the cultural and historical orientation of his own hermeneutical approach and engages in a form of the "originary" thinking for which he rebukes Heidegger. The turn to an "original" meaning of a term is especially problematic in the present instance, even if one maintains the hermeneutical sophistication that prevents the confusion of retrieved meanings with a literally understood original sense. Terms such as *Being* are distant enough from the general cultural sphere to allow hermeneutically retrieved meanings to function disclosively in the present. A term such as *prejudice*, however, carries too much immediate cultural significance to be so treated.

If hermeneutics is to remain relevant to the existential sphere, it must take the everyday-language meaning of terms seriously. Here, the term *prejudice* refers to a biased, ungrounded, and unfair attitude toward particular individuals, groups, or sets of ideas. The prejudiced person remains closed to alternate and opposing facts and perspectives. Therefore, "prejudice" may be described as a prejudgment which has become rigidified and which remains irrationally closed to dialogue and transformation. As such, prejudice must continue to be a pejorative term, designating one of the more reprehensible aspects of human reality.

Despite Gadamer's unfortunate attempt to rehabilitate the

term, his form of hermeneutics works toward the dissolution of prejudiced standpoints. Thus Gadamer argues that "we have continually to test all our prejudices."[79] Hence "the hermeneutical task becomes automatically a questioning of things."[80] This is not a unidirectional questioning of the standpoints of others but a reflexive questioning based upon a serious and open encounter with the otherness of the text. Hermeneutical questioning impels a process that involves "the conscious appropriation of one's own fore-meanings and prejudices . . . so that the text may be able to . . . assert its own truth against one's own fore-meanings."[81] Therefore hermeneutics recoils back upon the standpoint of the inquirer, disclosing prejudgments so that they may become subject to rational transformation. One must become conscious of the functioning of prejudgments before they can be "brought into play" and "placed at risk."[82]

Gadamer rightly emphasizes that all judgments will be conditioned by historically formed prejudgments. This awareness is part of a procedure that seeks to *overcome* the closure and reification of prejudgments lest they harden into what are commonly called prejudices. The use of the latter term to refer to prejudgments obscures the nature of the argument. Therefore we must reject Gadamer's conflation of *prejudice* and *prejudgment* and maintain a clear differentiation of the significance of the two terms.

A related argument of Gadamer's likewise suffers from a misplaced use of the term *prejudice*. This appears in the question: "What distinguishes legitimate prejudices from all the countless ones which it is the undeniable task of critical reason to overcome?"[83] At the moment, we need only note that Gadamer responds to his own query by arguing that "temporal distance" is the key to distinguishing "true prejudices, by which we understand, from the false ones by which we misunderstand."[84] Temporal distance is directly related to effective history, by which the differences between past and present create the tension necessary to critical reflection.

However, it is not so much the answer, but rather the question itself that remains problematic. As Habermas asks, "Does it follow from the unavoidability of hermeneutic anticipation *eo ipso* that there are legitimate prejudices?"[85] For Habermas, it certainly does *not* follow, for to speak of "legitimate prejudices" implies that particular finite standpoints are privileged and secured from hermeneutical criticism. We must concur with Habermas and reject any thus-conceived legitimation of prejudices *or* of prejudgments.

Nevertheless, Habermas's remarks are wide of the mark in relation to the meaning of Gadamer's argument. This is indicated in the latter's statement that it is "the prejudice against prejudice which deprives tradition of its power."[86] A change of focus occurs with the connection of "legitimate prejudgments" to tradition. Any tradition is itself a conditioned historical product and embodies the finite perspectives and conditions within which it takes shape. Because of this, the uncritical privileging of forms of tradition serves to ossify limited perspectives and impede the growth of awareness and understanding. On the other hand, Gadamer's point is that the contemporary inquirer *needs* the prejudgments embodied in traditions in order to develop a historically-based dialogical inquiry.

This argument emphasizes that understanding does not occur by means of the unilateral judgments of the autonomous rational subject but rather in communicative interchange. The basis for the processes that constitute understanding is the willingness to allow that the "other" may represent a standpoint that possesses a degree of validity. That is, hermeneutical inquiry is predicated upon an acknowledgment of the *legitimacy* of alternate perspectives so that fruitful dialogue might ensue.

The inquirer's interpretive standpoints and biases will themselves be the result of the influence of traditions that are constitutive of cultural reality. If this is repressed, then the prejudgments inherent in these traditions become fixed and work covertly to produce misunderstanding.[87] The consciously developed dialogue with tradition can disclose these conditioning factors in the interpreter and transform the way in which tradition is apprehended. Therefore, "to stand within a tradition does not limit the freedom of knowledge, but makes it possible."[88] The increase in reflexive awareness that derives from the hermeneutical encounter produces the kind of freedom that Heidegger connects with truth. This is the freedom that accompanies an increased awareness of how one's modes of disclosure are conditioned by interpretive frameworks.

The increase in awareness that emerges through the encounter with tradition means that repressed or unthought aspects of cultural history may be brought to light. Insight into the prejudgments that determine disclosure allows for the opening of vision and understanding, enabling alternate possibilities to be realized. This point is given a succinct formulation not by Gadamer but by Lonergan: "The general bias of common sense involves the disregard of timely and fruitful ideas; and this disregard not only excludes their implementation but also deprives subsequent stages both of the further ideas, to which they would give rise, and of the correction that they and their retinue would bring to the ideas that are implemented."[89]

Repeated repression and disregard of fruitful developments throughout the course of history mean that there are hidden dimensions of tradition yet to be disclosed. The hermeneutical dialogue with tradition, by means of the text, does not serve to substantiate the present status quo, nor does it seek to reestablish antiquated cultural forms. It discloses perspectives and insights in a creative and transformative manner through dialogue and interaction.

Gadamer's attention to the historical and interpretive nature of understanding militates against the rigidification of fixed cultural forms. Tradition exists only in terms of its interpretive reception and appropriation by ensuing historical periods. Therefore, hermeneutics does not seek to return to immutable truths that are legitimated as such. Rather, as Hart argues, "tradition is the potency established in the past which yet bears upon our unfinished being." As part of the process by which human being continues to be disclosed, "tradition transcends the merely ontic, unrepeatable past and enters into historical causality."[90]

The hermeneutical encounter with tradition, which transforms both past and present, is articulated as a "fusion of horizons" (horizontverschmelzung).[91] Gadamer defines his use of the term horizon as "the range of vision that includes everything that can be seen from a particular vantage point."[92] The concept of horizons indicates that human beings, in their existential finitude, have access to a limited interpretive apprehension of reality at any given time. In the process of fusion, the nature of the horizon within which interpretation occurs is itself transformed by the encounter: "The historical movement of human life consists in the fact that it is never bound to any one standpoint, and hence can never have a truly closed horizon. . . . Thus the horizon of the past, out of which all human life lives and which exists in the form of tradition, is always in motion. It is not the historical consciousness that first sets the surrounding horizon in motion, but in it this motion becomes aware of itself."[93] This movement or

alteration in horizons occurs with the transformations of historical existence. In historical hermeneutics, the interpretive distance created by historical change is articulated in new encounters with the alterity of tradition.

There is an inherent tension in historical hermeneutics that
precipitates ongoing disclosure and the transformation of horizons. The text, which is the embodiment of tradition with which
Gadamer is primarily concerned, remains an "other" that cannot
be fully absorbed by an interpretive standpoint. The text discloses
itself only in the hermeneutical act, only within the horizon of
the interpreter, and hence through a "fusion." Yet the text maintains an alterity, what Heidegger would call a concealment, that
prevents the closure of particular horizons. Therefore, "this process of fusion is continually going on."[94] The perpetually unfinished nature of the hermeneutical process, when made conscious as a guide to inquiry, acts as a critical check against the
closure of fixed interpretations.

The "tension between the text and the present" is the product
of the alterity of the text that allows creative disclosure to occur.
Therefore, "the hermeneutic task consists in not covering up this
tension by attempting a naive assimilation but consciously bringing it out."[95] Every time the tension of the text as "other" is experienced, the horizon of the inquirer undergoes a transformation to
accommodate new insight. Since the hermeneutically engaged
tradition is embodied in the form of texts, "the fusion of horizons
that takes place in understanding is the proper achievement of
language."[96] It is precisely because of its linguistic nature that the
process can transcend the domination of the inquirer. Since language is constitutive of the cultural universes inhabited by human beings, its disclosive capacities exceed the grasp of particular
standpoints within those worlds. This is a point that is pivotal to
Gadamer's thought.

Sensus Communis *and* Phronesis

Gadamer's approach to tradition emphasizes a form of knowledge
that derives from collective historical experience and is embodied
in its linguistic achievements. This dimension of knowledge is
inaccessible to individual rational procedures. Gadamer explicates this point in his discussion of *sensus communis*, "the sense
that founds community."[97] Gadamer cites with approval Vico's
statement that "what gives the human will its direction is not the

abstract generality of reason, but the concrete generality that represents the community of a group, a people, a nation, or the whole human race."[98] This "concrete generality," embodied in cultural traditions, does not appear suddenly in fully articulated forms. Rather, the *sensus communis* takes shape through the collective experiences of historical existence. It is not representative of universal rational laws but instead embodies something of the particular and conditioned forms of wisdom that emerge from practical engagement with existential situations. Moreover, because the *sensus communis* derives from communal responses to communal problems, it possesses an interpersonal and ethical dimension.

Sensus communis as a source of moral knowledge tended to decline into obscurity in the history of thought. For example, Gadamer refers to Kant as advocating a theory of moral knowledge that "excluded the idea of the *sensus communis* from moral philosophy."[99] The Kantian categorical imperative is a rational and universal law of moral judgment that opposes theories that are mutable in relation to existential contingencies. Gadamer argues that, in Kant's formulations, "the character of moral law totally excludes any comparative reflection about others."[100]

Kant characterizes the moral law by the categorical imperative, the law of pure practical reason: "I should never act in such a way that I could not also will that my maxim should be a universal law."[101] Actually, on an abstract level, this imperative *does* seek to establish an ethic of reciprocity. To will that one's maxims be made into universal laws means, for Kant, that one grants to others the right to act reciprocally in relation to oneself. However, the abstract and universal nature of the Kantian moral imperative does not allow for the possibility of attending to the specificity of individual cases. The fixity of the universal law cannot take into account the qualifying factors that complexify existential judgments. Kant emphasizes this in arguing that "for reason to be legislative, it is required that reason presuppose only itself, because the rule is objectively and universally valid only when it holds without any contingent subjective conditions which differentiate one rational being from another."[102] Kant's rational ethic is not truly capable of acknowledging the specificity of the other and of attending to the complex combinations of factors and forces endemic to existential situations.

In contradistinction to Kant, Gadamer emphasizes the unique nature of experience on both the individual and sociohistorical levels. Because human experiences have a contextualized, diversified, and unrepeatable quality, they resist the uniform application of universal laws of moral behavior. Hence, Gadamer develops a dialogical approach to understanding that mediates between normative standpoints and the specificity of historical and personal situations. "Understanding" in this case does not represent merely a process of epistemological enhancement but affects the modes of being that are determinative of our experiences of and relations with others. The link between Gadamer's hermeneutical project and a concern with ethics is expressed in his argument that "understanding is a modification of the virtue of moral knowledge. It appears in the fact of concern, not about myself, but about the other person." [103]

This linking of moral wisdom with understanding draws upon Aristotle's *Nichomachean Ethics*. Gadamer articulates the historically-formed avenue to moral knowledge represented by *sensus communis* by relating it to Aristotle's conception of *phronesis*, or "practical wisdom." As noted in Chapter 1, this concept applies to the problem of truth within the sphere of social and interpersonal relationships and has a distinctly ethical significance. "Practical knowledge, *phronesis*, is another kind of knowledge. Primarily it means that it is directed toward the concrete situation." [104] *Phronesis* provides a model for a type of rationality that is not predicated upon the self-transparent subject and does not presume access to universal norms of behavior. "This type of reflection," states Habermas with reference to Gadamer's use of *phronesis*, "is no longer blinded by the illusion of an absolute, self-grounded autonomy and does not detach itself from the soil of contingency on which it finds itself." [105] Rather than turning to universal laws for guides to moral action, *phronesis* addresses itself to cultural forms that have been forged within historical existence.

What is the nature of these disclosed historical forms and institutions? Following Aristotle, Gadamer argues that traditions represent an *ethos* that differs from *physis*. Since "man becomes what he is through what he does and how he behaves," that is, through historical existence, there come into being "human institutions and human attitudes that can be changed and have the quality of rules only to a limited degree." [106] While the ethos embodied in historically formed institutions and traditions provides guiding insight for social and moral activity and understanding, these disclosed forms are not inalterable laws. Because historical reality continues to be reinterpreted as it evolves, traditions do not abide as fixed forms. The practical wisdom inherent in these traditions cannot be applied in a predetermined manner. A uniform and unmediated application of historically derived forms of *phronesis* would be equivalent to a historicized version of the categorical imperative.

Since traditions are not immutable universal structures, the heart of the hermeneutical problem "is that the same tradition must always be understood in a different way."[107] This is the nature of the problem of hermeneutical "application," and it indicates what may be called a second stage of *phronesis*. The first stage of *phronesis*, from the point of view of hermeneutics, appears in the historical-cultural processes by which the practical wisdom of *sensus communis* becomes distilled and articulated in traditions. The second stage involves the contemporary hermeneutical task of establishing a critical dialogue between the embodiments of *phronesis* in texts and the contemporary cultural reality.

Gadamer does not explicitly establish such a second stage of *phronesis*, yet it is implied in his discussion of hermeneutical application and its parallels with moral knowledge. He points out that "we can only apply something that we already possess; but we do not possess moral knowledge in such a way that we already have it and then apply it to specific situations."[108] Therefore the very nature of *phronesis* requires that it take shape as it is interpretively applied within varying existential situations.

We have noted that, in opposition to theorists such as Hirsch, Gadamer argues that understanding and interpretation are inseparable. In fact, he further transgresses the traditional boundaries not only between *subtilitas intelligendi* and *subtilitas explicandi* but between these and *subtilitas applicatio* as well.[109] Application is not a secondary or tertiary procedure, because the interpreter is already placed within historical loci that create frames of reference to which a text is related. Understanding is intrinsically a relation between past and present that impinges upon the interpreter's sense of immediacy. Therefore, "application is neither subsequent nor a merely occasional part of the phenomenon of understanding, but codetermines it as a whole from the beginning."[110] For Gadamer, the choice facing hermeneutics is not between an "applied" understanding and an "original" one but between a conscious and an unconscious process of application.

One may discern in the mediation of hermeneutical application a "moral task." This involves subjecting the prejudgments of the interpreter to questioning and transformation in a reflexive encounter with the historical matrices that contribute to the formation of those prejudgments. This is what I have called the second stage of *phronesis*. It draws upon the forms of *phronesis* derived from *sensus communis* and its historical articulations and engages in a critical hermeneutical application in light of contemporary concerns and problems. This is a form of *phronesis* unfamiliar to the world of Aristotle, which could presuppose a relatively stable polis and which was not heir to the diversity of historical traditions available to contemporary inquiry.

The establishment of two forms or stages of *phronesis*, the one inherent in traditions and the other a contemporary task, does not mean that we ever have one without the other. But it does clarify the nature of hermeneutical inquiry, and this may help to address some of the issues raised by Bernstein in his reflections upon *phronesis*.

Bernstein notes that according to both Aristotle and Gadamer, "*phronesis* presupposes the existence of *nomoi* (funded laws) in the community."[111] Without a basis in a historical community, "practical wisdom" is likely to degenerate "into the mere cleverness or calculation that characterizes the *deinos* (the clever person)."[112] The problem related to these observations is that contemporary Western culture appears to lack the communal bases of *phronesis* evident in such previous cultural formations as the Greek polis. As Bernstein argues, "We are living in a time when the very conditions required for the exercise of *phronesis*—the shared acceptance and stability of universal principles and laws— are themselves threatened (or do not exist)."[113]

The problem of the lack of contemporary sources for communal and interpersonal forms of understanding is seen by Bernstein to have a number of implications for Gadamer's hermeneutics:

> When Gadamer tells us that practice is conducting oneself, and acting, in solidarity, that *phronesis* requires a type of community in which there is an *ethos* and the shared acceptance of *nomoi*, that practical and political reason can be realized and transmitted only through dialogue, he *presupposes*, at least in an incipient form, the existence of the very sense of community that such practical and political reason is intended to develop.[114]

In essence, Bernstein is arguing that hermeneutics must predicate its dialogical inquiry upon the form of community that represents the goal toward which it strives. If this is the case, then Gadamer's hermeneutical approach is trapped in a vicious circle.

Yet when the two dimensions of *phronesis* are considered, it appears that Bernstein's critique derives from a misapprehension. *Phronesis*, as Gadamer employs the notion, does not presuppose present forms of integrated community and universally accepted laws. Rather, the actualization of practical reason in the contemporary world is effected through the encounter with those expressions of *phronesis* that are historically given. The cultural embodiments of *phronesis* are presented through the text, and the contemporary enactment of practical wisdom consists in the hermeneutical engagement with those texts.

This is not to say, for example, that Plato or Aristotle have already produced the solutions to contemporary problems. Instead, hermeneutical dialogue with such texts can allow the contemporary inquirer to attain a differentiation of understanding that counteracts the immersion within prevalent frameworks of disclosure. This complexification contributes to the liberation of the inquirer's modes of thinking from closed interpretive structures, disclosing alternate possibilities for approaching problems. Moreover, the encounter with the text might itself be the source for new ideas and perspectives that will be applicable to contemporary concerns.

Bernstein seems to desire the establishment of communities of open communication *prior* to the critical task of hermeneutics. Gadamer, by contrast, conceives of hermeneutics as a means of addressing some of the problems of ethical self-understanding in a disrupted and fragmented cultural world. Hermeneutics does not presuppose extant contemporary forms of *phronesis;* it functions as a means of introducing a constructive critique into a world that lacks *phronesis.* "Only when our entire culture for the first time saw itself threatened by radical doubt and critique," states Gadamer, "did hermeneutics become a matter of universal significance."[115]

It is precisely because strong and integrated cultural communities are lacking, being replaced by mass-produced commercial conditioning, that hermeneutics must disrupt the present as it discloses repressed and unthought dimensions of tradition. In this respect Gadamer's thought takes account of the negative as well as the positive dimensions of social existence. Community, as a creative and nurturing social environment that stimulates the development of human potential, is less in evidence than one could desire. Yet this does not mean that there are not other, less desirable collective forces operative in the contemporary world. As Gadamer stresses, "We are always dominated by conventions. In every culture a series of things is taken for granted and lies fully beyond the explicit consciousness of anyone, and even in the greatest dissolution of traditional forms, mores, and customs the degree to which things held in common still determine everyone is only more concealed."[116]

It becomes essential to take account of the ideological determinations of the public realm; what Heidegger calls *das Man* and Lonergan refers to as "group bias." These indicate forces which produce conformity and lack of differentiation and which rigidify socially determined worldviews and modes of being. To privilege "solidarity," as Bernstein does, is to neglect the *critical* dimension hermeneutics introduces into culture by opening access to sources of differentiation and reflection.

The other side of this issue is the danger of cultivating an elite of sophisticated individuals isolated from society. Bernstein argues that while in any society "there can always be those individuals who exemplify the virtues of the *phronimos*," it is a different matter to confront the question of "what material, social, and political conditions need to be concretely realized in order to encourage the flourishing of *phronesis* in all citizens."[117] Such a collective flourishing must be considered our preeminent task and goal. If it can be achieved, it will not be by conceptual thought alone. However, insofar as critical thinking can contribute to a commonly shared *phronesis*, it will do so by means of a historically based reflexive opening of worldviews rather than by the imposition of fixed ideals.

Gadamerian hermeneutics, as the antithesis of those forms of thought that presume the self-sufficiency of reason, seeks to foster openness and dialogue rather than the hegemony of the individual. As Bernstein notes, "Gadamer softens this elitist aura by blending his discussion of *phronesis* with the analysis of the type of dialogue and conversation that presupposes mutual respect, recognition, and understanding."[118] To this it should be added that not only is such reciprocity presupposed by hermeneutics, it is, moreover, the result and effect that its reflexive inquiry seeks to foster.

Problems in the Dialogical Model

Something of the general manner in which Gadamerian hermeneutics can be applied in the critical analysis of cultural reality has now been explicated. It remains to inquire into some of the limitations evident in Gadamer's specific dialogical model of understanding.

The dialogical model is predicated upon an image of the text as a "Thou" with which the interpreter interacts. This analogy is based on the linguistic nature of tradition, which prevents it from being subject to determinative objectifications. Gadamer emphasizes that "tradition is not simply a process that we learn to know and be in command of through experience; it is language, i.e., it expresses itself like a 'Thou.'"[119] In Gadamer's view, the linguisticality of the text has an expressive force that resists being exhausted by a single interpretive framework. The "Thou" quality indicates the reflexive potential inherent in the polysemous nature of language, which allows the text to address and challenge the standpoints of the interpreter.

Because of the reflexive nature of the hermeneutical encounter with the text, there is a moral quality to the interpretive experience. As we have seen, Gadamer explicates this dimension in terms of *phronesis* as a form of moral knowledge that relates to the particularity of diverse life situations. This moral quality, like the dialogical structure of hermeneutical experience, is traced by Gadamer to the text's capacity to function as a "person." He argues that "since here the object of experience has itself the character of a person, this kind of experience is a moral phenomenon, as is the knowledge acquired through experience, the understanding of the other person."[120]

One may concur with Gadamer's critique of attempts to objectify and delimit the meaning of the text, as seen in methodological objectivism or in hermeneutical approaches based upon authorial intent. Likewise, one may agree that there is a potentially transformative and moral dimension to the hermeneutical experience. But it does not follow that this experience is best expressed by an analogy with interpersonal encounters or that the text need be "personified." This issue becomes important because the model the inquirer brings to the text will shape the nature and results of hermeneutical inquiry. At this point we must consider the possibility that the personification of the text works to undermine some of the potential for critical and reflexive inquiry inherent in hermeneutics.

The resistance of the text to objectification indicates the nature of the problems facing the dialogical model. There is a tension in Gadamer's formulations that appears in his discussions of the text as a Thou. The latter must possess an independent source of volition and self-expression. Yet the inseparability of the text from the interpretive process belies its capacity to function like an autonomous Thou. Gadamer's inability to resolve this difficulty in an adequate manner appears in a number of passages in which he is led, despite himself, toward subject-oriented standpoints.

Gadamer presents a series of illustrations serving to indicate resemblances between understanding and conversation; for example, the reciprocal relationship between interpreter and text and the emergence of a "common language" shared by each. Yet in the course of this argument Gadamer acknowledges that the hermeneutical situation does differ considerably from interpersonal dialogue because "one partner in the hermeneutical conversation, the text, is expressed only through the other partner, the interpreter. Only through him are the written marks changed back into meaning. Nevertheless, by being changed back into intelligible terms, the object of which the text speaks finds expression."[121] With the final statement, Gadamer is able to sustain his position by arguing that the "object" expressed by the text "unites the two partners, the text and the interpreter."[122] Yet while noting the "inequality" in the relationship between text and reader, and indeed the radically divergent nature of the two conversationalists, Gadamer makes little attempt to address seriously the issues raised by these matters. The text does *not* possess the qualities of animation and direct responsiveness required to assert itself against the appropriations of the reader or to react spontaneously to the new interpretive contexts into which it is placed.

Gadamer accepts a traditional paradigm that conceives of language as locked into a relationship of dependency upon the presence of human beings. The conversational model imposes the priority of the subject upon the text, leading to the argument that "precisely because it entirely detaches the sense of what is said from the person saying it, the written word makes the reader, in his understanding of it, the arbiter of its claim to truth."[123] Such passages indicate that Gadamer has not fully developed his repudiation of authorial intent and that he has not consistently worked out the consequences of that repudiation.

While emphasizing the expressive capacities of language over the fixed origin of the author, Gadamer contradicts himself on those occasions when he reduces language to a dependency upon the interpreter. His thinking remains informed, at least partially, by an either-or paradigm in which either author or reader determines meaning. This appears in his stating that "all the meaning of what is handed down to us finds its concretion, in which it is understood, in its relation to the understanding 'I'—and not in the reconstruction of an 'I' of the original meaning."[124]

To be sure, we have seen that Gadamer develops a number of arguments that refute subjectivism and seek to maintain the alterity of the text in relation to the perspectival interpretations of the reader. For example, Gadamer repeatedly emphasizes the "priority of the question," which has the form of "the knowledge of not knowing."[125] The text cannot be reduced to a single interpretive grasp and so continues to disclose itself on the basis of repeated interrogative procedures. "To ask a question means to bring into the open."[126] Such continued opening or disclosure subverts and supersedes the hegemony of the "interpretive I." This critical subversion does not occur because the text responds to questioning as does a person but rather, as Winquist notes, because "the text can never exhaust its potential for meaning through multiplication or repetition."[127]

It now appears that there are two divergent models of understanding copresent in Gadamer's work: a model based on disclosure and a model based on conversation. The disclosure model resists the domination of the "I" and provides the basis for Gadamer's arguments concerning the critical and transformative nature of hermeneutics. It is because language has a disclosive capacity, and is not simply a tool, that the critical and ethical developments of which Gadamer speaks can occur within hermeneutical inquiry. However, this disclosive capacity becomes distorted and curtailed by the model of understanding based upon the conversation between individuals.

There is a contradiction inherent in Gadamer's hermeneutics. He emphasizes that language transcends subjectivity, and yet he continues to view understanding through a model based on the conversational interaction of subjects. On the one hand Gadamer asserts that "in linguistic communication, 'world' is disclosed."[128] On the other hand he maintains "that language has its true being only in conversation, in the exercise of understanding between people."[129] The priority of the subject that derives from the latter formulation is incompatible with the disclosive transformation of the former, and this serves merely to highlight the nature of the problem. The disclosive model, which potentially can give expression to the historical, supraindividual, and critical nature of hermeneutics, becomes constrained and curtailed by a conversational model dependent upon the presence of individuals to one another.

Gadamer's work has allowed us to extend our inquiry into truth as disclosure beyond the limits of Heidegger's ahistoricism. We need now to extend Gadamer's insights into hermeneutics and disclosure, while relinquishing his allegiance to a model of understanding based upon conversation. In order to accomplish this task, and to provide further articulation of the relationships between hermeneutics, historicity, and truth as disclosure, we shall draw upon the work of Paul Ricoeur.

5

LANGUAGE AND THE
DISCLOSURE OF WORLDS:
RICOEUR

The Depersonification of Alterity

GADAMER CONTRIBUTES to an approach to truth as disclosure by developing the hermeneutical and historical dimensions of understanding that are constitutive of the human experience of truth. He accomplishes this development by linking truth-disclosure to a reflexive hermeneutics that effects a critical interaction of contemporary understanding with textual forms of historically produced *phronesis*. However, in attempting to formulate the relational process of understanding based upon this historical interaction, Gadamer relies upon a problematic notion of the text as a Thou.

In the main, Gadamer emphasizes that it is language itself, or the text itself, rather than the author or the reader, that forms the focal point of hermeneutical disclosure. Yet these insights into the disclosive nature of language, and hence of truth, become compromised and restricted through the imposition of a "dialogical" model of hermeneutics based upon the personification of the text. By framing his hermeneutics within the parameters of a person-to-person model of interaction, Gadamer delimits the possibilities of disclosure within the confines of a notion of response. The hermeneutical problems that derive from the incapacity of the text to function responsively like an actively present individual remain unresolved by Gadamer.

The later work of Paul Ricoeur provides a guide for continuing the development of our central arguments concerning hermeneutics and truth as disclosure but seeks to avoid the shortcomings of Gadamer's dialogical model. We may gain entry into

Ricoeur's work by attending to his specific opposition to dialogical models of hermeneutical understanding. Clearly, approaching Ricoeur's thought from the vantage point of this issue produces a contextualization of a very definite kind. This means that we forgo an overview of the line of development of Ricoeur's work, including the schools of thought and areas of concern that have contributed to his intellectual genealogy. Instead, aspects of Ricoeur's later work will be introduced into an argument that has taken shape up to this point primarily through an analysis of the work of Heidegger and Gadamer. Both of these thinkers stand prominently among those whose thought has been influential upon Ricoeur, and many aspects of his later work take the form of direct responses to, critiques of, and extrapolations from their insights.

Ricoeur concurs with Gadamer's arguments that interaction with textual embodiments of historically produced wisdom provides the dynamic basis for reflexive and disclosive forms of understanding. However, he argues that the functional mode of this process is ill-represented by a personification of the text as a conversation partner. The basis for this divergence is that "with writing, the conditions of direct interpretation through the interplay of question and answer, hence through dialogue, are no longer fulfilled."[1] The necessary condition of a dialogue is the presence of the interlocutors to one another. Such a condition of presence is constitutive of dialogue in a far more essential and intrinsic manner than is immediately evident. *Presence* means more than simply that two or more individuals are in a condition of direct or indirect vocal proximity that allows for linguistic interaction. Presence also serves to *contextualize* the conversation in such a manner as to provide both a referential matrix for interpretation and the motive force directing the development of the dialogue. "It is the 'here' and 'now,' determined by the situation of discourse, which provides the ultimate reference of all discourse."[2] In any genuine dialogue, the statements of each of the interlocutors will develop in response to the immediately preceding statements of the other, as well as in relation to the bearing of the conversation to that point. The referential situation provided by the emergent disclosure of meaning through statements and responses provides both the focus and the stimulus for continuing the dialogue.

According to Ricoeur, the problem is not simply that the immediate presence presupposed by the dialogical model of understanding is *unattainable* in hermeneutical inquiry. In addition, the model of presence is too limiting and constraining to encapsulate the complexity of the encounter with the text. An orientation toward presence, and the neglect of historical context that is its concomitant, suppresses the complex problems of reference in hermeneutics. This serves to limit arbitrarily the possibilities of meaningful disclosure because "conversation, i.e., ultimately the dialogical relation, is contained within the limits of a *vis-à-vis* which is a *face-à-face*. The historical connection which encompasses it is singularly more complex."[3]

The matter of the "historical connection" involved in hermeneutics, by introducing a new dimension of contextuality that is not based upon immediate presence, severely qualifies the validity of the dialogical model. While in a facile sense the text may be said to be present to the reader, the semantic disclosure of the text produces meaningful worlds that are not fully assimilable to existential and historical immediacy. This serves to split the referential function of the text, producing a critical moment in the reader's conceptualization of the real.

In thus relinquishing the dialogical model, Ricoeur separates his hermeneutics from the vestiges of the paradigm of authorial intent remaining in Gadamer's work. While Gadamer's hermeneutical approach is far removed from that represented by, for example, Hirsch, the notion of the text as a Thou remains conditioned by the model of human presence. By contrast, Ricoeur's more consistent development of a disclosure model of hermeneutics avoids the reliance upon an authorial subject as the basis for the truth of the text. "Insofar as the meaning of a text is rendered autonomous with respect to the subjective intention of its author, the essential question is not to recover, behind the text, the lost intention, but to unfold, in front of the text, the 'world' which it opens and discloses."[4] Therefore, the hermeneutical encounter with the text is not analogous to a dialogue with a personified Thou but is rather a process in which the linguistic disclosure of the text opens worlds of meaning before the reader.

In a manner parallel to the transcending of authorial intent, the text's disclosive capacities operate critically in relation to the reader's frameworks of understanding. Because of this, the disclosure model avoids lapsing into a compliance with the domination of the subject in either of its guises. "The text thus produces a double eclipse of the reader and the writer. It thereby replaces the relation of dialogue, which directly connects the voice of one to the hearing of the other."[5] The text is not simply a medium of communication between two subjects or a substitute for the authorial partner in a conversation. Rather, the text is the source of a disclosive process that supersedes and transforms the subjectivity of both author and reader.

To be sure, this transformative process could not occur without an author and a reader. Yet there is a profound difference between viewing the linguisticality of the text as mediating between two otherwise autonomous and unchanging subjects, and understanding the text as constitutive of modes of subjectivity. The meaning disclosed by the text transcends the subject and challenges the interpretive frameworks of understanding derived from the manner in which reality (or, in Heidegger's language, Being) is disclosed to the subject. The critical and transformative effects of hermeneutics are predicated upon this potential for a "clash" of disclosed worlds.

There is an essential tension that characterizes Ricoeur's hermeneutical project. This derives from the conjunction of the task of liberating language from the limitations of traditional conceptions of representation and reference, with the task of retrieving and reformulating these representational and referential functions. As a means of executing these two sides of his project, Ricoeur repudiates conceptions of representation, or mimesis, as a secondary process of "copying." Likewise, he argues that reference cannot be confined to the descriptive denomination of extralinguistic entities that are posited "in themselves." Yet the problems of mimesis and reference cannot be ignored, for they are essential to the capacity of hermeneutics to operate critically and disclosively in relation to modes of being-in-the-world.

At this point, it is necessary to develop a more detailed analysis of these issues. The problem of mimesis will be approached first, beginning with a general discussion of the issue of representation. Following this, we turn to an analysis of Ricoeur's reformulations of mimesis, and then to the problem of reference.

Plato and Mimesis

Traditional conceptions of mimesis that view all artistic and linguistic production as derivative and secondary may be traced back to Plato's *Republic* and *Phaedrus*. The most influential position has been that proposed by Socrates in the *Republic*, wherein he argues that the artist is at "third remove" from reality because he imitates things, such as the products of craftsmanship, which are themselves but imitations of the forms.[6] This tertiary status means that artistic products are very low in rank of valuation because they are far distanced from the originary sources of Being and truth. As Socrates concludes, "Poetry, and in general the mimetic art, produces a product that is far removed from truth in the accomplishment of its task, and associates with the part in us that is remote from intelligence, and is its companion and friend for no sound and true purpose."[7]

These arguments are straightforward, if perhaps unconvincing. However, in the light of the analysis of the *Republic* developed in chapter 3 of this work, it becomes possible to question the viability of taking Socrates at his word in any of his proposals for an ideal state. If, as Randall and Wolz argue, the portrayal of the ideal state in the *Republic* has an ironic quality designed to highlight the *undesirability* of such a state, then the attitude toward the mimetic arts that is intrinsic to this state cannot automatically be assumed to be Plato's position.

Nevertheless, these considerations do not alter the fact that a literal interpretation of the *Republic* has had an enormous influence upon the cultural history of the Western world. This "effective history," to use Gadamer's term, has its own reality that cannot be dismissed, even if the status of its origin is opened to question. To advance the discussion, we need to explicate some of the issues involved in the question concerning the status of mimesis.

In the *Phaedrus*, particularly at 274e–277e, there is a more detailed indictment of imitation as it manifests itself specifically in the form of writing. These arguments are also paradigmatic of the view that defines mimetic activity as productive of qualitatively diminished reflections of "original" being. Socrates argues that written words cannot provide true knowledge, but can do little more "than remind one who knows that which the writing is concerned with."[8] Thus writing can serve only as a mnemonic device stimulating the recall of knowledge previously acquired through nonwritten means. Writing cannot contribute to the creative development of new knowledge and insight. Moreover, continues Socrates, writing is "truly analogous to painting" because while seeming to be "alive," each of these art forms is actually "dead" and "mute." If one attempts to address them in order to elicit some response, "they maintain a most majestic silence."[9] Here Socrates indicates a problem that will still trouble the fundamental figure of Gadamer's hermeneutics: the text does not respond as does an animate conversation partner.

The most serious problem related to the muteness of writing, and of all mimetic forms, is that the essential nature and truth of an idea or set of ideas becomes subject to obfuscation and distortion. Socrates argues that "once a thing is put in writing . . . [it] drifts all over the place, getting into the hands not only of those who understand it, but equally of those who have no business with it." [10] Again, this argument is based upon the premise that writing cannot *produce* knowledge or transform those who encounter it. The reader must already be wise in order to make proper use of written transcriptions of ideas. The unwise, who have no business becoming involved in these matters, will simply abuse ideas if they are granted unguided and unrestricted access to them through texts.

Because writing is simply derivative and has no autonomy or "voice" of its own, it easily becomes the victim of manipulation. In Socrates' words, "When it is ill-treated and unfairly abused," that is, when it becomes subjected to misinterpretation and questionable application, "it always needs its parent to come to its help, being unable to defend or help itself." [11] Thus we are directed to the author, who is possessed of "another sort of discourse that is brother to the written speech, but [is] of unquestioned legitimacy." [12] The author, as the "parent" of the text, possesses an alternate form of discourse which is "living" and which "goes together with knowledge, and is written in the soul of the learner." [13] Unlike the mute writing of the text, this "living speech" in the soul of the author "can defend itself, and knows to whom it should speak and to whom it should say nothing." [14]

Jacques Derrida points out that "Plato thinks of writing, and tries to comprehend it, on the basis of *opposition* as such." [15] Derrida indicates a series of antitheses that appear to govern the text of the *Phaedrus*, such as "good/evil, true/false, essence/appearance, inside/outside, etc." [16] It is this predominant principle of opposition that guides Plato's central division of writing into "legitimate discourse," which is written in the soul, and the secondary, deficient writing, which is inscribed "in water or that black fluid we call ink." [17] These antitheses governing the *Phaedrus*'s condemnation of writing are also those, according to Derrida, that govern Western metaphysics in general. The *Phaedrus*, therefore, may be understood to be operating within and sustaining this set of metaphysical paradigms.

However, the matter is not so simple as it may initially appear
to be. The focus of Derrida's analysis of the *Phaedrus* derives
from Socrates' frequent likening of writing or the text to a *pharmakon*.[18] The point here is that this term has a plurality of possible translations, which Derrida lists as follows: "'remedy,' 'recipe,' 'poison,' 'drug,' 'philter,' etc."[19] When writing is likened to a
pharmakon, it would seem to be granted an inner ambivalence,
and even a self-contradictory nature. "If the *pharmakon* is 'ambivalent,' it is because it constitutes the medium in which op-
posites are opposed, the movement and the play that links them
among themselves, reverses them, or makes one side cross over
into the other."[20] Indeed, it is this inherent ambiguity which
makes the *pharmakon*, and writing as well, so dangerous and sus-
pect. As Derrida notes, mimetic activity such as writing, or, in his
terms, "the supplement," both "is" and "is not." Writing is not
itself "a being (*on*)," but neither is it "a simple nonbeing (*me on*),"
either. Its slidings slip it out of the simple alternative presence/
absence. *That* is the danger."[21]

The potential reversals inherent in the ambivalence of the
pharmakon begin to emerge when Derrida notes that "Socrates in
the dialogues of Plato often has the face of a *pharmakeus*
[magician or wizard]."[22] This attribution is related to Socrates'
constant overturning of the fixed perspectives and presuppositions of his interlocutors. He frequently constructs spurious arguments precisely so that he may overturn them; consequently, an
iconoclastic form of illumination is initiated. This is the core of
Socratic irony, which is inseparable from the Platonic texts in
which it appears.

> Irony does not consist in the dissolution of a sophistic charm or in
> the dismantling of an occult substance or power through analysis
> and questioning. It does not consist in undoing the charlatanesque
> confidence of a *pharmakeus* from the vantage point of some obsti-
> nate instance of transparent reason or innocent *logos*. Socratic
> irony precipitates out one *pharmakon* by bringing it in contact
> with another *pharmakon*. Or rather, it reverses the *pharmakon*'s
> powers and turns *its* surface over.[23]

Does this ironic reversal shared by writing as a *pharmakon* and
Socrates as a *pharmakeus* reflect back upon the *Phaedrus*'s condemnation of mimesis? We cannot follow Derrida's analyses in
their entirety, but the following point is pivotal. As we have seen,

Plato describes the higher form of knowledge of which writing in ink is a mere semblance as "writing in the soul." It is remarkable, Derrida argues, that "the so-called living discourse should suddenly be described by a 'metaphor' borrowed from the order of the very thing one was trying to exclude it from, the order of its simulacrum."[24] If we take this metaphor as seriously as we take the overt arguments of the text, we may conclude, with Derrida, that "the *Phaedrus* is less a condemnation of writing in the name of present speech than a preference for one sort of writing over another, for the fertile trace over the sterile trace."[25]

An even more pervasive irony appears in the fact that the means of the condemnation of writing is itself writing. Emphasizing this inherent irony, Derrida inquires "why Plato, while subordinating or condemning writing and play, should have written so much, . . . *indicting* writing in writing, lodging against it that complaint (*graphe*) whose reverberations even today have not ceased to sound."[26] Indeed, the enduring reverberations of the Platonic texts have granted to the "author's voice" a power and scope otherwise unattainable. Because of this, Derrida concludes that there is a pervasive tension inherent in the *Phaedrus* that complexifies and reverses literal readings, forcing the reader beyond immediate and obvious levels of interpretation.[27]

Derrida's analysis of the *Phaedrus* shares with the work of Gadamer and Ricoeur a refusal to attempt to instate contemporary interpretations in the role of "authorial intent." Derrida explicates something of the "system" or "chain of significations" operative in the text itself. He emphasizes, however, that "the system here is not simply that of the intentions of an author who goes by the name of Plato. The system is not primarily that of what someone *meant-to-say* [*un vouloir-dire*]."[28] Derrida allows that some of the links in such a chain of significations may have been intended by Plato and are deliberately inscribed in the text. In other cases, however, "Plato can *not* see the links, can leave them in the shadow or break them up. And yet these links go on working of themselves."[29]

Thus, even in one of the central texts that has operated historically as a source for the condemnation of mimesis, the mimetic nature of language exhibits a creative and disclosive capacity to produce new meaning and insight. Language frees itself from the mind of the author, extending beyond his or her intentions through its capacity to speak freshly to historically changing loci of appropriation.

Reformulations of Mimesis

Derrida's deconstruction of the Platonic texts that, interpreted literally, provide arguments for the disparagement of mimetic activity brings to light some of the complexities involved in the relationship between mimesis and hermeneutics. Through interpretation the creative capacities of the text may be disclosed in a variety of ways. Because mimesis in the form of writing has this potential, hermeneutics becomes a creative and critical undertaking. However, while Derrida provides a deconstruction, he does not undertake the reconstruction of mimesis that his work implies.

Some attempt at a reconstruction of mimesis has been contributed by Gadamer. We noted in the previous chapter that the historical orientation of Gadamer's hermeneutics reflects critically upon notions of an "original" place of truth, whether this is formulated on the level of Heidegger's "Being" or Schleiermacher's and Hirsch's "authorial intent." Within Gadamer's development of a historical and hermeneutical approach to truth there resides an understanding of mimesis that views it as disclosive rather than reproductive. Gadamer argues that "representation is an ontological event and belongs to the ontological level of what is represented. Through being represented it experiences, as it were, an increase in being."[30] Representation is not simply "added on" to preexistent entities determinable as such but rather divulges aspects of things heretofore obscured.

The creative and productive nature of mimesis is a necessary aspect of the historical and disclosive dimensions of hermeneutics. However, the reconstruction of mimesis indicated by the passage quoted above, among others, is not adequately developed by Gadamer. The main problem requiring analysis derives from the implications of the displacement of the notion of a fixed "original" for a theory of the relationship between world and representation (particularly representation in language). The original is not final or closed in its nature, for it continues to "become" through representation. That is, the original has a "rift in its self-identity"[31] and therefore cannot properly function as a fixed reference point for processes of reduplication. Indeed, the logical conclusion to be drawn from Gadamer's arguments concerning the *interpretive* nature of human being-in-the-world is that all "originals" are themselves in some sense mimetic.

This is a line of inquiry Gadamer does not develop, although his notion of "double representation" would seem to lend itself to a treatment of this issue. Yet when this notion is analyzed, it is actually less penetrating than it might be. As an example of double representation, Gadamer refers to the "interpretive arts," in which "both the piece of writing and its reproduction, say on the stage, are representation."[32] While this is an important point, it fails to address the broader issues of the mimetic nature of existence itself, the relationship between the mimetic arts per se and this encompassing existential dimension.

At this point we may rejoin Ricoeur at the place where he addresses these problems by developing a reconstruction of the notion of mimesis. In many of Ricoeur's later writings he will employ the term mimesis in ways that, upon close scrutiny, appear to have slightly different connotations. This diversification of the concept of mimesis is given a clear articulation in *Time and Narrative*.

Ricoeur differentiates the functions of mimesis into the threefold structure of mimesis$_1$, mimesis$_2$, and mimesis$_3$. The significance of this development should not be underestimated on account of its cumbersome appearance. Threefold mimesis is far more complex than Gadamer's extension of the mimetic process to cover different stages of artistic activity. Ricoeur provides a preliminary definition of the three dimensions of mimesis as "a reference back to the familiar pre-understanding we have of the order of action; an entry into the realm of poetic composition; and finally a new configuration by means of this poetic refiguring of the pre-understood order of action."[33] The central term in this triad, mimesis$_2$, indicates what is commonly understood as the representational arts per se. The innovation of threefold mimesis resides in the expansion of the notion of representation to include both the pregiven cultural worlds inhabited by human beings and activity transformative of those worlds.

This development allows Ricoeur to address issues surrounding the relationship of representational structures, specifically texts, to the "existential" realm. That is, mimesis$_1$ and mimesis$_3$ provide the means for articulating the referential dimensions of representational acts, without requiring the positing of nonrepresentational referents. Representation per se refers to a being-in-the-world that is culturally and linguistically formed and hence is itself mimetic. It is this interaction of the hermeneutics of the text with the existential sphere that we will be concerned with. Thus we shall have relatively little to say concerning mimesis$_2$, although Ricoeur devotes considerable attention to an analysis of this level of representation as manifested in historical narrative and in the novel. For our present purposes, mimesis$_2$ will be presumed in the existence of texts of all types, including conceptual works such as those of Plato. Our primary concern is the operation found in mimesis$_3$, which intersects with the hermeneutical process. Since these processes are predicated upon memesis$_1$, however, we need to examine this stage of representation before turning to a more specific analysis of Ricoeur's hermeneutics.

The notion of mimesis$_1$ hinges upon the irreducible temporality and linguisticality of human being-in-the-world. Narrative and other linguistic and mimetic forms, which are grouped under the heading of mimesis$_2$, are not extrinsic formations glossing an existence defined by uninterpreted sensory-level, or "raw feel," relationships to reality. Rather, human existence is carried out within linguistically formed temporal worlds from which representation per se emerges in distilled and heightened forms of creative expression. Human activity is expressed in narration "because it is always already articulated by signs, rules, and norms. It is always already symbolically mediated."[34]

This intrinsic symbolic and linguistic nature of human existence characterizes all cultural reality. Ricoeur does not define mimesis$_1$ in terms of preliterary cultural periods; nor does threefold mimesis lend itself to linear developmental notions of historical progress. Indeed, while the application of the concept of mimesis$_1$ to cultural reality gives expression to an irreducible dimension of being-in-the-world, the differentiation of threefold mimesis is to some extent heuristic. If, for matters of expediency, we confine ourselves to modern cultures, it is clear that any manifestation on the level of mimesis$_1$ is already permeated by innumerable operations on the levels of mimesis$_2$ and mimesis$_3$.

Mimesis$_1$ is best understood in the light of Heidegger's formulations concerning the temporal and linguistic nature of existence. Ricoeur himself develops his arguments with specific reference to Heidegger, whom he summarizes in stating that "within-timeness is defined by a basic characteristic of Care, our being thrown among things."[35] The human experience of temporality occurs within a set of relational activities with others and with "things" in the world. These relational modes of being are defined by Heidegger as *care*, as seen in chapter 2. If we become aware of our "thrownness," we do so only subsequent to our existential modes having taken shape within determined social matrices and relations. Because of this prior conditioning, it is automatic for us to become immersed in unreflective relational modes to things as ready-to-hand. This is where the problem of mimesis₁ comes into play. In an unreflective condition, the linguistic determinations of being-in-the-world, which are endemic to cultural worlds, are taken as value-neutral tools of operation, and their specific interpretive and mimetic nature is suppressed. Such immersion within the immediacy of dominant modes of being and acting, Ricoeur argues, "tends to make our description of temporality dependent on the description of the things about which we care."[36]

To become submerged in a relationship to things founded upon the presumed immediacy of the given and the linearity of temporal activities within a prestructured world is to obscure and repress the representational nature of existence. For Ricoeur, existential temporality can be called "narrative," and hence mimetic, because it is always mediated and organized by linguistically formed cultural structures. Because of this, an attention to the problems of language and representation provides the means of counteracting the closure of specific cultural worlds. "It is language, therefore, with its store of meanings, that prevents the description of Care, in the mode of preoccupation, from becoming prey to the description of things we care about."[37]

Ricoeur refers to Heidegger's analysis of the relations between the interpretive modes in which human beings interact with reality and the temporal structures of those modes. By explicating the temporality of being-in-the-world in terms of the retention and protention that characterize the apprehension of the "now," Heidegger reveals the interpretive basis of temporal experience. This analysis of within-time-ness serves to effect a break with "the linear representation of time, understood as a simple succession of nows."[38] The introduction of complex notions of the temporality of existence is related to the disruption of the immersion in "present things." This places us in a position to see that "the existential now is determined by the present of preoccupation, which is a 'making present,' inseparable from 'awaiting' and 'retaining.'"[39] It is here that the interpretive and representational structures of culture are operative in the apprehension of "immediate" reality.

Ricoeur further argues that this complexified and differentiated understanding of temporal existence means that "a bridge is constructed for the first time between the narrative order and Care."[40] Temporal existence as analyzed by Heidegger indicates that Care, that is, active relational engagement with others in the world, occurs within linguistically formed frameworks of representation. Existence itself is formed by linguistic practice, which means, as noted above, that the operations of mimesis$_2$ and mimesis$_3$ have already contributed to the constitution of mimesis$_1$. "Being-in-the-world according to narrativity is a being-in-the-world already marked by the linguistic (*langagiére*) practice leading back to this preunderstanding."[41] The linguisticality of temporal existence may be termed *narrative* because it involves action, language, and meaning. This allows us to conclude, with Ricoeur, that "narrative configurations and the most elaborated forms of temporality corresponding to them share the same foundation of within-time-ness."[42] It should be emphasized that to say that human existence is characterized by an inherent "narrativity" does not involve the imposition of an artificial logical order upon it. Behind Ricoeur's formulations there lurks no teleology or chronology of beginning-middle-end that seeks to encapsulate the flux of experience into neat prefabricated structures. Indeed, the value of the differentiations involved in threefold mimesis is that it avoids the error of attributing the more deliberate, distilled, and highly-organized configurations of mimesis$_2$ to the more contingent and open-ended narrativity of mimesis$_1$.

The inherent linguisticality and narrativity of temporal existence makes possible the emergence of narrative per se (mimesis$_2$): "We can see the richness in the meaning of mimesis$_1$. To imitate or represent action is first to preunderstand what human acting is, in its semantics, its symbolic system, its temporality. Upon this preunderstanding, common to both poets and their readers, emplotment is constructed and, with it, textual and literary mimetics."[43] Moreover, it is the intrinsic narrativity of cultural existence that makes efficacious the critical reflection of forms of mimesis$_2$ back upon reality by means of mimesis$_3$. In order to clarify and articulate this process, we need to turn specifically to the problem of reference. For Ricoeur, a reconstructed notion of reference is no more dispensable than is a reconstructed notion of mimesis. This reconstruction will involve attention both to metaphor and to hermeneutics.

The Problem of Reference

Ricoeur's reconstruction of the concept of mimesis provides the conceptual framework for understanding language as creatively disclosive of Being rather than simply as providing significations of things in their preexistent forms. Moreover, the notions of mimesis₁ and mimesis₃ reveal that language use is not limited to specific acts within an otherwise nonlinguistic existential world. Language is constitutive of human being-in-the-world.

However, because the cultural-historical worlds inhabited by human beings are themselves the product of mimetic and interpretive activity, this does not necessitate or validate the dissolution of the distinctions between these worlds and the specific acts of configuration in texts which Ricoeur calls mimesis₂. There are clear processes of transformation operative within the movement from mimesis₁ to mimesis₂. Ricoeur uses the general term *configuration* to designate these transformations, which include the operations endemic to literary production. The transformative dimension of configuration prevents the collapse of the threefold differentiation of mimesis into an undifferentiated notion of language.

Here, once again, an essential tension is evident in Ricoeur's formulations. His inquiry is situated at the intersection between the establishment of analytic distinctions and the need to involve hermeneutics in a critical reflection upon existence. The differentiations of threefold mimesis cannot be such as to segregate these modes into watertight compartments. In this respect Ricoeur may be seen to be continuing a vital dimension of Heidegger's ontological inquiry. For this form of inquiry, as for hermeneutics, language is not closed in on itself, trapped within its own structures, but is instead the "house of Being."

Ricoeur articulates the relationship between language and Being, and hence the critical and transformative dimensions of hermeneutics, by a reconstruction of the notion of reference. The disclosive and creative nature of language does not derive from, or result in, an abolishing of the functions of reference. Rather, with the reformulation of mimesis and all that this implies, we are led to a complexification of our understanding of reference. In order to act meaningfully and disclosively upon human existence, language must point beyond itself. "In the phenomenon of the sentence, language passes outside itself; reference is the mark of the self-transcendence of language."[44]

Ricoeur seeks to maintain the connectedness of language and Being while avoiding a collapse of the differentiation that allows language to function. Being as such cannot be dirempted and isolated from the disclosive capacity of language. Yet neither does the nature of Being allow of a total absorption into language. A sense of the alterity of Being and the difference between language and Being maintains the tension necessary to creative and critical reflection. Based on this difference, the minimalist argument for the irreducibility of the referential function of language is that "something must be for something to be said."[45]

The employment of such tradition laden terminology as *being* and *reference* may create the impression that Ricoeur is positing an extralinguistic reality accessible to human understanding. It is not surprising that Ricoeur has been criticized for "referring to a non-linguistic referent as if this notion were immediately self-evident."[46] However, a careful examination of Ricoeur's arguments, both in *The Rule of Metaphor* and elsewhere, reveals that his insistence upon the referential function of language is not predicated upon the self-evidence of a nonlinguistic referent. Ricoeur acknowledges that "there is no standpoint outside language" and that "it is and has always been *in* language that men claim to speak *about* language."[47] Nevertheless, "language possesses the *reflective* capacity to place itself at a distance and to consider itself . . . in relation to the totality of what is. Language designates itself and its other."[48] Clearly, Ricoeur is not accepting a rigid dichotomy that imposes a choice between positing human access to "things as such" or positing closed linguistic universes incapable of self-transcending referential functions. It remains to be seen how successful he is in subverting this dichotomy and maintaining the essential tension that characterizes his reformulations of reference.

The full extent of Ricoeur's innovations can only gradually become clear, since a key component of these will be an extended analysis of the problem of metaphor. For the moment, however, there is an initial point that, while perhaps obvious to some, nevertheless needs to be stressed. In analyzing mimesis₁, we saw that Ricoeur develops his arguments concerning the representational nature of human existence in the light of an understanding of the linguisticality of being-in-the-world that is in accordance with the formulations of both Heidegger and Gadamer. It follows from these arguments that human interaction with reality is shaped by language. At the same time, through the course of linguistically shaped historical existence, cultural worlds come into being and take on a considerable degree of independence from existing individuals. To indicate that the referential function of language operates within such cultural worlds, Ricoeur differentiates between *Welt* and *Umwelt*.[49] While the latter represents an "environment" in a naturalistic sense, the former gives expression to the encompassing cultural contexts that shape human existence.

Cultural worlds, in all their variety, antecede individuals and operate as formative matrices within which life is carried out. While not "original," "objective," or "nonlinguistic," cultural worlds nevertheless provide the contexts for the referential structures through which discourse functions meaningfully. As Thompson expresses the matter, "The referential function in everyday speech cannot be divorced from a theory of the social-psychological conditions of action."[50] It is because cultural worlds take on this independence and this role of matrix of existence and speech that a differentiation between mimesis$_1$ and mimesis$_2$ is required. The latter may be said to operate referentially in relation to the former, without the former itself being posited as nonlinguistic.

Moreover, it is because existential worlds are themselves constituted linguistically (i.e., mimetically and interpretively) that linguistic acts have transformative potential. While culture is composed of material as well as nonmaterial forces, the structuring of these forces is governed by the dominant interests and worldviews shaping the culture. In other words, "many an aspect which we uncritically attribute to 'social reality' are in fact organizing principles of our being-in-the-world."[51] These organizing principles are hermeneutical in nature and may be subjected to disclosure and transformation by a reflexive hermeneutical analysis.

Ricoeur describes the critical relationship between linguistic disclosure (mimesis$_2$) and cultural reality (mimesis$_1$) as a referential operation. He maintains that it is the referential function that allows language in general and hermeneutics in particular to operate critically in relation to cultural worlds. "If you suppress this referential function," he argues, "only an absurd game of errant signifiers remains."[52] Like Gadamer, Ricoeur discerns an ethical dimension to hermeneutics, and this is inseparable from the capacity of linguistic disclosure to speak *to* existential worlds.

Here the basic issues involved in Ricoeur's critique of structuralist linguistics become relevant to the argument. The crux of the matter is that Ricoeur insists upon a differentiation between the sense and the reference of the text.[53] He emphasizes that it is in the latter phenomenon that the meaning of the sentence or text is manifested. This distinction between sense and reference means "that what is *intended* by discourse [*l'intente*], the correlate of the entire sentence, is irreducible to what semiotics calls the signified, which is nothing but the counterpart of a sign within the language code."[54] In this way Ricoeur rejects the primacy of what Saussure calls *langue*, the linguistic codes that are intrinsic to the structures of languages independently of any instance of language use or "speech" (*parole*).[55]

The structuralist focus upon langue is also a focus upon the synchronic and simultaneous nature of the closed internal relations of a sign system. This focus means that the synchronic aspect of language "can be isolated from its diachronic or successive and historical aspect."[56] In opposition to this position, Ricoeur argues that there are artificial restrictions at work in this isolation of the sign-signified relation from the contextuality of actual linguistic usage. In line with the temporal-disclosive ontology of Heidegger and the historical hermeneutics of Gadamer, Ricoeur reverses the primacy of the synchronic over the diachronic. This reversal places the emphasis upon the nature of language as discourse, that is, as it is employed expressively within specific referential contexts:

> Not only are the two planes of the sign and the discourse distinct, but the first is an abstraction of the second; in the last analysis, the sign owes its very meaning as sign to its usage in discourse. How would we know that a sign *stands for* . . . if its use in discourse did not invest it with the scope that relates it to that very thing *for which* it stands? To the extent that it restricts itself to the closed world of signs, semiotics is an abstraction from *semantics*, which relates the internal constitution of the sign to the transcendent aims of reference.[57]

Here it becomes clear that Ricoeur, in agreement with such diverse figures as Wittgenstein and Foucault, understands the reality of language to be inseparable from its instances of use.[58] Linguistic meaning cannot be determined in any full and final sense apart from its operations within specific contexts. This means that while linguistic meaning cannot be given an absolute determination "in itself," neither is it bound to any one context of interpretation. The transcendent dimension of language does not involve the positing of "ideal" meaning but rather derives from the inexhaustible variety of personal and historical contexts of interpretation.

The shifts in focus from sense to reference and from langue to parole reflect a parallel movement from the "internal" structure of a work to the world which it discloses in the interpretive process. "The structure of the work is in fact its sense, and the world of the work its reference."[59] The notion of the world of the work is central to Ricoeur's reconstruction of the notion of reference. This transfers the focus of the problem of reference from the ostensive designation of nonlinguistic entities to the "disclosure of worlds" that are themselves linguistically constituted. There are two seemingly unrelated linguistic phenomena Ricoeur conjoins to explicate the "non-ostensive" reference that is integral to semantic disclosure. The first, metaphor, actually provides a model for the second, interpretation.

Metaphor

The creative disclosure of meaning through metaphor derives from a tension between the form of disclosure or vision effected by metaphorical utterances and the anterior worldviews governing the hearer or reader. It is because of this tensive relationship between the textual and existential worlds that metaphorical disclosure, hermeneutics, and the cultural critique of mimesis$_3$ are intertwined in Ricoeur's articulation of the experience of truth.

In some of the initial discussions in *The Rule of Metaphor*, Ricoeur attempts to articulate the nature of the tension endemic to metaphor without reference to the existential and hermeneutical contexts of understanding. For example, Ricoeur argues that this tension derives from the relationship between the components of a phrase or sentence. Following I. A. Richards, Ricoeur distinguishes between words that, in a specific instance of language, are functioning "literally" and those that are functioning "metaphorically." Ricoeur summarizes Richards's position that in a metaphorical sentence some words are used metaphorically and some literally. He views this trait as distinguishing "metaphor from proverb, allegory, and riddle, in which all the words are used metaphorically."[60]

Ricoeur notes Richards's use of the terms *tenor* and *vehicle* to designate the constituent elements of metaphorical tension. At the same time, he expresses a preference for the terms *focus* and

frame derived from Max Black, which he views as equivalent to
tenor and vehicle. The focus indicates the word or words used
"metaphorically," and the frame indicates "the rest of the sentence."[61] Giving as a standard example of a metaphorical sentence
"The chairman *plowed* through the discussion," Ricoeur notes
that "plowed" acts as the focus, that is, as the "metaphorical
word."[62] The word *plowed* can be designated in this manner since
it "clashes" with the rest of the sentence because of its reference
to an activity that, literally understood, is completely removed
from the topic of the sentence as a whole. However, the metaphorical nature of the word *plowed* is dependent upon its relation
to the frame or vehicle. Because of this relation, the entire sentence becomes a metaphor. The sentence is meaningless if
plowed is taken literally, and this provokes a metaphorical troping that changes both the meaning of the focus and the nature of
the frame.

Ricoeur's linking of the terminology of Richards and Black, and
the understanding of metaphorical tension this indicates, has
come under some criticism. In her important analysis of theories
of metaphor, Soskice has argued that Richards's "interanimation
theory" of metaphor views the trope as emerging from "the interplay of the interpretive possibilities of the whole utterance."[63]
This means that metaphor cannot be produced by "individual
words in isolation" but rather requires the interplay (or interanimation) of the components of complete utterances, *including
context*. Therefore, Soskice argues that Ricoeur's equation of
Richards's tenor and vehicle with Black's focus and frame is mis-
construed.[64] It is Black's terms that lend themselves to theories of
metaphor as involving "two subjects," for example, the subject
man being understood in terms of the subject wolf in "man is a
wolf."[65] This position lapses into a "comparison" theory rather
than interaction or interanimation theory of metaphor and fails
to account for the metaphorical nature of utterances such as
"giddy brink."[66]

Soskice argues that "metaphor has one true subject which
tenor and vehicle conjointly depict and illumine in full."[67] The
operating feature of this capacity to depict a subject metaphorically derives not from the conjunction of two "subjects" but
from the act of "speaking of one thing in terms which are seen to
be suggestive of another."[68] This conjunction of two modes of
speaking of a single subject matter necessarily involves the context, particularly the reader or hearer as the point of reference for

notions of literality and the fit of expressive suggestion. This interanimation, not only of words or subjects but of utterances and interpretive contexts, produces "a new understanding, a new referential access . . . new possibilities of vision."[69]

While Soskice is correct in taking Ricoeur to task for some of his formulations, it would seem that rather than refuting his overall position, Soskice helps both to reveal inconsistencies within and to clarify the nature of Ricoeur's arguments. Ricoeur's overall theory of metaphor is in fact an interanimation theory, one that understands metaphor as disclosing a unique dimension of a single subject, and doing so in such a way as to involve a tension that incorporates the entirety of the utterance, including the context. Indeed, it is precisely the involvement of reader and context in the process of metaphorical troping that links Ricoeur's theory of metaphor to his disclosive hermeneutics.

The relation between metaphorical tension and hermeneutics begins to be evident when Ricoeur speaks of the tension produced by the conjunction of words and phrases that cannot fit together meaningfully on a literal level as "semantic impertinence" (l'impertinence sémantique, derived from Jean Cohen).[70] Because this impertinence produces a transformation to a new level of meaning not otherwise accessible, Ricoeur also speaks of a "semantic innovation" (une innovation sémantique) in this connection.[71] The trope in the semantic function of the focus word or words produces a related troping of the sentence as a whole, making it metaphorical. "Accordingly, metaphor is a semantic event that takes place where several semantic fields intersect. It is because of this construction that all the words, taken together, make sense. Then, and only then, the metaphorical twist is at once an event and a meaning, an event that means or signifies, an emergent meaning created by language."[72] The metaphorical event may be understood as an innovation in meaning emerging from the tension of semantic impertinence. Metaphor, therefore, cannot be reduced to the impertinence itself or to the incommensurable components that establish it. Rather, metaphor and its transformation in meaning "is the answer of discourse to the threat of destruction represented by semantic impertinence."[73] Metaphor emerges from the violation of the literal, and from the "ruins" of this violation creates new meaning.

The notion of semantic impertinence seems to be based upon the presupposition that there are determinable meanings on a "literal" level that can be troped through their conjunction with "metaphorical" words. However, one of the implications of Ricoeur's analysis of language is that the notion of a foundational "literal" meaning of words is insupportable. In accordance with this view, he formulates an argument concerning an "initial metaphorical impulse." The development of "proper" and "literal" meanings occurs through the habituation to uses that were initially metaphorical. "The idea of an initial metaphorical impulse destroys these oppositions between proper and figurative, ordinary and strange, order and transgression. It suggests the idea that order itself proceeds from the metaphorical constitution of semantic fields, which themselves give rise to genus and species."[74]

Does this argument serve to invalidate Ricoeur's formulations concerning semantic impertinence? Such a possibility is raised by some of the work of Derrida. Without himself developing a notion of an "original metaphorical impulse," Derrida, on the basis of a series of illustrations drawn from Mallarmé, establishes that no "proper" meaning remains in metaphorical statements. Because "everything becomes metaphorical," Derrida, in stark contrast to Ricoeur, argues that "there is no longer any literal meaning and, hence, no longer any metaphor either."[75] The point of departure for this conclusion is an understanding of metaphor as a figure that "claims to procure access to the unknown and to the indeterminate by the detour of something recognizably familiar."[76] If the familiar is robbed of its literal standing, therefore, the metaphorical operations that are parasitically dependent upon the literal are sapped of vitality.

With this interpretation of metaphor, Derrida aligns himself with Heidegger against Ricoeur. He refers to Heidegger's expression "Language is the house of Being," wherein traditionally the metaphor would seem to operate by means of the "familiar" term *house* granting meaning to the unfamiliar term *Being*. Reversing this order, Derrida argues that "Being says more to us, or promises more about the house than the house about Being."[77] However, the term *Being* retains a quality of mystery, and hence "Being has not become the proper of this supposedly known, familiar, nearby being."[78] Here the "metaphorical" structure of the familiar reflecting meaningfully upon the unfamiliar is no longer operative. "We are therefore no longer dealing with a metaphor in the usual sense, nor with a simple inversion permutating the places in the usual tropical structure."[79] In this way, the concept of metaphor is overshadowed and displaced as a disclosive process.

The real problem Derrida perceives in metaphor is that it is linked to a notion of the apprehension of reality as "natural" and "present." This would seem to be presumably uninterpreted apperception of the "thing in itself," a notion the present work has continually sought to call into question. "Like *mimesis,* metaphor *comes back* to *physis,* to its truth and its presence. There, nature always refinds its own, proper analogy, its own resemblance to itself, takes increase only from itself."[80] Derrida denies that metaphor is representative of the truly creative and disclosive process Ricoeur claims it is. Rather, metaphor is bound to a notion of the natural and literal and can only reflect back upon this same pregiven nature. "Does not such a metaphorology, transported into the philosophical field, always, by destination, rediscover the same?" inquires Derrida. He continues in the same vein, asking "What *other* than this return of the same is to be found when one seeks metaphor?"[81]

Such counterarguments allow us to gain a clearer understanding, in this case, of what Ricoeur is and *is not* saying. Misconceptions can be avoided if one remembers that Ricoeur is arguing within the context of a historically and culturally grounded notion of discourse. That is, Ricoeur's analyses of language are not semiotic but semantic and, as we shall see, hermeneutic. For him, the notion of the "literal" is predicated upon the cultural matrices articulated in the notion of mimesis$_1$. Thus Ricoeur maintains that "the metaphorical use of a word could always be opposed to its literal use; but literal use does not mean proper in the sense of originary, but simply correct, 'usual.' The literal sense is the one that is lexicalized."[82]

The tension of metaphor is based upon the historical use of terms, rather than upon a notion of the proper on the synchronic level of langue. This does not privilege the linguistic component of the metaphorical statement that is more familiar or is used literally. It means that the literal is itself the product of cultural interpretations. The difference between the literal and the nonliteral, the familiar and the strange, occurs in relation to the interpretive standpoint of the culturally located reader.

This means that metaphorical tension is relative to hermeneutical context and is directly linked to the perspectives representative of cultural frames of reference. "All our words being polysemic to some degree, the univocity or plurivocity of our discourse is not the accomplishment of words but of contexts."[83] The interpretive framework brought to bear upon the sentence is the basis for semantic impertinence, but the impertinence itself is

disruptive of the literal and hence potentially of the very interpretive standpoint that makes it possible. Since, as Ricoeur repeatedly stresses, *all* the components in a metaphorical statement undergo troping, there remains no fixed anchor to keep the
metaphorical meaning chained to the literal and the present. One
must begin from *some* standpoint, since this is the nature of human understanding, but that standpoint is itself subjected to disruption and transformation through metaphorical reversal.

A statement such as "Language is the house of Being" *is* metaphorical, but not because "being" or "language" derive their
meaning from the familiarity of "house." Rather, the conjunction
of these incommensurables transforms the meaning of each component of the statement and makes something new of the statement in its entirety. In the creative disclosure produced by metaphor, "house" is no more familiar than "being," and indeed takes
on its meaning through the relationship of "being" and "language." "In other words, it is in the region of unusual syntagmatic
liaisons, of new and purely contextual combinations, that the se-
cret of metaphor is to be sought."[84] To answer Derrida, then, there
is an "otherness" operative in metaphorical processes. It is a historically derived other, introduced through the interaction of the
diversity and variety of linguistic forms and historical contexts.
To follow Soskice, it is the interanimation of discourse with historical contextuality, mediated through the reader, that produces
the troping and semantic disclosure of the metaphorical event.

The differentiation between living and dead metaphor also has
a historical basis. Once a metaphor becomes incorporated into
cultural use, it loses the tension productive of its disruptive and
creative properties. This, however, is not simply a process of en-
tropy but according to Ricoeur is constitutive of linguistic structures and laws. Saussure's dichotomy between langue and parole
is again challenged, this time because language *use*, in the creation of metaphors, contributes to the lexicalized meanings of
words. "The circle can be described in the following manner.
Initial polysemy equals 'language,' the living metaphor equals
'speech,' metaphor in common use represents the return of speech
towards language, and subsequent polysemy equals language. This
circle is a perfect illustration of the untenability of the Saussurean
dichotomy."[85]

The dependency of the polysemic and transformative dimensions of metaphor upon usage and context returns us to the problem of reference. In explicating this point, Ricoeur develops the

differentiation between the sense and the reference of the text, which was discussed earlier, and applies it to metaphor. There is a referential moment operative in metaphor, but it is one that displaces literal reference. This "second order" reference is produced by the capacity of metaphorical statements to display worlds through the suspension of descriptive discourse. "Just as the metaphorical statement captures its sense as metaphorical midst the ruins of the literal sense, it also achieves its reference upon the ruins of what might be called . . . its literal reference."[86]

Ricoeur employs the expression "metaphorical reference" to describe the disclosure of aspects of human being-in-the-world that do not lend themselves to descriptive or literal reference. This includes the interpretive modalities which are operative on the level of mimesis$_1$ but which, not being "objects," cannot be designated or apprehended in themselves. The transference from the literal to the metaphorical discloses the nature of the literal and the interpretive constraints upon perception, understanding, and being it exercises. Established frameworks and modes of being become disclosed as they are relativized and displaced.

Nevertheless, we might inquire how the notion of semantic impertinence actually functions referentially. What is the nature of this referential disclosure, and how does it incorporate a critical moment? An indication of the line of development Ricoeur's argument follows is provided when he states that in order to fulfill "the claim of the metaphorical statement to reach reality in some particular manner . . . tension must be introduced into metaphorically affirmed being."[87] The nature of the tension inherent in metaphor is further developed in terms of the referential operations occurring in hermeneutical understanding, and by means of understanding to an application in the existential sphere. Pursuing this problem, Ricoeur asks: "Does not the tension that affects the copula in its relational function also affect the copula in its existential function? This question contains the key to the notion of *metaphorical truth*."[88] In his attention to the problem of the referential relation of metaphorical disclosure to the existential sphere, Ricoeur's concern becomes explicitly focused upon the truth of existential interpretations.

Here, as well, we return to the problem of articulating an approach to truth that is not locked within fixed interpretive frameworks of disclosure. Such an approach addresses the level of the ontological rather than the ontic and acts critically in relation to ontic modes of thinking and being. This critical dimension, which subverts closed frameworks of disclosure, is operative in metaphor by virtue of what Ricoeur calls *split reference* (*référence dédoublée*).[89] This expresses metaphorical reference as including a negative or critical element in its disclosure. "The paradox consists in the fact that there is no other way to do justice to the notion of metaphorical truth than to include the critical incision of the (literal) 'is not' within the ontological vehemence of the (metaphorical) 'is.'"[90] Because metaphor subverts the literal and the familiar, it reflects critically upon these ontic "givens" concurrently with its disclosure of new meaning.

We have argued that the notions of proper and improper, and therefore the tension between them, are context-dependent and hence interpretation-dependent. The relationship between the operations of metaphor and those of hermeneutics becomes even more apparent when we pursue the problem of the realization and application of the split reference disclosed by metaphor. For "it will be the task of interpretation to elaborate the design of a world liberated, by suspension, from descriptive reference."[91] Through hermeneutics the split reference engendered by metaphor is applied in specific cultural-historical locations. At the same time, it is metaphor that provides the model for the tension inherent in, and the disclosure made manifest by, hermeneutical inquiry. The hermeneutics Ricoeur formulates does not only put into practice the critical and disclosive force of metaphor. It is a metaphorical operation in its own right, functioning on a level where the three forms of mimesis intersect.

Distanciation and Hermeneutical Disclosure

There is a parallelism in the structures of the metaphorical and the hermeneutical disclosure of truth. Indeed, "the case of metaphor is only a particular case for a general theory of hermeneutics."[92] The tension between identity and difference, familiarity and strangeness, that produces metaphorical disclosure through semantic impertinence is reflected in hermeneutical understanding.

Ricoeur expresses the enabling tension essential to hermeneutics by means of the concept of *distanciation*. This is related to Gadamer's notion of effective-historical consciousness by virtue of its expressing the irreducible yet attenuated operation of the past upon the present. "The history of effects is precisely what occurs under the condition of historical distance. It is the nearness of the remote . . . , it is the efficacy at a distance. There is thus a paradox of otherness, which is essential to historical consciousness."[93] Attention to the distanciation involved in this historical efficacy maintains the creative tension between proximity and alterity in the hermeneutical relation. This means that "the play of difference is included in the processes of convergence"[94] and that the collapse into "fusion" that characterizes many of Gadamer's remarks is avoided. The difference expressed in the concept of distanciation prevents Ricoeur's hermeneutics from presuming "unbroken historical continuity." As Fackenheim has indicated, such a presumption is unwarranted in light of the shattering nature of recent historical events.[95] Yet although Fackenheim argues that a presupposition of historical continuity is inherent in contemporary hermeneutics, this need not be the case. The concept of distanciation puts into practice the Heideggerian notion of the "disturbed assignment," by which the disruption of brokenness reveals to us the nature of our projects and orientations. If history reveals to us the failure of some of our governing paradigms, this is disclosed and articulated by the distanciation operative in critical hermeneutics.

There is a multiple application of the concept of distanciation. One form is operative in the production of the text itself whereby it becomes disengaged from the author's intentionality and the immediacy of cultural-historical contexts. Distanciation is intrinsic to the functioning of language; that is, "distanciation is not the product of methodology and hence something superfluous and parasitical; rather it is constitutive of the text as writing."[96] The text, as we have argued, is not context-free or "ideal" in its constitution. Yet it transcends the specificity of particular sociohistorical contexts because it relates itself differently to varying interpretive standpoints and matrices of understanding.

A process of "double distanciation"[97] is operative here, by which the text maintains an alterity in relation to both author and interpreter. In terms of the latter, this means that it is not the subjectivity of the interpreter that need dominate and determine the outcome of hermeneutical inquiry. The concept of distanciation allows Ricoeur to develop a notion of hermeneutical appropriation that is not founded upon the primacy of the subject. "Appropriation is the *response* to this double distanciation which is linked to the matter of the text, as regards its sense and as regards its reference."[98] The notion of distanciation in hermeneutics provides the key to maintaining the alterity of the text, stimulating the critical and reflexive transformation of subjective modes of knowing and being.

In order to develop the critical side of distanciation, it is necessary to elaborate on the nature of textual disclosure, which, while related to contexts of appropriation, retains an alterity in relation to them. Here the links between the split reference of metaphor and that of hermeneutics become evident. Just as semantic impertinence functions to introduce a creative tension in metaphor, so in a similar manner does distanciation function as the source of creative tension in hermeneutics. Distanciation maintains a pluralism of the referential sphere, preventing a collapse of the field of understanding into a single delimited historical matrix. Likewise, this tension, by its subversion of familiar frames of reference, will be productive of a new *form* of referentiality. Ricoeur describes the transformed reference that appears in hermeneutics as *nonostensive reference* and develops this by means of the related notion of "the world of the text."[99]

By means of nonostensive reference, the text discloses meaningful worlds that may be appropriated in the existential sphere. The reference that occurs here is a creative one that is founded on the formative nature of mimetic activity. The disclosed meaning does not refer back to some preestablished frame of reference but produces a "futural" referentiality characterized by the possibility of alternate interpretive modes. "The meaning is not something hidden but something disclosed. What gives rise to understanding is that which points toward a possible world, by means of the non-ostensive references of the text. Texts speak of possible worlds and of possible ways of orienting ourselves in these worlds."[100]

The language of "disclosed worlds" counteracts tendencies toward the reification of interpretive frameworks conditioned by the worldview of the inquiring subject. This critical dimension is predicated upon the insight, evident in Heidegger's work but frequently obscured in Gadamer's, that the subject is itself the product of worlds of meaning. Against "the tradition of the cogito" and "the pretension of the self to know itself by immediate intuition," Ricoeur argues that the self is not constituted as autonomous and self-transparent. Rather, "we understand ourselves only by the long detour of the signs of humanity deposited in cultural works."[101] As temporal and relational beings, we become what we are by active participation with others in linguistically constituted cultural worlds. Hence self-understanding and self-transformation occur with the disclosure and analysis of these worlds.

The tension and the creative split in the referential function, which allows for creative or nonostensive disclosure, is not predicated upon an interaction of subjects. Rather, it emerges from a tensional interaction of divergent contexts and frames of reference, that is, through a clash of worlds. "In short, the work *decontextualizes* itself, from the sociological as well as the psychological point of view, and is able to *recontextualize* itself differently in the act of reading. It follows that the mediation of the text cannot be treated as an extension of the dialogical situation."[102] This parallels the split reference of metaphor, by which it functions simultaneously in "two referential fields."[103] Because the subject is constituted *within* these referential fields, or worlds, a critical transformation of subjectivity is effected by nonostensive reference.

As with the split reference of metaphor, the critique involved in the hermeneutical disclosure of worlds is not simply "destructive." Closed interpretive frameworks, or worlds, are not adequately critiqued simply by being shown to be based upon uncertain or spurious premises or by being revealed as incomplete and inadequate. A more effective critique will include a constructive, that is, a creatively disclosive, dimension. The conjunction of critique with the opening of possibility is evident in Ricoeur's statement that "the mode of being-in-the-world opened by the text is the mode of the possible, or better of the power-to-be: therein resides the subversive force of the imaginary."[104] It is the disclosure of the possible, in a referential relation to the real, that simultaneously discloses the limitations and distortions of the actual.

Here Ricoeur's long-standing project of mediating between "iconoclastic" and "restorative" hermeneutics bears fruit.[105] The hermeneutics that produces the "destruction of idols" and the "reduction of illusions" and the hermeneutics that seeks to "restore meaning" each involves a "shift in the origin of meaning" away from the ego.[106] This relativizes the hegemony of the "present" and the "familiar" and effects a critique of the closure of modes of being-in-the-world. Again, this is not a matter of "shattering" the ego but rather of "exposing ourselves to the text and receiving from it an enlarged self" based upon "the world proposed."[107] This enlarging is not an "inflation" but a transcendence of previously fixed boundaries of knowing and being. It emerges from a reflexive encounter that occurs *between* the self and the other, opening the self by disclosing its relational and dependent nature.

There is yet a third form of distanciation that becomes manifest directly in the displacement of the closed world of the ego. Hermeneutics, by introducing critical complexification into the world of the self, distances the self from its prior modes of disclosure. In addition to the distanciation between text and author, and that between the text's world and reader's world, there is also effected a "distanciation in the relation of self to itself."[108] This is not as paradoxical as it may seem, since Ricoeur formulates his argument in terms of a notion of the self as constituted within the worlds of meaning it inhabits.

Hermeneutical distanciation liberates the self from the initial interpretive frameworks or modes of disclosure that form and condition its being. This produces a complexification of the self that is both creative and critical. The self's identification with specific worlds or interpretive frameworks is, in a deep sense, *self-denying*. The closure of worlds limits the self to specific ontic engagements with reality. Since the self is constituted in its relations, this closure limits the growth of potential experience and understanding. This is why "the subjectivity of the reader comes to itself only insofar as it is placed in suspense, unrealized, potentialised. . . . As reader, I find myself only by losing myself."[109] The familiar and habitual self-identity with established modes of being must be overturned in order for repressed and uncultivated aspects of the self to be realized.

The transformation of the self as reader is a moment in the critical reflection of hermeneutics upon the existential-historical sphere. This is lucidly expressed by Kristeva, who argues that "textual experience represents one of the most daring explorations the subject can allow himself, one that delves into his constitutive process. But at the same time and as a result, textual experience reaches the very foundation of the social—that which is exploited by sociality but which elaborates and can go beyond it, either destroying or transforming it."[110] Just as the representational configurations of the text emerge from worlds marked by language, so too do they reflect back upon these worlds by hermeneutical inquiry. In Ricoeur's terms, "mimesis$_3$ marks the intersection of the world of the text and the world of the hearer or reader."[111] The "configuration" of mimesis$_2$ moves toward the "refiguration" of mimesis₃ by means of the act of reading, which is synonymous with interpretation. For Ricoeur, however, this refiguration is fulfilled only "beyond" reading, in the "effective action" in the world instructed by the disclosure of the text.[112]

The displacement and expansion of the world of the reader, as the basis for a transformed activity in the world, provides the means whereby hermeneutics operates on an ontological level. Hermeneutical transformation is ontological rather than ontic because it addresses the level of interpretive modes of disclosure. It transforms the way we apprehend on the level of "worlds," rather than simply in relation to specific things we encounter that are already determined by prior, encompassing, interpretive worlds.

The refiguration operative on the ontological level is modeled after the process of "metaphorical redescription."[113] Speaking of the notions of metaphorical tension and split reference, Ricoeur argues that "the dynamism of meaning allowed access to the dynamic vision of reality which is the implicit ontology of the metaphorical utterance."[114] The disclosure of worlds of meaning, which enables the active transformation of being, is a dynamic process that occurs in the clash of semantic worlds effected by hermeneutical inquiry. Moreover, this clash has a historical basis that is itself dynamic. "We are never at the beginning of the process of truth," Ricoeur argues.[115] Rather, the quest for truth in the present is both conditioned by and given an existential basis in historical traces of being-in-the-world. Historicity is involved because the referential matrices of meaning, the tension between which provides the dynamism of disclosure, are based upon historical usage. "This semantic dynamism, proper to ordinary language, gives a 'historicity' to the power of signifying. New possibilities of signifying are opened up, supported by meanings that have already been established."[116] Historicity is dynamic both because it is the product of active being-in-the-world and because it is subject to continuing transformation through hermeneutical appropriation.

Furthermore, the ontology of hermeneutical disclosure is dynamic because the appropriation of the world of the text effects a critical transformation of the interpretive matrices of knowing and doing. As Ricoeur argues, this dynamic form of disclosure takes into account the linguisticality and historicality of human existence, which "require a concept of truth other than that of truth-verification, the correlate of our ordinary concept of reality."[117] Truth verification simply confirms specific ontic experiences within the frameworks governing the appearances of things. The dynamic and disclosive approach to truth developed by Heidegger, Gadamer, and Ricoeur displaces the closure of interpretive frames and opens our understanding to repressed and unthought dimensions of existence.

The approach to truth that has been traced from Heidegger through Ricoeur is hermeneutical, critical, and disclosive. It is not predicated upon the immediate apprehension of unanalyzed "ordinary" reality. Hermeneutics moves from the unreflexive ontic and apophantic to the level of disclosed frameworks of interpretation that condition any experience of immediacy *as* this or that.[118] In so doing, it incorporates a critical *is not* within the creative disclosure of the *is*. The quest for truth, on this level, leads us to rethink the interpretive patterns that govern our existential activity. It carries us beyond the false immediacy of the subjective appropriation of objects to the processes that are constitutive of subjectivity. In this way there is engendered an "unrestricted inquiry" that stimulates the ongoing supersession of distorted and closed modes of disclosure.

CONCLUSION

THE DISCLOSURE APPROACH to truth does not provide final resolutions to all of the problems that remain unresolved by traditional truth theories. What has been presented, however, is a form of inquiry that functions to prevent the blocking and distorting of truth as a process. The disclosure approach provides a means of access to an inquiry into truth on levels of analysis neglected by traditional theories. This approach attends to the existential, historical, and linguistic constitution of human experience and understanding. It constructs a historically generated and linguistically structured model of truth that avoids the curtailments and contradictions of traditional theories.

We have seen that the main problems besetting correspondence theories of truth when they attempt to function on the level of everyday experience and judgment derive from the predication of truth upon statements concerning "immediate" sense perception. In other words, as Toulmin notes, "it is implicitly assumed in any statement of the 'correspondence' theory of truth that all our significant utterances are intended as *descriptions*."[1] The restriction of attention to immediately (ontically) presented phenomena has as its concomitant a limitation to descriptive (or "assertive") discourse.

Yet for human beings experience does not occur in an immediate manner without the influence of interpretive factors. Perceptions and judgments are shaped by a variety of cultural and personal forces that delimit and interpret phenomena. Moreover, linguistic usage contributes to the formation of cultural worlds, and its mimetic force is irreducibly creative and transformative. The interpretive nature of language and of human experience is not simply a fetter constraining the pure activity of the mind directed toward the apodictic determination of truth. Instead, it is by means of linguistic expression and interpretation that human existence takes shape and develops.

In relation to the problem of truth, the interpretive nature of human experience takes on increased significance as one moves from simple perceptual givens to more complex social and existentially relevant judgments. The further one moves from questions of truth that are restricted to static objects situated before an observer, the greater becomes the interpretive influence of social worlds. By ignoring the linguistic and contextual factors operative in any descriptive statement, correspondence approaches foster the relativism they attempt to overcome. With the positing of truth as a closed descriptive relationship between perceiver and perceived, they forgo the reflexivity necessary to mediate variant standpoints and to overcome reductions to finite perspectives.

Coherence theories attempt to resolve the problem of the derivative nature of presented phenomena by focusing on the context that conditions and informs immediate experience. For traditional coherence theories, however, this leads to an infinite regress. Since every particular is determined by its fit within a greater whole, truth cannot be attained without the positing of human access to the absolute whole that conditions all. The coherence approach leads to the construction of metaphysical systems positing an absolute knowledge that is unwarranted in light of the finite, perspectival, and temporal nature of human existence. This last attribute means not only that we are trapped in time but also that through time, through historical existence, and through language, reality is disclosed in new and unforseen ways that defy the completion of systems. Therefore, coherence theories not only fail to come to grips with negative aspects of existence—such as error, contingency, and limitation—they also deny positive characteristics such as freedom and creativity. Finally, by creating complete, encompassing systems of knowledge, coherence theories reify specific perspectives under the guise of formulating or discovering objective contexts of understanding. Hence the closure and limitation of correspondence approaches is simply transferred to another level and given another form. Truth is no longer founded upon the direct perceptions and judgments of a finite human intellect but upon a system created by this same subject.

The hermeneutical approach to truth as disclosure parallels coherence theories in one major respect. Each seeks to supersede "immediate" observations on the level of correspondence and attend to the interpretive contexts that inform our experience. However, truth as disclosure does not posit a complete coherence of understanding, nor does it involve the requirement of "knowing the whole." Instead, following the ontological formulations of Heidegger, the disclosure approach articulates a model of reality that is dynamic, emergent, and necessarily unfinished. It sees in the historical and conceptual activities of humanity an ongoing process of the productive disclosure of reality, although it does not idealize this disclosure as automatically a condition of progress and refinement.

Hermeneutics draws upon the historical differentiation of interpretive experiences and expressions. However, this does not indicate an uncritical acceptance of those forms but rather an emphasis upon reflexive critique. Hermeneutics addresses the problems of relativism inherent in the finite, interpretive, and perspectival nature of human existence. It does so not by positing an apodictic truth that is beyond contingency but by seeing truth in the emergent awareness engendered by the critical interchange of finite stances. Hermeneutics does not embrace historical formations in the static and unreflective manner of "traditionalism." It engages the problems of language and history by turning to the inherent differentiation of language and history as the means of avoiding the curtailments of closed frameworks of understanding. It provides a historical and linguistic rather than an ideal basis for truth, and in so doing it articulates the critical-transcendental dimensions of the experience of truth.

The pursuit of truth shifts radically in several important respects in the transition from traditional theories of truth to the disclosure-oriented approach. In the latter, truth has the nature of a process. It has to do with the "modes of being" that shape human existence. Hence, truth appears within temporality, action, and relationality. Truth is no longer taken to be synonymous with a theory of knowledge but addresses modes of human existence. The quest for truth appears at the intersection of epistemology and ontology, at the point where knowing and being codetermine one another. Therefore, by asking not only how our existence limits and determines what we know but also how our modes of knowing and seeing determine how we act, we are led to a dimension of truth with profoundly ethical significance. To ask about truth is, simultaneously, to ask about the structures that inform our modes of being-in-the-world.

The hermeneutical orientation penetrates more deeply into the structures of being-in-the-world than would an inquiry into ways of being on a normative and prescriptive level. Granted, the latter forms of inquiry have made seminal contributions to the problems of ethics. Yet they tend to operate *within* the temporal-linguistic structures which I have called *frameworks of disclosure* and *worlds* (and which might also be called *interpretive paradigms*). A prescriptive ethics will be limited because the standpoints upon which its norms are based will be finite and conditioned. If it does not attend to the interpretive structures that delimit its orientation, it will run the risk of reifying a limited perspectival formation. Such a rigidification of ethical stances involves more than the curtailment of inquiry: it can provide the basis for acts of intolerance and repression in the cultural sphere.

The reflexive hermeneutics that provides the dynamic for an inquiry into disclosure, by contrast, allows interpretive structures to be revealed and transformed. It approaches the ethical dimension of truth on the level at which the ontological modes and interpretive paradigms informing human activity take shape. Therefore, it works to offset the closure of frameworks governing standards of judgment and to expose these hidden standards to critical reflection. It offers a caveat to tendencies to absolutize finite individual and cultural perspectives, without forgoing the pursuit of a more encompassing understanding.

The hermeneutical approach has an in-built reflexivity that derives from the pluralism and differentiation of cultural reality and provides the catalyst for critique and transformation of the self. Because of its dynamic and reflexive nature, it becomes clear that *disclosure* has a threefold application.

First, disclosure gives expression to the way in which existential worlds allow particulars to be disclosed or interpretively presented in delimited ways. The worlds we inhabit are already permeated by a series of historically formed and transmitted motivations, projects, and preconceptions that inform the cultural sphere. Since the encompassing cultural worlds inhabited by individuals provide the referential matrices for interpretation, the "particulars" we encounter in our lives are determined by antecedently operative hermeneutical constructs. As Heidegger argues, the immediate apprehension of things in an ontic manner, which is the basis of correspondence theories, is founded upon a prior process of disclosure. This is the reason for Heidegger's fusing of an inquiry into disclosure with ontology. The latter, through its attention to time and language, moves beyond immediacy to the ways in which things have come to be presented. The modes of being that shape human existence are correlated with modes in which reality is disclosed. Gaining an awareness of the interpretive structures that delimit the presentation of things is the first step in critically transforming our patterns of existence.

Secondly, truth as disclosure seeks to address the problem that these temporal-interpretive structures are largely unconscious and need to be brought into the open. One cannot directly grasp ontological and interpretive formations that are constructed and transmitted through cultural history. These formations, as they operate in any present circumstance, require disclosure. To achieve this, hermeneutics introduces an alterity by means of the encounter with texts. For Gadamer, the disclosive process takes the form of a dialogical encounter with the otherness of the text. The "fusion of horizons" that occurs in this encounter may be understood as an interplay of alternate standpoints disclosed through the reader's engagement with the text. This interplay allows the interpretive foremeanings and prejudgments of the inquirer to be disclosed in the interpretive process. Hermeneutics is reflexive because, as it discloses the text, it concurrently discloses the interpretive standpoints of the inquirer.

While Ricoeur employs the same reflexive principle predicated upon the encounter with linguistic forms of alterity, he transforms the hermeneutical model by means of which this is effected. Rather than enframing hermeneutics within the narrow paradigm of the interpersonal dialogue, Ricoeur articulates it in terms of the clash of semantic worlds. Yet despite the significant points of divergence in the hermeneutics of Gadamer and Ricoeur, in each case disclosure has a distinctly *critical* dimension. It reveals the limitations and biases inherent in fixed worldviews and subjects them to critique and transformation. Only by being disclosed can interpretive worldviews be subjected to comparative rational analysis.

The disclosure of truth functions negatively in relation to fixed standpoints, or positions. It does not see truth in the positing of statements concerning reality but in the critical supersession of closed frameworks of understanding. Thus the pursuit of truth turns from what is given to what is hidden and unthought within previously disclosed insights and in this way serves to further ongoing reflexivity. This model of understanding and the pursuit of truth emerges from the possibility of interactional encounters within a pluralistic universe. While truth does not appear as the final answer, it provides the impetus for continuing interchange, reflection, and transformation. "Truth, in this case, is the norm which guides the search for agreement."[2] This "norm" is never attained in itself but is rather the process of critique and transcendence that stimulates the growth of understanding.

The third dimension of disclosure appears in Ricoeur's argument that the clash of worlds in hermeneutical inquiry parallels the metaphorical operations of semantic impertinence. In metaphor the clash of incommensurable literal meanings in relationship to interpretive contexts impels a troping that produces new meaning and insight. Here, disclosure has an irreducibly creative function, expressing meaning on a level that transcends the literal and the familiar. Ricoeur draws upon the polysemous nature of language, the very imprecision that is a liability to descriptive orientations, as a means of superseding fixed interpretive boundaries. In a parallel manner, hermeneutical inquiry employs the clash of semantic worlds to disclose dimensions of understanding and existing that are repressed by dominant interpretive frameworks. Therefore, the cultural critique produced by hermeneutics will be inherently constructive.

In its third form, disclosure expresses the articulation of existential possibilities that challenge the cultural frameworks that delimit human existence. It sees language not as a veil that obscures reality or ideation in their pristine forms but as offering a means whereby finite cultural stances can be revealed and transformed. Language, as the creative and disclosive matrix of human existence, provides the means for the supersession of closed and repressive modes of being.

Hermeneutics does not foster the illusion that human understanding can fully transcend the perspectival nature of existence within language and historicality. The critique of closure and the liberation of understanding that hermeneutics offers remain within language and history. Yet by drawing upon the pluralism and alterity produced by the varieties of cultural existence, hermeneutics provides a means of transcending specific interpretive frameworks. What curtails and distorts the human experience of truth is not plurality and finitude as such but rather the fixation upon closed perspectives by the finite mind. Such fixation derives from a fusion of subjective needs and perspectives with an objective ideal. Moreover, fixation upon static truths seems to be associated with orientations aiming at mastery and control. "Only if I can be sure that what I have grasped is from now on immutable and immune to contingencies of fate, can my knowledge give me the feeling of genuine mastery over the object."[3] Such "mastery," however, is an illusion in the face of the radically temporal and interpretive nature of our existence. Fixations upon apodictic forms of knowledge create a closure of understanding that diminishes an individual's and a culture's capacities for growth and transformation.

The hermeneutical acceptance of history and language as the matrices of human existence and understanding indicates much more than a resignation to the impossibility of realizing the idealist dreams of previous cultural epochs. Rather, the hermeneutical approach to truth challenges the presuppositions inherent in the removal of truth from the realm of pluralism and contingency. It does not accept that differentiation and change are a falling away from a purer noetic status. Instead, it embraces the sphere of cultural and historical activity as the place where reality is disclosed. In doing so, hermeneutics challenges us to come to grips with the responsibilities of our role as cocreators of the worlds we inhabit.

This is not meant to instill humanity with a false and destructive hubris. Rather, the disclosive nature of existence indicates that we need to take seriously our participation in reality and to reflect more deeply upon the paradigms that govern this participatory activity. As long as truth remains "out there," inscribed within a notion of the object as such, or projected upon an ideal realm that transcends the flux of experience, the truth of our *actions* is easy to ignore.

However, especially in the contemporary world, it is inadequate to describe things as they appear because such descriptive discourse and the activity within which it is inscribed are always determined by prior structures of interpretation. These structures are shaped by historically contingent interests and attitudes. They are determined by specific means-ends orientations and cannot be presumed to be balanced and unbiased. The experience of truth will be distorted if it appears within the confines of habitual and unreflected paradigms. However, truth does not consist in an escape from interpretive perspectives but rather in a critical and reflexive attention to the ways in which such interpretations govern our activity.

Finally, the hermeneutical approach to truth reveals the interdependency of finite beings. It denies that truth can appear in any instance where a hegemonic repression of plurality and alterity governs thinking and acting. Truth occurs by a continuing openness to otherness and to transformation. Its pursuit requires the free and critical interchange of divergent standpoints rather than the imposition of fixed standards. It is abrogated by the closure of worlds and the denial of plurality, eluding the grasp of our controlling motivations. "For in this world of lies, Truth is forced to fly like a scared white doe in the woodlands; and only by cunning glimpses will she reveal herself."[4]

NOTES

BIBLIOGRAPHY

INDEX

NOTES

1. Aspects of the Problem of Truth
in the History of Thought

1. Martin Heidegger, *Being and Time*, trans. John Macquarrie and Edward Robinson (New York: Harper and Row, 1962), pp. 257–58 (hereafter *BT*), and idem, *Basic Writings*, ed. David Farrell Krell (New York: Harper and Row, 1977), p. 120 (hereafter *BW*).
2. Richard Rorty, *Philosophy and the Mirror of Nature* (Princeton: Princeton Univ. Press, 1979), p. 12.
3. *Sophist* 263a, trans. F. M. Cornford, *Collected Dialogues*, ed. Edith Hamilton and Huntington Cairns (Princeton: Princeton Univ. Press, 1961), pp. 957–1085.
4. Ibid. 263b. A similar definition is found at *Sophist* 240d–240e.
5. *Sophist* 243c, 246a, 249d.
6. Ibid. 247e.
7. Ibid. 248e.
8. Ibid. 249a.
9. Ibid. 249d.
10. Precedents for this position are found in a number of comparatively recent works of scholarship on Plato. These works agree that the dramatic and open-ended nature of the dialogues is the key to their meaning, rather than something that must be bracketed in order to distill the real arguments. See, for example, Herman L. Sinaiko, *Love, Knowledge, and Discourse in Plato* (Chicago: Univ. of Chicago Press, 1965), pp. 7–8, and John Herman Randall, Jr., *Plato: Dramatist of the Life of Reason* (New York: Columbia Univ. Press, 1970), p. 34.
11. Randall, *Plato*, p. 34.
12. *Theaetetus* 160c, trans. F. M. Cornford, *Collected Dialogues*, pp. 845–919.
13. Ibid. 156e–157a.
14. Ibid. 161d. Cf. ibid. 170c and 171c.
15. Ibid. 164b.
16. Ibid. 187a.
17. Ibid. 188d.

18. Ibid. 189a.
19. Ibid. 189b.
20. Ibid. 196b–196c.
21. A. E. Taylor, *Plato* (Indianapolis: Bobbs-Merrill, 1956), p. 848.
22. *Theaetetus* 149a, 157c.
23. Cf. Randall, *Plato*, p. 144.
24. *Metaphysics* 4.7.1, trans. Hugh Tredennick (New York: G. P. Putnam's Sons, 1933) (Loeb ed., pp. 199–201).
25. Ibid. 4.7.1 (Loeb ed., p. 201).
26. Ibid. 4.7.8 (Loeb ed., p. 203).
27. Ibid. 4.7.4 (Loeb ed., p. 201).
28. Aristotle, "On Interpretation" 1.16a, 11–12, *Organon* 1, trans. Harold P. Cooke (Cambridge: Harvard Univ. Press, 1938) (Loeb ed., pp. 115–17).
29. *Metaphysics* 6.4.3 (Loeb ed., pp. 307–9).
30. *Nichomachean Ethics* 6.2.1, trans. H. Rackham (Cambridge: Harvard Univ. Press, 1962) (Loeb ed., pp. 327–29).
31. Ibid. 6.2.2–3 (Loeb ed., p. 329).
32. *Nichomachean Ethics* 3.1.3:1112a 14–18; 1113a 9–13, quoted in John Herman Randall, Jr., *Aristotle* (New York: Columbia Univ. Press, 1960), p. 76.
33. Ibid. 6.8:1141b 24–1142a 12, quoted in Randall, *Aristotle*, p. 76.
34. Randall, *Aristotle*, p. 77.
35. Ibid.
36. *Nichomachean Ethics* 6.5:1140a 25–1140b 8, quoted in Randall, *Aristotle*, p. 78.
37. St. Thomas Aquinas, *Summa Theologiae* 1a.16.1, trans. Thomas Gornall, S. J. (New York: McGraw-Hill, 1964), 4:75.
38. Ibid., p. 77.
39. Ibid., p. 77.
40. Ibid., p. 79.
41. Ibid., p. 81. For a careful analysis of these points, see Patrick Lee, "Aquinas on Knowledge of Truth and Existence," *New Scholasticism* 60 (1986): 46–71.
42. *Summa Theologiae*, p. 87.
43. St. Thomas Aquinas, *On the Truth of the Catholic Faith: Summa Contra Gentiles*, book 1.58.1, trans. Anton C. Pegis (New York: Image Books, 1955), p. 199.
44. See ibid., chaps. 46, 55.
45. Ibid., p. 198.
46. *Summa Theologiae* 1a.16.6, p. 89.
47. Ibid., p. 91.
48. Ibid., 1a.16.8, p. 97.
49. Ibid., 1a.16.8, p. 99.
50. Immanuel Kant, *Critique of Pure Reason*, trans. Norman Kemp Smith (1929, reprint New York: St. Martin's, 1965), pp. 97, 220.
51. *BW*, p. 120.
52. D. J. O'Connor, *The Correspondence Theory of Truth* (London: Hutchinson, 1975), p. 24.
53. H. H. Joachim, *The Nature of Truth* (1906, reprint New York: Greenwood Press, 1969), pp. 7–8.
54. Ibid., pp. 10–11.
55. Ibid., p. 17.
56. Ibid., p. 76.
57. Brand Blanshard, *The Nature of Thought* (New York: Macmillan, 1940), 2:228.
58. Ibid., p. 259.

59. Joachim, *Nature of Truth*, p. 148.
60. Benedict de Spinoza, *Ethics* 1, axiom 6, in *The Collected Works of Spinoza*, vol. 1, trans. Edwin Curley (Princeton: Princeton Univ. Press, 1985), p. 410.
61. *Ethics* 1, prop. 30, dem. (p. 434). As Curley notes with general reference to Spinoza's system, "In our complete description of the world, the ideal of a unified science is realized. Every true singular proposition about extended objects has its scientific explanation, and every nomological proposition has its place in a system analogous to Newton's *Principia*" (E. M. Curley, *Spinoza's Metaphysics* [Cambridge: Harvard Univ. Press, 1969], p. 53).
62. *Ethics* 1, def. 3.(p. 408).
63. *Ethics* 1, def. 6 (p. 409).
64. Joachim, *Nature of Truth*, p. 149.
65. *Ethics* 1, prop. 28, scholium 2 (p. 433).
66. *Ethics* 1, prop. 29 (p. 433).
67. *Ethics* 2, prop. 7 (p. 451).
68. Ibid., p. 472.
69. Stuart Hampshire, *Spinoza* (Harmondsworth: Penguin, 1951), p. 87.
70. *Ethics* 2, prop. 40, scholium 2 (p. 478).
71. Hampshire, *Spinoza*, p. 103.
72. Spinoza, *Ethics* 2, prop. 47 (p. 482).
73. Alexandre Kojève, *Introduction to the Reading of Hegel*, trans. J. H. Nicholas (New York: Basic Books, 1969), p. 120.
74. *Ethics* 2, prop. 35 (p. 108).
75. Joachim, *Nature of Truth*, p. 160. Cf. Curley, *Spinoza's Metaphysics*, pp. 134–36.
76. G. W. F. Hegel, *The Phenomenology of Spirit*, trans. A. V. Miller (New York: Oxford Univ. Press, 1977), p. 11.
77. Kant, *Critique of Pure Reason*, p. 74.
78. Hegel, *Phenomenology of Spirit*, p. 486.
79. Ibid., p. 487.
80. Ibid., p. 490.
81. Mark C. Taylor, *Altarity* (Chicago: Univ. of Chicago Press, 1987), p. 19.
82. Hegel, *Phenomenology of Spirit*, p. 489.
83. Ibid.
84. Ibid.
85. Ibid.
86. Jacques Derrida, *Margins of Philosophy*, trans. Alan Bass (Chicago: Univ. of Chicago Press, 1982), pp. 120–21.
87. Hegel, *Phenomenology of Spirit*, p. 489.
88. Ibid., p. 492.
89. Ibid., p. 493.
90. Jean Hyppolite, *Genesis and Structure of Hegel's Phenomenology of Spirit*, trans. S. Cherniak and J. Heckman (Evanston: Northwestern Univ. Press, 1974), p. 221.
91. J. N. Findlay, *Hegel* (Oxford: Oxford Univ. Press, 1976), p. 230.
92. Ibid., p. 257.
93. Ibid., p. 230.
94. Emil Fackenheim, *The Religious Dimension of Hegel's Thought* (Chicago: Univ. of Chicago Press, 1967), p. 18.
95. Ibid.
96. Findlay, *Hegel*, pp. 222–23.
97. G. W. F. Hegel, *Science of Logic*, trans. A. V. Miller, (New York: Humanities Press, 1969), p. 586.
98. Findlay, *Hegel*, p. 223.

99. Ibid., p. 224.
100. G. W. F. Hegel, *Lectures on the History of Philosophy*, trans. E. S. Haldane and F. H. Simson (New York: Humanities Press, 1968), 3:467.
101. Haig Khatchadourian, *The Coherence Theory of Truth* (Beirut: American Univ. Press, 1961), pp. 18–19.
102. Joachim, *Nature of Truth*, p. 170.
103. Findlay, *Hegel*, p. 97.
104. Joachim, *Nature of Truth*, p. 171.
105. Søren Kierkegaard, *Concluding Unscientific Postscript*, trans. David F. Swenson and Walter Lowrie (Princeton:Princeton Univ. Press, 1941), p. 176.
106. Blanshard, *Nature of Thought*, 2:264.
107. Ibid., p. 271.
108. Ibid., p. 272.
109. William James, *Essays in Pragmatism* (New York: Hafner, 1948), p. 161 (emphasis in original).
110. William James, *The Varieties of Religious Experience* (1902, reprint New York: Macmillan, 1961), p. 266.
111. Ibid.
112. William James, *Pragmatism* (1907, reprint New York: Longman's, Green, 1943), p. 76.
113. Bertrand Russell, *Philosophical Essays* (London: Longman's, Green, 1910), p. 135.
114. Ibid., p. 136.

2. An Ontology of Disclosure: Heidegger

1. See *BT*, p. 29 (Martin Heidegger, *Gesamtausgabe*, Band 2, *Sein und Zeit* [Frankfurt a.M.: Vittorio Klostermann, 1976], p. 12 [hereafter *SZ*]); idem, *Early Greek Thinking*, trans. David Farrell Krell and Frank A. Capuzzi (New York: Harper and Row, 1975), p. 22 (hereafter *EGT*) [*Holzwege* [Frankfurt a.M.: Vittorio Klostermann, 1963], p. 328); idem, *What is Called Thinking?* trans. Fred D. Wieck and J. Glenn Gray (New York: Harper and Row, 1968), pp. 221, 227. I have chosen to retain the capitalization of the term *Being* to indicate its unique status as expressing "modes of being."
2. Martin Heidegger, *Poetry, Language, Thought*, trans. Albert Hofstadter (New York: Harper and Row, 1971), p. 131 [hereafter *PLT*) ("Von solcher art ist das Sein, so zwar, das dieses keine besondere Art unter anderen ist, sondern die Weise des Seienden als solchen" [*Holzwege* p. 285]).
3. Martin Heidegger, *Nietzsche*, vol. 4, *Nihilism*, trans. Frank A. Capuzzi (New York: Harper and Row, 1982), p. 217 (*Nietzsche* 2 [Pfullingen: Verlag Günther Neske, 1961], p. 357).
4. *BT*, p. 25 (*SZ*, p. 7).
5. Martin Heidegger, *The Basic Problems of Phenomenology*, trans. Albert Hofstadter (Bloomington: Indiana Univ. Press, 1982), p. 327.
6. Ray L. Hart, *Unfinished Man and the Imagination* (New York: Herder and Herder, 1968), p. 110.
7. See Martin Heidegger, "Overcoming Metaphysics," in *The End of Philosophy*, trans. Joan Stambaugh (New York: Harper and Row, 1973).
8. See Hans-Georg Gadamer, *Truth and Method*, trans. Garrett Barden and John Cumming (New York: Seabury, 1975), p. 228 [hereafter *TM*) (*Wahrheit und Methode*, Zweite Auflage [Tübingen: J. C. B. Mohr, 1965], p. 243) (hereafter *WM*).
9. Werner Marx, *Heidegger and the Tradition*, trans. Theodore Kisiel and Murray Green (Evanston: Northwestern Univ. Press, 1971), p. 112.

10. Ibid., pp. 37, 81–82, 105.
11. *BT*, p. 125 (*SZ*, p. 123).
12. René Descartes, *Principia Philosophica* 1, par. 51, quoted in *BT*, p. 125 (*SZ*, p. 123).
13. Ibid.
14. See *BT*, pp. 130–31.
15. *BT*, p. 125 (*SZ*, p. 124) (emphasis original).
16. *BT*, p. 130 (*SZ*, pp. 130–31).
17. He argues,for example, that all traditional logic "has its foundation in an ontology of the present at hand" (*BT*, pp. 166–67 [*SZ*, pp. 171–72]).
18. A somewhat indirect connection between taking things as "handy" and taking them in an "ontic" manner is made in *Basic Problems*, pp. 305–6. The relationship between these terms becomes clearer in Heidegger's use of them.
19. *BT*, pp. 102–4 (*SZ*, pp. 97–99).
20. *BT*, pp. 140–41 (*SZ*, pp. 141–42).
21. See "TheThing," in *PLT* ("Das Ding," in *Vorträge und Aufsätze*, Teil 2 [Pfullingen: Günther Neske,1967]).
22. *BT*, p. 127 (*SZ*, pp. 125–26).
23. See Martin Heidegger, *What Is a Thing?* trans. W. B. Barton, Jr., and Vera Deutsch (South Bend: Gateway, 1967), p. 104, and *Nietzsche*, 4:120, 238.
24. Heidegger, *Nietzsche*, 4:117 (*Nietzsche 2*, p. 166).
25. *BT*, p. 23 ("'Sein' kann in der Tat nicht als Seiendes begriffen werden" [*SZ*, p. 5]).
26. Theodor Adorno, *Negative Dialectics*, trans. E. B. Ashton (New York: Continuum Books, 1973), pp. 76, 91,104.
27. Ibid., pp. 75, 87,101.
28. Ibid., p. 87.
29. Ibid., p. 115.
30. Ibid., p. 86.
31. Ibid., p. 119.
32. This point concerning Heidegger's inconsistency on the relation of Being to beings and to historical existence is developed at the end of chapter 3.
33. *BT*, p. 32 (*SZ*, p. 16).
34. See *BT*, p. 27 (*SZ*, p. 10). Heidegger states that the term *Dasein* refers explicitly to human beings. This is slightly different from the interpretation given by William Richardson, who states that *Dasein* represents an ontological structure that is "prior to man" (*Heidegger* [The Hague: Martinus Nijhoff, 1967], p. 45). Richardson's position represents an unwarranted multiplication of entities, and it obscures Heidegger's argument that the ontological structures of being-in-the-world are both disclosed through human activity and are constitutive of the human.
35. *BT*, p. 32 (*SZ*, p. 16).
36. Ibid.
37. *BT*, p. 255 (*SZ*, p. 281).
38. "Letter on Humanism," *BW*, p. 216.
39. Martin Heidegger, *Identity and Difference*, bilingual ed. with English trans. by Joan Stambaugh (New York: Harper and Row, 1969), pp. 31–32 ("Mensch und Sein sind einander übereignet. Sie gehören einander" [ibid. p. 95]).
40. Heidegger, *What Is Called Thinking?* p. 79.
41. Ibid.
42. Calvin O. Schrag, *Experience and Being* (Evanston: Northwestern Univ. Press, 1969), p. 87.
43. Ibid.
44. Heidegger, *Basic Problems*, p. 11.
45. *BT*, p. 191 (*SZ*, p. 199).

46. Ibid.
47. *BT*, p. 191 (*SZ*, pp. 199–201).
48. *BT*, pp. 191–92 (*SZ*, p. 200).
49. *BT*, p. 372 (*SZ*, p. 430).
50. Cf. Hart, *Unfinished Man*, p. 113.
51. *PLT*, pp. 179–82 (*Vorträge und Aufsätze* 2, pp. 52–55).
52. Schrag, *Experience and Being*, p. 98.
53. *PLT*, pp. 63 ff. (*Holzwege*, pp. 51 ff.); cf. David L. Miller, *Christs* (New York: Seabury, 1981), pp. 146–47.
54. *Holzwege*, p. 47.
55. *BT*, p. 152 (*SZ*, p. 155).
56. Gregory Schufreider, "Art and the Problem of Truth," *Man and World* 13 (1980): 58.
57. *BT*, p. 174 (*SZ*, p. 180).
58. See, e.g., Langdon Gilkey, *Naming the Whirlwind* (Indianapolis: Bobbs-Merrill, 1969), p. 43.
59. John Macquarrie, *An Existentialist Theology* (New York: Macmillan, 1955), pp. 87, 75.
60. For an analysis of the domination of subjectivity and the obliteration of alterity, particularly as manifested in its most extreme form in contemporary technology, see Martin Heidegger, *The Question concerning Technology*, trans. William Lovitt (New York: Harper and Row, 1977), esp. pp. 107, 129–30.
61. *BT*, p. 176 (*SZ*, p. 182) (emphasis original). Also cf. *BT*, p. 171: "Dasein is its disclosedness" (*SZ*, p. 177) (emphasis removed).
62. Martin Heidegger, *On Time and Being*, trans. Joan Stambaugh (New York: Harper and Row, 1972), p. 12 (*Zur Sache des Denkens* [Tübingen: Max Niemeyer Verlag, 1969], p. 12).
63. *BT*, p. 377 (*SZ*, p. 435) (emphasis removed).
64. Ibid.
65. Heidegger, *On Time and Being*, p. 16 (*Zur Sache des Denkens*, p. 16).
66. *BT*, p. 376 (*SZ*, p. 434).
67. *On Time and Being*, p. 13 (*Zur Sache des Denkens*, p. 13).
68. *BT*, p. 378 (*SZ*, p. 436).
69. *BT*, p. 287 (*SZ*, p. 323).
70. *BT*, p. 279 (*SZ*, p. 314) (emphasis removed).
71. Hart, *Unfinished Man*, p. 167 (emphasis original). Cf. *BT*, p. 185: "Dasein *is* its possibilities."
72. Martin Heidegger, "What Is Metaphysics," trans. R. F. C. Hull and Alan Crick, in *Existence and Being*, ed. Werner Brock (Chicago: Henry Regnery 1949), p. 337, and idem, *The Essence of Reasons*, bilingual ed. with English trans. by Terrence Malick (Evanston: Northwestern Univ. Press, 1969) p. 109.
73. Richardson, *Heidegger*, pp. 56–58.
74. *BT*, p. 236 (*SZ*, p. 255).
75. *BT*, p. 156 (*SZ*, p. 161).
76. Cf. Peter L. Berger and Thomas Luckmann, *The Social Construction of Reality* (Garden City: Doubleday, 1966), p. 51, and Clifford Geertz, *The Interpretation of Cultures* (New York: Basic Books, 1971), p. 47.
77. *BT*, p. 156 (*SZ*, p. 161).
78. *BT*, p. 157 (*SZ*, p. 162).
79. Ibid.
80. *BT*, p. 158 (*SZ*, p. 163).
81. Ibid.
82. Cf. Thomas Langan, *The Meaning of Heidegger* (New York: Columbia Univ. Press, 1958), p. 230; Richardson, *Heidegger*, p. 92.

83. John Fowles, *The Magus*, rev. version (New York: Dell, 1978), p. 570.
84. *BT*, p. 213 (*SZ*, p. 225).
85. *BT*, p. 167 (*SZ*, p. 172).
86. *BT*, p. 219 (*SZ*, p. 233).
87. *BT*, p. 211 (*SZ*, pp. 222–23).
88. *BT*, p. 213 (*SZ*, p. 225).
89. *BT*, p. 167 (*SZ*, p. 172).
90. *BT*, p. 312 (*SZ*, p. 356).
91. *BT*, p. 343 (*SZ*, p. 393).
92. *PLT*, p. 67 (*Holzwege*, p. 55).
93. *PLT*, p. 67 (translator's note).
94. *BT*, p. 213 (*SZ*, p. 225).
95. *BT*, p. 42, cf. ibid, p. 278 (*SZ*, pp. 28, 312).
96. *BT*, pp. 443–44 (*SZ*, p. 517).
97. *BT*, pp. 42–43 (*SZ*, p. 24).
98. Ferdinand de Saussure, *Course in General Linguistics*, trans. Wade Baskin (New York: McGraw-Hill, 1966), pp. 9–13.
99. *BT*, pp. 196–98 (*SZ*, pp. 205–6).
100. *BT*, p. 199 (*SZ*, p. 208).
101. *BT*, p. 199 (*SZ*, p. 209).
102. *BT*, pp. 200–201 (*SZ*, pp. 209–10); and cf. Richard E. Palmer, *Hermeneutics* (Evanston: Northwestern Univ. Press, 1969), p. 138.
103. *BT*, p. 201 (*SZ*, p. 210).
104. Otto Pöggeler, "Heidegger's Topology of Being," in *On Heidegger and Language*, ed. Joseph J. Kockelmans (Evanston: Northwestern Univ. Press, 1972), p. 111.
105. Martin Heidegger, *On the Way to Language*, trans. Peter D. Hertz (New York: Harper and Row, 1971), p. 29 (hereafter *WL*) (*Unterwegs Zur Sprache* [Pfullingen: Verlag Günther Neske, 1959], p. 122).
106. Heidegger, *Existence and Being*, p. 275.
107. *WL*, p. 160 (*Unterwegs*, p. 38).
108. *WL*, p. 86 ("Ein Ding ist erst und nur, wo das Wort nicht fehlt, mithin da ist" [*Unterwegs*, p. 191]).
109. *WL*, p. 87 (*Unterwegs*, p. 193).
110. *WL*, p. 88 (*Unterwegs*, p. 193).
111. Ernst Cassirer, *The Philosophy of Symbolic Forms*, vol. 1, *Language*, trans. Ralph Manheim (New Haven: Yale Univ. Press, 1955), p. 286.
112. *WL*, p. 133 (*Unterwegs*, p. 264).
113. *WL*, p. 112 (*Unterwegs*, p. 241).
114. *WL*, p. 107 (*Unterwegs*, p. 214).
115. *PLT*, p. 132 (*Unterwegs*, p. 286).
116. *WL*, p. 124 (*Unterwegs*, p. 255).

3. Truth as Disclosure: Heidegger

1. José Ortega y Gasset, *Meditations on Quixote*, trans. Evelyn Rugg and Diego Marín (New York: Norton, 1961), p. 67.
2. *BT*, p. 262 (*SZ*, pp. 290–91). We shall return to Heidegger's analysis of *aletheia* in some detail later in this Chapter.
3. *BW*, p. 123 (Martin Heidegger, *Wegmarken* [Frankfurt a.M.: Vittorio Klostermann, 1978], p. 181).
4. *BW*, pp. 123–24 ("Dieses Erscheinen des Dinges im Durchmessen eines Entgegen vollzieht sich innerhalb eines Offenen, dessen Offenheit vom

Vorstellen nicht erst geschaffen, sondern je nur als ein Bezugsberiech bezogen und übernommen wird" [*Wegmarken*, pp. 181–82]).

5. Joseph J. Kockelmans, *On the Truth of Being* (Bloomington: Indiana Univ. Press, 1984), p. 7.

6. *BW*, pp. 124–25 ("was die Richtigheit erst ermöglicht, mit ursprünglicherem Recht als das Wesen der Wahrheit gelten" [*Wegmarken*, p. 182]).

7. Reiner Schürmann, *Heidegger on Being and Acting*, trans. Christine-Marie Gros in collaboration with the author (Bloomington: Indiana Univ. Press, 1987), p. 74.

8. Ibid., p. 51.

9. Richardson, *Heidegger*, p. 163.

10. Ibid., p. 268. Cf. Heidegger, *The Essence of Reasons*, p. 117.

11. *BT*, p. 268 (*SZ*, pp. 297–98).

12. H. Pietersma, "Heidegger's Theory of Truth," in *Heidegger's Existential Analytic*, ed. Frederick Elliston (The Hague: Mouton, n.d.), p. 223.

13. Cf. W. B. Macomber, *The Anatomy of Disillusion* (Evanston: Northwestern Univ. Press, 1967). Macomber argues that truth as correspondence obscures the fact that "Dasein is rather a *way* of being than a being" (p. 31).

14. *BT*, p. 267 (*SZ*, p. 297).

15. *BW*, p. 125 ("Das Sich-freigeben für eine bindende Richte ist nur möglich als Freisein zum Offenbaren eines Offenen" [*Wegmarken*, p. 183]).

16. Ibid. (emphasis original).

17. Macomber, *Anatomy of Disillusion*, p. 99.

18. *BW*, p. 127 ("Die Freiheit zum Offenbaren eines Offenen lässt das jeweilige Seiende das Seinde sein, das es ist. Freiheit enthüllt sich jetzt als das Seinlassen von Seiendem" [*Wegmarken*, p. 185]).

19. Cf. Erik Erikson, *Insight and Responsibility* (New York: Norton, 1964), p. 234.

20. Palmer, *Hermeneutics*, p. 217.

21. Emil Fackenheim, *To Mend the World: Foundations of Future Jewish Thought* (New York: Schocken, 1982), p. 190.

22. Macomber, *Anatomy of Disillusion*, p. 102 (emphasis original).

23. *BW*, p. 128 ("Das Sein-lassen, d.h. die Freiheit ist in sich aus-setzend, ek-sistent. Das auf das Wesen der Wahrheit hin erblickte Wesen der Freiheit zeigt sich als die Aussetzung in die Entborgenheit des Seienden" [*Wegmarken*, p. 186]).

24. *BW*, p. 135.

25. Cf. *BT*, p. 270 (*SZ*, p. 301).

26. *BT*, p. 105 (*SZ*, p. 100).

27. Ibid. (emphasis original).

28. *BT*, p. 105 (*SZ*, p. 101).

29. *BT*, p. 265 (*SZ*, p. 295).

30. *BW*, p. 132.

31. *PLT*, p. 53 (*Holzwege*, p. 42).

32. *PLT*, p. 54 (*Holzwege*, p. 42).

33. *PLT*, pp. 54–55 (*Holzwege*, pp. 42-43).

34. *BT*, p. 301 (*SZ*, p. 341).

35. *BT*, p. 265 (*SZ*, p. 294).

36. *PLT*, p. 55 ("Eine dieser Weisen, wie Wahrheit geschieht, ist das Werksein des Werkes" [*Holzwege*, p. 41]).

37. *PLT*, p. 44 ("In-sich-aufragend eröffnet das Werk eine Welt und hält diese im waltenden Verbleib" [*Holzwege*, p. 29]).

38. Joseph J. Kockelmans, *Heidegger on Art and Artworks* (Dordrecht: Martinus Nijhoff, 1985), p. 187.

39. Joel Weinsheimer, *Gadamer's Hermeneutics* (New Haven: Yale Univ. Press, 1985), p. 98.

40. *PLT*, p. 17 (*Holzwege*, p. 7).
41. Schufreider, "Art and the Problem of Truth," p. 72.
42. *PLT*, p. 62 (*Holzwege*, p. 51).
43. *PLT*, p. 42 (*Holzwege*, p. 31).
44. *PLT*, p. 76 (*Holzwege*, p. 63).
45. *PLT*, p. 63 (*Holzwege*, p. 51).
46. Albert Hofstadter, *Truth and Art* (New York: Columbia Univ. Press, 1965), p. 209.
47. Walter Biemel, *Martin Heidegger*, trans. J. H. Mehta (New York: Harcourt, Brace, Jovanovich, 1976), p. 112.
48. Hofstadter, *Truth and Art*, p. 35 (emphasis removed).
49. Robert P. Scharlemann, *The Being of God: Theology and the Experience of Truth* (New York: Seabury, 1981), pp. 13–14.
50. Loren Eiseley, *The Night Country* (New York: Charles Scribner's Sons, 1947), p. 137.
51. Ibid.
52. *Truth and Art*, p. 39.
53. Schufreider, "Art and the Problem of Truth," p. 70.
54. *EGT*, p. 16 ("Oder verbirgt sich in der chronologisch-historischen Entfernung des Spruches eine geschichtliche Nähe seines Ungesprochenen, das in das Kommende hinausspricht?" [*Holzwege*, p. 321]).
55. *EGT*, pp. 59–60 (*Vorträge* 3, p. 3).
56. Ibid.
57. Ibid. Here, and in subsequent passages, I have transliterated the Greek of Heidegger's text.
58. Ibid.
59. *EGT*, pp. 61–62 (*Vorträge* 3, pp. 6–7).
60. Ibid., p. 63 (*Vorträge* 3, p. 8).
61. *BT*, pp. 262–63 (*SZ*, pp. 290–91).
62. *EGT*, p. 70 (*Vorträge* 3, p. 16).
63. Ibid., p. 71 (*Vorträge* 3, p. 17).
64. This point is made by Richardson, *Heidegger*, p. 484.
65. *EGT*, p. 104 (*Vorträge* 3, p. 55).
66. *EGT*, pp. 112–13 (*Vorträge* 3, p. 66).
67. *EGT*, p. 109 (*Vorträge* 3, pp. 61–62).
68. *EGT*, p. 120 (*Vorträge* 3, p. 75). These hermeneutical arguments are developed extensively in chapters 4 and 5.
69. "Plato's Doctrine of Truth," in *Philosophy in the Twentieth Century*, ed. William Barrett and Henry D. Aiken (New York: Random House, 1962), p. 251 (hereafter cited as *PDT*) ("Platons Lehre von der Wahrheit," in *Wegmarken*, p. 201).
70. *PDT*, p. 265 (*Wegmarken*, p. 228). The passage is from *Republic* 517c. Compare the translation by Paul Shorey: "The idea of the good . . . is indeed the cause for all things of all that is right and beautiful, giving birth in the visible world to light, and the author of light and itself in the intelligible world being the authentic source of truth and reason" (*Collected Dialogues*, pp. 749–50). Although this is significantly different from Heidegger's rendition, it likewise conveys the sense of the Idea of the Good determining the nature of truth.
71. *PDT*, p. 265 (*Wegmarken*, p. 228).
72. *PDT*, p. 265 ("Wahrheit wird zur orthotes, zur Richtigkeit des Vernehmens und Aussagens" [*Wegmarken*, p. 229]).
73. *PDT*, p. 265 ("Als Richtigkeit des 'Blickens' aber wird sie zur Auszeichnung des menschlichen Verhaltens Seienden" [*Wegmarken*, pp. 228–29]).
74. *PDT*, p. 267 (*Wegmarken*, pp. 230–31).

164   NOTES

75. *PDT*, p. 267 (*Wegmarken*, p. 232).
76. Cf., for example, Derrida's emphasis upon the need "to save Nietzsche from a reading of the Heideggerian type" (Jacques Derrida, *Of Grammatology*, trans. Gayatri Chakravorty Spivak, [Baltimore: Johns Hopkins Univ. Press, 1974], p. 19).
77. Schürmann states that "Heidegger's writings may be read in their entirety as a quest for the origin. They can never be read, however, as a quest for the *fons et origo*, a mythical source of all things" (*Heidegger on Being and Acting*, p. 120). This expresses the general orientation of Heidegger's work, yet it fails to attend to the profound ambiguity which haunts that work, and fails also to account for the interpretation of Plato's thought as a loss of a temporally antecedent experience of truth.
78. *Rep.* 6, 484b; cf. Henry G. Wolz, *Plato and Heidegger* (Lewisburg: Bucknell Univ. Press, 1981), p. 189.
79. *Rep.* 6, 484c; Wolz, *Plato and Heidegger*, p. 190.
80. *Rep.* 6, 500d; Wolz, *Plato and Heidegger*, p. 190.
81. *Rep.* 6, 501a; Wolz, *Plato and Heidegger*, p. 196.
82. *Rep.* 7, 541a; Wolz, *Plato and Heidegger*, p. 197.
83. Randall, *Plato*, p. 162. Gadamer also argues that Plato's definition of the ideal Republic is clearly one which "cannot be actualized," and that this serves to "demonstrate its impossibility" (Hans-Georg Gadamer, *The Idea of the Good in Platonic-Aristotelian Philosophy*, trans. P. Christopher Smith [New Haven: Yale Univ. Press, 1986], p. 70).
84. Randall, *Plato*, p. 170.
85. Wolz, *Plato and Heidegger*, p. 197.
86. *Rep.* 10, 619b–619c.
87. *Rep.* 10, 619c.
88. Wolz, *Plato and Heidegger*, p. 204. Randall makes a similar point concerning the function of the myth of Er (*Plato*, pp. 163–64).
89. Randall, *Plato*, p. 165.
90. Cf. William A. Galston, "Heidegger's Plato: A Critique of *Plato's Doctrine of Truth*," *Philosophical Forum* 13 (Summer 1982): 381.
91. Wolz, *Plato and Heidegger*, p. 19.
92. Paul Friedländer, *Plato*, trans. Hans Meyerhoff (Princeton: Princeton Univ. Press, 1969), pp. 223 ff.
93. Heidegger, *On Time and Being*, pp. 70–71 (*Zur Sache des Denkens*, p. 78).
94. Heidegger, *Nietzsche*, 4:212 (*Nietzsche* 2, p. 352).
95. Ibid., p. 227 (*Nietzsche* 2, p. 370).
96. Ibid., p. 239 (*Nietzsche* 2, p. 383).
97. Heidegger, *On Time and Being*, p. 2 ("Sein ohne das Seiende zu denken" [*Zur Sache des Denkens*, p. 2]).
98. Cf. Paul Ricoeur, *The Rule of Metaphor*, trans. Robert Czerny (Toronto: Univ. of Toronto Press, 1977), p. 311; Jürgen Habermas, *Philosophical-Political Profiles*, trans. Thomas McCarthy (Cambridge: MIT Press, 1981), p. 194; Hans-Georg Gadamer, *Reason in the Age of Science*, trans. Frederick G. Lawrence (Cambridge: MIT Press, 1981), pp. 56–57, 58, 62–63, and idem, "Heidegger and the History of Philosophy," *The Monist* 64 (Oct. 1981): 444. By contrast, Schürmann, on the basis of his exposition of Heidegger's notion of "origin" as "coming forth" and "presencing," criticizes the positions of Ricoeur and Habermas as stemming from inadequate comprehension (*Heidegger on Being and Acting*, p. 316 n. 10). Yet while Schürmann's analyses of "origination" give profound expression to disclosive ontology, Heidegger's notion of a literal "original" truth and the view of history derived from this remain a separate issue. In the view of history which accompanies his critique of metaphysics, Heidegger conflates "originary presenc-

ing" with a "loss of origins." In doing so, he undertakes a hermeneutical project that impedes reflexive encounters with historical forms.

99. *TM*, p. 227 (*WM*, p. 242).
100. Allan Megill, *Prophets of Extremity* (Berkeley and Los Angeles: Univ. of California Press, 1985), p. 119. It should be noted that Megill tends to focus rather one-sidedly on the reactive dimension of Heidegger's work, without attending to the contrary dimensions of futurity and progressiveness that are likewise essential to it.
101. I believe that this skewed notion of history provides a clue to understanding the conceptual side of Heidegger's brief but horribly misguided political involvements of the 1930s. It should be evident that the disclosure approach to truth, in stark contrast to these political involvements, has an orientation that is antithetical to and disruptive of any form of totalitarianism and bigotry.

Historical Hermeneutics as a Process of Disclosure: Gadamer

1. *TM*, p. 232 (*WM*, p. 247).
2. Ibid.
3. Ibid.
4. *TM*, p. xviii (*WM*, p. xvi).
5. *TM*, p. 274 (*WM*, p. 291).
6. *TM*, p. 267 (*WM*, p. 283).
7. *TM*, p. 253 (*WM*, p. 269).
8. Ibid.
9. *TM*, p. 89 (*WM*, p. 95).
10. Richard J. Bernstein, *Beyond Objectivism and Relativism* (Philadelphia: Univ. of Pennsylvania Press, 1983), pp. 151–52.
11. *TM*, p. 267 (*WM*, p. 283).
12. *TM*, pp. 267–68 (*WM*, p. 284).
13. *TM*, p. 268 (*WM*, p. 285).
14. *TM*, p. 164 (*WM*, pp. 174–75). It may be appropriate to note that the use of author's names such as "Heidegger" "Gadamer" and "Schleiermacher" to designate the works written by those individuals does not function to reduce the work to the thoughts of the author.
15. Heinz Kimmerle, Introduction, Friedrich Schleiermacher, *Hermeneutics: The Handwritten Manuscripts*, trans. James Duke and Jack Forstman (Missoula: Scholars Press, 1977), p. 27.
16. Ibid., p. 29.
17. Ibid., p. 42, also cf. pp. 64, 112.
18. Ibid., p. 97.
19. Ibid.
20. Palmer, *Hermeneutics*, p. 93.
21. *TM*, pp. 166–67 (*WM*, p. 177).
22. TM, p. 168 (*WM*, p. 179).
23. *TM*, p. 264 (*WM*, p. 280).
24. *TM*, p. 170 (*WM*, p. 181).
25. *TM*, p. 172 (*WM*, p. 184).
26. E. D. Hirsch, Jr., *Validity in Interpretation* (New Haven: Yale Univ. Press, 1967), p. 249.
27. Bernstein, *Beyond Objectivism and Relativism*, p. 19.
28. Hirsch, *Validity in Interpretation*, p. 170.
29. Ibid.

30. Ibid., pp. 170–71.
31. Ibid., p. 46.
32. Ibid., p. 48.
33. Ibid., p. 46.
34. Ibid., p. 129.
35. Ibid. For Gadamer's argument see *TM*, p. 274 (*WM*, pp. 290–91).
36. Hirsch, *Validity in Interpretation*, p. 8.
37. Ibid.
38. Ibid., p. 138.
39. Ibid., p. 49.
40. Ibid.
41. Ibid., p. 66.
42. Ibid.
43. Ibid., p. 76.
44. Ibid., p. 68.
45. Ibid., p. 207.
46. *TM*, p. 211 (*WM*, p. 225).
47. Ibid.
48. Cf. Heidegger, *The Question concerning Technology*, pp. 36 ff.
49. David Tracy, *The Analogical Imagination* (New York: Crossroad, 1981), p. 136 n.8.
50. Weinsheimer, *Gadamer's Hermeneutics*, p. 20.
51. Bernstein, *Beyond Objectivism and Relativism*, p. 31.
52. Ibid., p. 168.
53. John Dewey, *The Quest for Certainty* (New York: Minton, Balch, 1929), p. 165.
54. Ibid., p. 124.
55. Ibid., p. 128.
56. Ibid., p. 190.
57. *TM*, pp. 310–11 (*WM*, p. 329).
58. *TM*, p. 311 (*WM*, p. 330).
59. Weinsheimer, *Gadamer's Hermeneutics*, p. 9.
60. *TM*, p. 212 (*WM*, p. 227).
61. *TM*, p. 423 (*WM*, p. 441).
62. *TM*, p. 214 (*WM*, p. 229).
63. *TM*, p. 423 (*WM*, pp. 441–42).
64. *TM*, p. 423 (*WM*, p. 442).
65. *TM*, p. 153 (*WM*, p. 162).
66. *TM*, p. xxiv (*WM*, p. xxii).
67. *TM*, p. 319 (*WM*, pp. 337–38).
68. *TM*, pp. 332–33 (*WM*, p. 351).
69. Rodolphe Gasché, *The Tain of the Mirror*, (Cambridge: Harvard Univ. Press, 1986), p. 101.
70. Ultimately we shall take issue with Gadamer's enframing of the hetero-nomous other within a dialogical model.
71. *TM*, p. 319 (*WM*, p. 338).
72. *TM*, p. 320 (*WM*, p. 340).
73. The relationship between Heidegger's notions of "thrownness" and "finding oneself" and Gadamer's historical hermeneutics is articulated by Tracy, *Analogical Imagination*, p. 103.
74. *TM*, p. 245 (*WM*, p. 360).
75. *TM*, p. 245 (*WM*, p. 261).
76. *TM*, p. 244 (*WM*, p. 260).
77. Hirsch, *Validity in Interpretation*, p. 260.
78. *TM*, p. 240 (*WM*, p. 255). Gadamer himself does not refer to the English word *prejudice* (this is added by his translators), but this does not affect my dis-

cussion of the need to address the contemporary cultural significance of this word.

79. *TM*, p. 273 (*WM*, p. 289).
80. *TM*, p. 238 (*WM*, p. 253).
81. Ibid. (translation modified).
82. *TM*, p. 266 (*WM*, p. 283).
83. *TM*, p. 246 (*WM*, p. 261).
84. *TM*, p. 266 (*WM*, p. 282).
85. Jürgen Habermas, "A Review of Gadamer's *Truth and Method*," in Fred R. Dallmayr and Thomas McCarthy, eds., *Understanding and Social Inquiry* (Notre Dame: Univ. of Notre Dame Press, 1977), p. 357.
86. *TM*, p. 240 (*WM*, p. 255).
87. *TM*, pp. 250, 324 (*WM*, pp. 265, 343).
88. *TM*, p. 324 (*WM*, p. 343).
89. Bernard J. F. Lonergan, *Insight* (New York: Philosophical Library, 1957), p. 229.
90. Hart, *Unfinished Man*, p. 283.
91. *TM*, p. 273 (*WM*, p. 290).
92. *TM*, p. 269 (*WM*, p. 286).
93. *TM*, p. 271 (*WM*, p. 288).
94. *TM*, p. 273 (*WM*, p. 289).
95. *TM*, p. 273 (*WM*, p. 290).
96. *TM*, p. 340 (*WM*, p. 359).
97. *TM*, p. 21 (*WM*, p. 18).
98. Ibid.
99. *TM*, p. 31, and cf. p. 32 (*WM*, p. 29, and cf. p. 30).
100. *TM*, p. 31 (*WM*, p. 29).
101. Immanuel Kant, *Foundations of the Metaphysics of Morals*, trans. Lewis White Beck (Indianapolis: Bobbs-Merrill, 1959), p. 18.
102. Immanuel Kant, *Critique of Practical Reason*, trans. Lewis White Beck (Indianapolis: Bobbs-Merrill, 1956), p. 19.
103. *TM*, p. 288 (*WM*, p. 306).
104. *TM*, p. 21 (*WM*, p. 18). Similarly, Alasdair MacIntyre describes *phronesis* as characterizing "someone who knows how to exercise judgment in particular cases" (*After Virtue* [Notre Dame: Univ. of Notre Dame Press, 1981], p. 144).
105. Habermas, "Review of *Truth and Method*," p. 357.
106. *TM*, p. 279 (*WM*, p. 296).
107. *TM*, p. 278 (*WM*, p. 295).
108. *TM*, p. 283 (*WM*, p. 300).
109. *TM*, p. 274 (*WM*, pp. 290–91).
110. *TM*, p. 289 (*WM*, p. 307).
111. Bernstein, *Beyond Objectivism and Relativism*, p. 157.
112. Ibid.
113. Ibid.
114. Ibid., p. 225.
115. Gadamer, *Reason in the Age of Science*, p. 100.
116. Ibid., p. 82.
117. Bernstein, *Beyond Objectivism and Relativism*, pp. 157–58.
118. Ibid., p. 164.
119. *TM*, p. 321 (*WM*, p. 340).
120. Ibid.
121. *TM*, p. 349 (*WM*, p. 365).
122. Ibid.
123. *TM*, p. 356 (*WM*, p. 372).
124. *TM*, p. 430 (*WM*, pp. 448–49).

125. *TM*, p. 325 (*WM*, p. 344).
126. *TM*, p. 326 (*WM*, p. 345).
127. Charles E. Winquist, *Epiphanies of Darkness* (Philadelphia: Fortress Press, 1986), p. 68.
128. *TM*, p. 404 ("als der sprachlicher Verständigung 'Welt' offenbar gemacht wird" [*WM*, p. 422]).
129. *TM*, p. 404 (*WM*, p. 422).

5. Language and the Disclosure of Worlds: Ricoeur

1. Paul Ricoeur, *Hermeneutics and the Human Sciences*, ed. and trans. John B. Thompson, (Cambridge: Cambridge Univ. Press, 1981), p. 45 (hereafter *HHS*) ("LaTache de L'Herméneutique," in François Bovon and Grégoire Rouiller, eds., *Exegesis* [Paris: Delachaux & Niestlé, 1975], p. 181).
2. *HHS*, p. 141 ("La Fonction Hermeneutique de la Distanciation, in *Exegesis*, p. 211).
3. *HHS*, p. 108.
4. Ibid., p. 111.
5. Ibid., p. 147.
6. *Republic* 597c.
7. *Republic* 603b.
8. *Phaedrus* 275d.
9. Ibid.
10. *Phaedrus* 275e.
11. Ibid.
12. *Phaedrus* 276a.
13. Ibid.
14. Ibid.
15. Jacques Derrida, "Plato's Pharmacy," in *Dissemination*, trans. Barbara Johnson (Chicago: Univ. of Chicago Press, 1981), p. 103.
16. Ibid.
17. *Phaedrus* 276c.
18. See, e.g., *Phaedrus* 230d, 274e, and cf. *Dissemination*, pp. 70, 75. Derrida's analysis hinges upon the ambivalence of the word *pharmakon*. In the Hackforth translation of the text, only one of the meanings, "recipe," is given, and hence the ironic dimension is lost.
19. Derrida, *Dissemination*, p. 71.
20. Ibid., p. 127.
21. Ibid., p. 109.
22. Ibid., p. 117.
23. Ibid., p. 119.
24. Ibid., p. 149.
25. Ibid.
26. Ibid., p. 158.
27. Ibid.
28. Ibid., p. 95.
29. Ibid., p. 96.
30. *TM*, p. 124 (*WM*, p. 133).
31. Weinsheimer, *Gadamer's Hermeneutics*, p. 122.
32. *TM*, p. 121 (translation modified) (*WM*, p. 130).
33. Paul Ricoeur, *Time and Narrative*, vol. 1, trans. Kathleen McLaughlin and David Pellauer (Chicago: Univ. of Chicago Press, 1984), p. xi (hereafter *TN*)

(*Temps et Reacit*, tome 1 [Paris: Editions du Seuil, 1983], p. 13) (hereafter *TR*).
34. *TN*, 1:57 (*TR*, 1:91). Compare MacIntyre: "It is not just that poems and sagas narrate what happens to men and women, but that in their narrative form poems and sagas capture a form that was already present in the lives which they relate" (*After Virtue*, p. 117).
35. *TN*, 1:62 (*TR*, 1:98).
36. Ibid.
37. Ibid.
38. *TN*, 1:63 (*TR*, 1:100).
39. *TN*, 1:63 (*TR*, 1:99); cf. *BT*, p. 473 (*SZ*, pp. 555–56).
40. *TN*, 1:64 (*TR*, 1:100).
41. *TN*, 1:81 (*TR*, 1:123).
42. *TN*, 1:64 (*TR*, 1:100).
43. Ibid.
44. Ricoeur, *Rule of Metaphor*, p. 74 (hereafter *RM*) (*La Métaphore Vive* [Paris: Editions du Seuil, 1975], p. 97) (hereafter *MV*).
45. *RM*, p. 304 (*MV*, p. 386).
46. Dominick LaCapra, "Who Rules Metaphor?" *Diacritics* 10 (1980):26.
47. *RM*, p. 304 (*MV*, p. 385).
48. Ibid.
49. *HHS*, p. 202.
50. John B. Thompson, *Critical Hermeneutics* (Cambridge: Cambridge Univ. Press, 1981), p. 204.
51. Zygmunt Bauman, *Hermeneutics and Social Science* (New York: Columbia Univ. Press, 1978), p. 183. Bauman is summarizing an argument of Alfred Schutz.
52. *HHS*, p. 202.
53. *RM*, p. 92 (*MV*, p. 119). This distinction is derived from Frege.
54. *RM*, p. 216 (*MV*, p. 273).
55. Cf. Saussure, *Course in General Linguistics*, p. 14 ff.
56. Paul Ricoeur, *Time and Narrative*, vol. 2, trans. Kathleen McLaughlin and David Pellauer, (Chicago: Univ. of Chicago Press, 1985), p. 30 (*Temps et Récit*, tome 2 [Paris: Editions du Seuil, 1984], p. 50).
57. *RM*, p. 217 (*MV*, p. 274). Cf. the analogous arguments in James M. Edie, *Speaking and Meaning* (Bloomington: Indiana Univ. Press, 1976), especially pp. 159, 184. Edie differentiates between *syntax* and *semantics*, arguing that we are forced to move from considerations of the former to the latter because words are "context dependent."
58. Cf. Ludwig Wittgenstein, *Philosophical Investigations*, trans. G. E. M. Anscombe, 3d ed. (New York: Macmillan, 1973), p. 109; Michel Foucault, *The Archaeology of Knowledge*, trans. A. M.Sheridan Smith (New York: Pantheon, 1972), pp. 101, 105, 117.
59. *RM*, p. 220 (*MV*, p. 278).
60. *RM*, p. 84 (*MV*, p. 110).
61. *RM*, p. 85 (*MV*, p. 111).
62. *RM*, p. 84 (*MV*, p. 110). This rather hackneyed example is better representative of what Ricoeur terms "dead metaphor" rather than the "live metaphor," which is the object of his inquiry. However, it serves to make the point, both for Ricoeur and for the present analysis.
63. Janet Martin Soskice, *Metaphor and Religious Language* (New York: Oxford Univ. Press, 1985), p. 45.
64. Ibid., p. 46.
65. Ibid., p. 43.
66. Ibid., p. 47.

67. Ibid.
68. Ibid., p. 49.
69. Ibid., p. 58.
70. *RM* 195 (*MV*, p. 246).
71. *RM*, p. 98 (*MV*, p. 126).
72. *RM*, pp. 98–99 (*MV*, p. 127).
73. *RM*, p. 152 (*MV*, p. 195).
74. *RM*, p. 23 (*MV*, p. 33).
75. Derrida, *Dissemination*, p. 258.
76. Jacques Derrida, "The *Retrait* of Metaphor," *Enclitic* 2, no. 2 (1978), p. 23.
77. Ibid., p. 24.
78. Ibid., pp. 24–25.
79. Ibid., p. 25.
80. Derrida, *Margins of Philosophy*, p. 244.
81. Ibid., p. 266.
82. *RM*, pp. 290–91 (*MV*, p. 369).
83. Paul Ricoeur, "Structure, Word, Event," trans. Robert Sweeney, in Ricoeur, *The Conflict of Interpretations*, ed. Don Ihde (Evanston: Northwestern Univ. Press, 1974), p. 94. Cf. *RM*, pp. 124–25 (*MV*, pp. 160–61).
84. *RM*, p. 180 (*MV*, p. 230).
85. *RM*, pp. 121–22 (*MV*, p. 156).
86. *RM*, p. 221 (*MV*, p. 279).
87. *RM*, p. 247 (*MV*, p. 311).
88. *RM*, p. 248 (*MV*, pp. 312–13) (emphasis original).
89. *RM*, p. 297 (*MV*, p. 376).
90. *RM*, p. 255 (*MV*, p. 321). Antecedents for this notion of a critical element in metaphor may be found in Julián Marías, "Philosophic Truth and the Metaphoric System," in *Interpretation: The Poetry of Meaning*, ed. Stanley Romaine Hopper and David L. Miller (New York: Harcourt, Brace and World, 1967), pp. 46 ff., and Beda Alleman, "Metaphor and Antimetaphor," ibid., pp. 103 ff.
91. *RM*, p. 229 (*MV*, p. 289).
92. *HHS*, p. 211.
93. *HHS*, p. 61(*Exegesis*, p. 199).
94. *HHS*, p. 62 (*Exegesis*, p. 200).
95. Fackenheim, *To Mend the World*, pp. 257, 260.
96. *HHS*, p. 139.
97. *HHS*, p. 113.
98. *HHS*, p. 113.
99. *HHS*, p. 180, and cf. p. 140.
100. *HHS*, p. 177.
101. *HHS*, p. 143 (*Exegesis*, p. 214).
102. *HHS*, p. 91.
103. *RM*, p. 299 (*MV*, p. 379).
104. *HHS*, p. 93.
105. Paul Ricoeur, *Freud and Philosophy*, trans. Denis Savage (New Haven: Yale Univ. Press, 1970), p. 27.
106. Ibid., p. 54.
107. *HHS*, p. 143 (*Exegesis*, p. 214).
108. *HHS*, p. 144 (*Exegesis*, p. 215).
109. Ibid.
110. Julia Kristeva, *Revolution in Poetic Language*, trans. Margaret Waller (New York: Columbia Univ. Press, 1984), p. 67.
111. *TN*, 1:71 (*TR*, 1:110).
112. Paul Ricoeur, *Temps et Récit*, tome 3 (Paris: Editions du Seuil, 1985), p. 230

("C'est seulement *dans* la lecture que le dynamism de configuration achève son parcours. Et c'est *au-delá* de la lecture, dans l'action effective, instruite par les oeuvres reçues, que la configuration du texte se transmute en refiguration").
113. Ibid., p. 226.
114. *RM*, p. 297 (*MV*, p. 376).
115. *TR*, 3:329 (my translation).
116. *RM*, p. 298 (*MV*, pp. 377–78).
117. *RM*, p. 305 (*MV*, p. 387).
118. Cf. *RM*, p. 306 (*MV*, p. 388).

Conclusion

1. Stephen E. Toulmin, *An Examination of the Place of Reason in Ethics* (Cambridge: Cambridge Univ. Press, 1950), p. 77.
2. Bauman, *Hermeneutics and Social Science*, p. 241.
3. Ibid., p. 231.
4. Herman Melville, "Hawthorne and His Mosses," in *The Portable Melville*, ed. Jay Leyda (New York: Viking, 1952), p. 408. Quoted in William Hamilton, *Melville and the Gods* (Chico, Calif.: The Scholar's Press, 1985), p. xi.

BIBLIOGRAPHY

Adorno, Theodor. *Negative Dialectics*. Trans. E. B. Ashton. New York: Continuum Books, 1973.

Aristotle. *Metaphysics*. Books 1–10. Trans. Hugh Tredennick. New York: G. P. Putnam's Sons, 1933.

———. *Nichomachean Ethics*. Trans. H. Rackham. Cambridge: Harvard Univ. Press, 1962.

———. "On Interpretation," *Organon* 1. Trans. Harold Cooke. Cambridge: Harvard University Press, 1938.

Barrett, William, and Henry D. Aiken, eds. *Philosophy in the Twentieth Century* vol. 3. New York: Random House, 1962.

Bauman, Zygmunt. *Hermeneutics and Social Science*. New York: Columbia Univ. Press,1978.

Berger, Peter L., and Thomas Luckmann. *The Social Construction of Reality*. Garden City: Doubleday, 1966.

Bernstein, Richard J. *Beyond Objectivism and Relativism: Science, Hermeneutics, and Praxis*. Philadelphia: Univ. of Pennsylvania Press, 1983.

Biemel, Walter. *Martin Heidegger: An Illustrated Study*. Trans. J. H. Mehta. New York: Harcourt, Brace, Jovanovich, 1976.

Blanshard, Brand. *The Nature of Thought*. Vol. 2. New York: Macmillan, 1940.

Bovon, François, and Grégoire Rouiller, eds. *Exegesis: Problèmes de Méthode et Exercices de Lecture*. Paris: Delachaux & Niestlé, 1975.

Cassirer, Ernst. *The Philosophy of Symbolic Forms*, Vol. 1, *Language*. Trans. Ralph Manheim. New Haven: Yale Univ. Press, 1955.

Curley, E. M. *Spinoza's Metaphysics: An Essay in Interpretation*. Cambridge: Harvard Univ. Press, 1969.

Dallmayr, Fred R., and Thomas McCarthy, eds. *Understanding and Social Inquiry.* Notre Dame: Univ. of Notre Dame Press, 1977.

Derrida, Jacques. *Dissemination.* Trans. Barbara Johnson. Chicago: Univ. of Chicago Press, 1981.

———. *Margins of Philosophy.* Trans. Alan Bass. Chicago: Univ. of Chicago Press, 1982.

———. *Of Grammatology.* Trans. Gayatri Chakravorty Spivak. Baltimore: Johns Hopkins Univ. Press, 1974.

———. "The *Retrait* of Metaphor." *Enclitic* 2 (Fall 1978): 5–33.

Dewey, John. *The Quest for Certainty: A Study in the Relation of Knowledge and Action.* New York: Minton, Balch, 1929.

Edie, James M. *Speaking and Meaning: The Phenomenology of Language.* Bloomington: Indiana Univ. Press, 1976.

Eiseley, Loren. *The Night Country.* New York: Charles Scribner's Sons, 1947.

Elliston, Frederick, ed. *Heidegger's Existential Analytic.* The Hague: Mouton, n.d.

Erikson, Erik H. *Insight and Responsibility.* New York: Norton, 1964.

Fackenheim, Emil. *The Religious Dimension of Hegel's Thought.* Chicago: University of Chicago Press, 1967.

———. *To Mend the World: Foundations of Future Jewish Thought.* New York: Schocken, 1982.

Findlay, J. N. *Hegel: A Re-examination.* New York: Oxford Univ. Press, 1958.

Foucault, Michel. *The Archaeology of Knowledge.* Trans. A. M. Sheridan Smith. New York: Pantheon, 1972.

Fowles, John. *The Magus.* Rev. version. New York: Dell, 1978.

Friedländer, Paul. *Plato: An Introduction.* Trans. Hans Meyerhoff. Princeton: Princeton Univ. Press, 1969.

Gadamer, Hans-Georg. "Heidegger and the History of Philosophy." *The Monist* 64 (October, 1981): 434–44.

———. *The Idea of the Good in Platonic-Aristotelian Philosophy.* Trans. P. Christopher Smith. New Haven: Yale Univ. Press, 1986.

———. *Reason in the Age of Science.* Trans. Frederick G. Lawrence. Cambridge: MIT Press, 1981.

———. *Truth and Method.* Trans. Garrett Barden and John Cumming. New York: Seabury, 1975.

———. *Wahrheit und Methode.* Zweite Auflage. Tübingen: J. C. B. Mohr, 1965.

Galston, William A. "Heidegger's Plato: A Critique of *Plato's Doctrine of Truth.*" *Philosophical Forum* 13 (Summer 1982): 371–84.

Gasché, Rodolphe. *The Tain of the Mirror: Derrida and the Philosophy of Reflection.* Cambridge: Harvard Univ. Press, 1986.

Geertz, Clifford. *The Interpretation of Cultures.* New York: Basic Books, 1973.

Gilkey, Langdon. *Naming the Whirlwind.* Indianapolis: Bobbs-Merrill, 1969.

Habermas, Jürgen. *Philosophical-Political Profiles.* Trans. Thomas Mc-
Carthy. Cambridge: MIT Press, 1983.
———. "A Review of Gadamer's *Truth and Method.*" In *Understanding
and Social Inquiry,* ed. Dallmayr and McCarthy, pp. 335–61.
Hamilton, William. *Melville and the Gods.* Chico, Calif.: Scholar's
Press, 1985.
Hampshire, Stuart. *Spinoza.* Harmondsworth: Penguin, 1951.
Hart, Ray L. *Unfinished Man and the Imagination.* New York: Herder
and Herder, 1968.
Hegel, G. W. F. *Lectures on the History of Philosophy.* Trans. E. S. Hal-
dane and F. H. Simson. New York: Humanities Press, 1968.
———. *The Phenomenology of Spirit.* Trans. A. V. Miller. New York: Ox-
ford Univ. Press, 1977.
———. *Science of Logic.* Trans. A. V. Miller. New York: Humanities
Press, 1969.
Heidegger, Martin. *Basic Problems of Phenomenology.* Trans. Albert
Hofstadter. Bloomington: Indiana Univ. Press, 1982.
———. *Basic Writings.* Ed. David Farrell Krell. New York: Harper and
Row, 1977.
———. *Being and Time.* Trans. John Macquarrie and Edward Robinson.
New York: Harper and Row, 1962.
———. *Early Greek Thinking.* Trans. David Farrell Krell and Frank A. Ca-
puzzi. New York: Harper and Row, 1975.
———. *The End of Philosophy.* Trans. Joan Stambaugh. New York:
Harper and Row, 1973.
———. *The Essence of Reasons.* Bilingual ed. with English translation by
Terrence Malick. Evanston: Northwestern Univ. Press, 1969.
———. *Existence and Being.* Ed. by Werner Brock. Chicago: Henry Reg-
nery, 1949.
———. *Holzwege.* Frankfurt a. M. Vittorio Klostermann, 1963.
———. *Identity and Difference.* Bilingual ed. with English translation by
Joan Stambaugh. New York: Harper and Row, 1969.
———. *Nietzsche* 2. Pfullingen: Verlag Gunther Neske, 1961.
———. *Nietzsche.* Vol. 4, *Nihilism.* Trans. Frank A. Capuzzi. New York:
Harper and Row, 1982.
———. *On the Way to Language.* Trans. Peter D. Hertz. New York:
Harper and Row, 1971.
———. *On Time and Being.* Trans. Joan Stambaugh. New York: Harper
and Row, 1972.
———. "Plato's Doctrine of Truth." in *Philosophy in the Twentieth Cen-
tury* Vol. 3. Ed. Barrett and Aiken.
———. *Poetry, Language, Thought.* Trans. Albert Hofstadter. New York:
Harper and Row, 1971.
———. *The Question concerning Technology and Other Essays.* Trans.
William Lovitt. New York: Harper and Row, 1977.
———. *Sein und Zeit. Gesamtausgabe.* Band 2. Frankfurt a. M.: Vittorio
Klostermann, 1977.

————. *Unterwegs Zur Sprache*. Pfullingen: Verlag Günther Neske, 1959.

————. *Vorträge und Aufsätze*. Pfullingen: Günther Neske, 1967.

————. *Wegmarken*. Frankfurt a. M.: Vittorio Klostermann, 1978.

————. *What Is a Thing?* Trans. W. B. Barton, Jr., and Vera Deutsch. South Bend: Gateway, 1967.

————. *What Is Called Thinking?* Trans. Fred D. Wieck and J. Glenn Gray. New York: Harper and Row, 1968.

————. *Zur Sache des Denkens*. Tübingen: Max Niemeyer Verlag, 1969.

Hirsch, E. D., Jr. *Validity in Interpretation*. New Haven: Yale Univ. Press, 1967.

Hofstadter, Albert. *Truth and Art*. New York: Columbia Univ. Press, 1965.

Hopper, Stanley Romaine, and David L. Miller, eds. *Interpretation: The Poetry of Meaning*. New York: Harcourt, Brace and World, 1967.

Hyppolite, Jean. *Genesis and Structure of Hegel's Phenomenology of Spirit*. Trans. S. Cherniak and J. Heckman. Evanston: Northwestern Univ. Press, 1974.

James, William. *Essays in Pragmatism*. New York: Hafner, 1948.

————. *Pragmatism: A New Name for Some Old Ways of Thinking*. 1907. Reprint. New York: Longman's, Green, 1943.

————. *The Varieties of Religious Experience*. 1902. Reprint. New York: Macmillan, 1961.

Joachim, H. H. *The Nature of Truth*. 1906. Reprint. New York: Greenwood Press, 1969.

Kant, Immanuel. *Critique of Practical Reason*. Trans. Lewis White Beck. Indianapolis: Bobbs-Merrill, 1956.

————. *Critique of Pure Reason*. Trans. Norman Kemp Smith. 1929. Reprint. New York: St. Martin's, 1965.

————. *Foundations of the Metaphysics of Morals*. Trans. Lewis White Beck. Indianapolis: Bobbs-Merrill, 1959.

Khatchadourian, Haig. *The Coherence Theory of Truth: A Critical Evaluation*. Beirut: American Univ. Press, 1961.

Kierkegaard, Søren. *Concluding Unscientific Postscript*. Trans. David F. Swenson and Walter Lowrie. Princeton: Princeton Univ. Press, 1941.

Kockelmans, Joseph J. *Heidegger On Art and Artworks*. Dordrecht: Martinus Nijhoff, 1985.

————, ed. *On Heidegger and Language*. Evanston: Northwestern Univ. Press, 1972.

————. *On The Truth of Being: Reflections on Heidegger's Later Philosophy*. Bloomington: Indiana Univ. Press, 1984.

Kojève, Alexandre. *Introduction to the Reading of Hegel*. Trans. J. H. Nicholas. New York: Basic Books, 1969.

Kristeva, Julia. *Revolution in Poetic Language*. Trans. Margaret Waller. New York: Columbia Univ. Press, 1984.

LaCapra, Dominick. "Who Rules Metaphor?" *Diacritics* 10, (1980): 15–28.

Langan, Thomas. *The Meaning of Heidegger.* New York: Columbia Univ. Press, 1958.

Lonergan, Bernard J. F. *Insight: A Study of Human Understanding.* New York: Philosophical Library, 1957.

MacIntyre, Alasdair. *After Virtue.* Notre Dame: Univ. of Notre Dame Press, 1981.

Macomber, W. B. *The Anatomy of Disillusion: Martin Heidegger's Notion of Truth.* Evanston: Northwestern Univ. Press, 1967.

Macquarrie, John. *An Existentialist Theology: A Comparison of Heidegger and Bultmann.* New York: Macmillan, 1955.

Marx, Werner. *Heidegger and the Tradition.* Trans. Theodor Kisiel and Murray Greene. Evanston: Northwestern Univ. Press, 1971.

Megill, Allan. *Prophets of Extremity: Nietzsche, Heidegger, Foucault, Derrida.* Berkeley and Los Angeles: Univ. of California Press, 1985.

Miller, David L. *Christs: Meditations on Archetypal Images in Christian Theology.* New York: Seabury, 1981.

O'Connor, D. J. *The Correspondence Theory of Truth.* London: Hutchinson, 1975.

Ortega y Gasset, José. *Meditations on Quixote.* Trans. Evelyn Rugg and Diego Marín. New York: Norton, 1961.

Palmer, Richard E. *Hermeneutics: Interpretation Theory in Schleiermacher, Dilthey, Heidegger, and Gadamer.* Evanston: Northwestern Univ. Press, 1969.

Pietersma, H. "Heidegger's Theory of Truth." In *Heidegger's Existential Analytic,* ed. Frederick Elliston, pp. 219–30.

Plato. *The Collected Dialogues.* Ed. Edith Hamilton and Huntington Cairns. Princeton: Princeton Univ. Press, 1963.

Pöggeler, Otto. "Heidegger's Topology of Being." In *On Heidegger and Language.* Ed. Kockelmans. Pp. 107–146.

Randall, John Herman, Jr. *Aristotle.* New York: Columbia Univ. Press, 1960.

———. *Plato: Dramatist of the Life of Reason.* New York: Columbia Univ. Press, 1970.

Richardson, William. *Heidegger: Through Phenomenology to Thought.* The Hague: Martinus Nijhoff, 1967.

Ricoeur, Paul. *The Conflict of Interpretations.* Ed. Don Ihde. Evanston: Northwestern Univ. Press, 1974.

———. *Freud and Philosophy: An Essay on Interpretation.* Trans. Denis Savage. New Haven: Yale Univ. Press, 1970.

———. *Hermeneutics and the Human Sciences.* Trans. and ed. John B. Thompson. Cambridge: Cambridge Univ. Press, 1981.

———. "La Fonction Herméneutique de la Distanciation," In *Exegesis.* Ed. Bovon and Rouiller. Pp. 201–15.

———. *La Métaphor Vive.* Paris: Editions du Seuil, 1975.

————. "La Tâche de L'Herméneutique," In *Exegesis*. Ed. Bovon and Rouiller. Pp. 179–200.

————. *The Rule of Metaphor*. Trans. Robert Czerny. Toronto: Univ. of Toronto Press, 1977.

————. *Temps et Récit*. Tome 1. Paris: Editions du Seuil, 1983.

————. *Temps et Récit*. Tome 2. Paris: Editions du Seuil, 1984.

————. *Temps et Récit*. Tome 3. Paris: Editions du Seuil, 1985.

————. *Time and Narrative*. Vol. 1. Trans. Kathleen McLaughlin and David Pellauer. Chicago: Univ. of Chicago Press, 1984.

————. *Time and Narrative*, Vol. 2. Trans. Kathleen McLaughlin and David Pellauer. Chicago: Univ. of Chicago Press, 1985.

Rorty, Richard. *Philosophy and the Mirror of Nature*. Princeton: Princeton Univ. Press, 1979.

Russell, Bertrand. *Philosophical Essays*. London: Longman's, Green, 1910.

Saussure, Ferdinand de. *Course in General Linguistics*. Trans. Wade Baskin. New York: McGraw-Hill, 1966.

Scharlemann, Robert P. *The Being of God: Theology and the Experience of Truth*. New York: Seabury, 1981.

Schleiermacher, Friedrich. *Hermeneutics: The Handwritten Manuscripts*. Trans. James Duke and Jack Forstman. Missoula: Scholars Press, 1977.

Schrag, Calvin O. *Experience and Being: Prolegomena to a Future Ontology*. Evanston: Northwestern Univ. Press, 1969.

Schufreider, Gregory. "Art and the Problem of Truth." *Man and World* 13 (1980): 53–80.

Schürmann, Reiner. *Heidegger on Being and Acting: From Principles to Anarchy*. Trans. Christine-Marie Gros in collaboration with the author. Bloomington: Indiana Univ. Press, 1987.

Sinaiko, Herman L. *Love, Knowledge, and Discourse in Plato*. Chicago: Univ. of Chicago Press, 1965.

Soskice, Janet Martin. *Metaphor and Religious Language*. New York: Oxford Univ. Press, 1985.

Spinoza, Benedict de. *The Collected Works of Spinoza*. Vol. 1. Trans. Edwin Curley. Princeton: Princeton Univ. Press, 1985.

Taylor, A. E. *Plato: The Man and His Work*. Indianapolis: Bobbs-Merrill, 1956.

Taylor, Mark C. *Altarity*. Chicago: Univ. of Chicago Press, 1987.

Thomas Aquinas, St. *On the Truth of the Catholic Faith: Summa Contra Gentiles*. Trans. Anton C. Pegis. Garden City: Image Books, 1955.

————. *Summa Theologiae*. Vol. 4. Trans. Thomas Gornall, S. J. New York: McGraw-Hill, 1964.

Thompson, John B. *Critical Hermeneutics: A Study in the Thought of Paul Ricoeur and Jürgen Habermas*. Cambridge: Cambridge Univ. Press, 1981.

Toulmin, Stephen E. *An Examination of the Place of Reason in Ethics.*
    Cambridge: Cambridge Univ. Press, 1950.
Tracy, David. *The Analogical Imagination.* New York: Crossroad, 1981.
Weinsheimer, Joel C. *Gadamer's Hermeneutics: A Reading of Truth and
    Method.* New Haven: Yale Univ. Press, 1985.
Winquist, Charles E. *Epiphanies of Darkness: Deconstruction in Theol-
    ogy.* Philadelphia: Fortress Press, 1986.
Wittgenstein, Ludwig. *Philosophical Investigations.* Trans. G. E. M.
    Anscombe. New York: Macmillan, 1968.
Wolz, Henry G. *Plato and Heidegger: In Search of Selfhood.* Lewisburg:
    Bucknell Univ. Press, 1981.

INDEX